Plays of the 70s

VOLUME 2

edited by Katharine Brisbane

Currency Press • Sydney

CURRENCY PLAYS
General Editor: Katharine Brisbane

First published 1999
Currency Press Ltd,
PO Box 2287, Strawberry Hills,
NSW, 2012, Australia
www.currency.com.au

A Hard God first published by Currency Methuen Drama, Sydney, 1974; *Coralie Lansdowne Says No* by Currency Methuen Drama, Sydney, 1974; *How Does Your Garden Grow* by Currency Methuen Drama, Sydney, 1974; *The Cake Man* by Currency Press, Sydney, 1978.

NATIONAL LIBRARY OF AUSTRALIA CIP DATA

Plays of the 70s.

ISBN 0 86819 552 9 (v.2).

1. Australian drama–20th century. I. Brisbane, Katharine.
II. Title: Plays of the seventies.

A822.308

Set by Dean Nottle.
Printed by Southwood Press, Marrickville, NSW.

Cover design by Mango Design.

Contents

Introduction

Katharine Brisbane

In Volume 1 of *Plays of the 70s* (1970–72) we explored a young theatre movement searching out new forms, and ideas about what it meant to be Australian. We noted that 'outdated' realistic character and motivation were abandoned in favour of archetypes, and presentational forms began to challenge the realistic theatre which had dominated for so long. This volume, which covers the period 1973–75, marks a consolidation of form, and the recognition of a sense of direction. While public and social issues were the preoccupation of the earlier plays, these plays display a strong move towards the domestic as expressive of community. Where previously the purpose of the protagonists had been to dramatise or lampoon the flaws in society, now the authors begin an examination of the way the individual is shaped by society.

In public life the years 1973–75 were also a discrete pocket of history, come to be known as 'the Whitlam period'. The heady election campaign which brought the Labor Party into office after 23 years of conservative government was followed by a breathtaking series of political decisions, received at first with exhilaration, and then by degrees, with increasing trepidation as inflation soared and the fundamentals of Australian society were challenged and (it was feared) undermined.

> Turn your back for five minutes and what happens? Rack and ruin, buggeration all round. Things fall apart, the centre cannot hold. Oh, my tree, my tree.

Coralie Lansdowne is inveighing against a dog which has pissed against the tree in her living room; but the reference to W.B. Yeats' poem 'The Second Coming' gives her feelings much wider reverberation.

> Things fall apart; the centre cannot hold;
> More anarchy is loosed upon the world,
> The blood-dimmed tide is loosed, and everywhere
> The ceremony of innocence is drowned;
> The best lack all conviction, while the worst
> Are full of passionate intensity.

The changes wrought by the Whitlam Government were necessary and overdue but the task of self-examination was too new to be undertaken by the electorate without the fear of anarchy and the loss of innocence. Middle-class reformers increasingly sought restraint and a middle way by joining groups like the Australia Party, a precursor of the Democrats, as Peter has in *Coralie Lansdowne Says No*. Finally, the moment came when voters concluded overwhelmingly that the best lacked all conviction and in 1976 the conservatives were re-elected. Revealingly, the plays in this volume reflect as much on the enduring need for commonplace emotional security and comfort as on the need for social progress.

What is reality? Should we follow our dreams? Is compromise the only path to happiness? The characters in these plays resolve these questions in different ways: some by accepting incomprehension, others by settling for the possible, some by defining the problem for the first time.

> He's a hard God, and our total ignorance of what he's about is what finally drives us to distraction. It would be unbearable if I wasn't sure he loved me. And I am sure of that. (*A Hard God*)

> I wanted to be brilliant in life, do you understand that, brilliant in life! (*Coralie Lansdowne*)

> Oh yeah, don't worry about me. I already woke up, today, when I seen what I've been away from. (*How Does Your Garden Grow*)

But it is Sweet William in *The Cake Man* who, at the close, defines the dilemma of the times:

> Two realities. An' I've lost one. But I want it back... I need it back. Not yours... mine.

The first of these plays, *A Hard God* (1973), is unquestionably one of the finest works to have been written for the Australian theatre. Coming from the previous generation of playwrights, its author Peter Kenna had the advantage of maturity; and he combined the opportunity to experiment in form with a desire to celebrate dramatically his own cultural heritage. In its early years the play was found remarkable for the density of the Irish-Australian language, its poetry and humour; the working-class detail and the sheer actability of the characters. The two time zones, conveying the slow progress of the old people and the emotional turmoil of the boys, were also seen as radical.

Today, nearly 30 years later, the text is a familiar one and the boundaries are blurred between 1946, when the play is set, and 1973 when it was first performed. But in fact the choice of the tail end of World War II, stale from rationing and deprivation; the year before the first 'displaced persons' began to pour into Australia to change it forever; seems a curious choice at a moment in history when Australia was undergoing another social revolution. It was Kenna's first work after his return from life in London in the roaring 60s; and the play has much more to do with his own coming to terms with changing Australia than with the rush for change being made to the theatre. *A Hard God*'s retreat back to Kenna's childhood provided him ground from which to begin to examine this newly-alien society. The play is a contemporary critique in that his portrait of a narrow, ignorant, rigidly sectarian community highlights the radical change wrought by the 60s. But, at the same time, a period which left lifetime scars on Kenna's body and mind is depicted with love, care and not a little nostalgia.

Looking back now the play takes on yet another perspective. The deracination of the characters—from Ireland, from their land, from their family—is less surprising in this more mobile world than the self-imposed self-restriction. The boys' social lives are bounded by Catholic school, club and the rules laid down by their elders. The elders' lives are bounded by poverty, familial duty, a low level of education and blind obedience to the Catholic Church. It is a closed community to which the immigrant today might better relate than contemporary Irish Catholic families.

For it is hard to give credence today to the sectarian wars of Australian schools, unions and political parties, which split the Labor Party in the 1950s; but they are a powerful part of our history. We must also remind ourselves that this time was well before the Second Vatican Council that swept away so many restrictions; and that in 1946 there was no Medicare. General practitioners took for granted their share of pro bono consultation; and the division between public and private hospitals was wide.

For the Cassidy family reality is tangible in the struggle of daily life. The extended family are bound together by a love which has nothing to do with liking, but is compounded from common memories—even resented memories—and common experience of life. Outside circumstances may uproot them but it is never their choice. Martin blames time, which he sees as a germ that everybody catches. 'You breathe in time and it gives you the wanderlust.' But Aggie has never caught the wanderlust: 'I'd always hoped I'd never have to leave Narrabri. Every person I knew in the world lived there.'

The pull of the family is everything: interdependence determines their every action. Even the boys do not question the dogma. Their awakening sexuality divides them without their coming to terms with the knowledge of good and evil; Jack escapes for no better reason than that his orphaned status sets him free.

Alex Buzo's *Coralie Lansdowne Says No* (1974) is very different; but equally a critique and more overtly an attempt to come to terms with the virtues and vices of a new society. Coralie is an upwardly-mobile 'high flying bird' in search of perfection. Her environment, like her life, has been artificially constructed to delete all reference to a past that does not accord with her view of herself. Like the characters in David Williamson's

Don's Party (1972), Coralie has arrived at the cusp of her thirtieth birthday and is disappointed. They are the new generation, who led the marches for change and are already disillusioned.

The play is also a critique of the new, liberated woman. A decade after the introduction of the contraceptive pill Coralie's freedom is revealed as lack of direction and control. She works at nothing and dismisses the achievement of others as 'bourgeois'. The ambition to be a wit has given her a bitter tongue and a conscious cultivation of the epithet; but her barbs are ill-considered and her targets undeserving. She is also an exhibitionist. In sharp contrast to the Cassidys' lives, nothing in Coralie's life has any tangible reality.

On the other hand the play is also a critique of the men who surround her. They are her willing audience; but they are conditioned to construct their women according to their needs. Because her presence assuages Peter's loneliness, he casts her as an accessory to his social life. Paul, because he and Coralie were once lovers, expects automatically to reassume his rights. Only Stuart, 'poet and public servant', sees clearly that the way to contentment lies in acknowledging ordinariness and interdependence. He also sees through Coralie's brilliance to her underlying fear:

> It's a question of coming to terms, it's not a question of what you want to achieve in life, it's a question of settling for what's available and reconciling fulfilment to an appropriate deal. (Sc. 3)

The two other women characters serve as a commentary on the possibilities and dangers inherent in 'liberation'. Coralie's sister Jill has seized the chance to build a career and is as tireless as Coralie is indolent. The challenge to Paul's wife Anne, on the other hand, has broken her spirit. The insecurities raised by the new social mores, combined with the unremitting traditional demands of being wife and mother, prove too much. With rather arcane symbolism she consigns her only 'valuables' to Coralie's erectile vase before throwing herself into the sea.

Just as *A Hard God* has strong links with the Irish theatre, so *Coralie Lansdowne Says No* owes a debt to the masters of comedy, William Congreve and Shakespeare. Buzo by this time had made his name as a chronicler of the vernacular and the coiner of smart epithets. Coralie is a personification of this, but in concept she has a passing resemblance to Mistress Millament in *The Way of the World*. The characters in that play are affluent and idle, preoccupied with sex and politics; and the style of *Coralie Lansdowne* depends for its effectiveness upon the presentational style of the comedy of manners. Millament's accommodations, however, are made within the manners of a mercantile society of extreme rigidity in which real emotion can only be expressed as metaphor; Coralie's subtext of misery and rootlessness is dense beneath her brittleness—a symptom of the social instability in which she finds herself.

Coralie appeared so new to the stage in 1974 that the moral critique of the author was less immediately apparent than her brilliance. Her early directors resolutely ignored the author's hints at slovenliness in his references to her 'bigness' and blowsiness. In fact, she is a direct descendent of Kate in *The Taming of the Shrew*; and her Petruchio, though no stormy merchant, is equally dogged and realistic in his methods. While at first it may appear that by settling for Stuart she will have her own way in marriage: 'I must be treated well' (Sc. 4), his gift to her is the freedom to be herself. Her coughing fit at the end of the play is an acknowledgment that it is all right to be vulnerable; to be damaged, like every other human being: and equally an acknowledgment that marriage is a partnership.

Millament and her Mirabell, like Katharine and Petruchio, face the task of achieving marital harmony within the constraints of their society. And so do Coralie and Stuart, perhaps rather more mundanely, as a public servant and his teacher wife. Society may shape the individual, all these plays are saying, but human nature changes little. The last two plays in this volume draw the same conclusion.

How Does your Garden Grow (1974) and *The Cake Man* (1975) have a close historical relationship. They were both written in the period 1973–74; and both owe no debt whatever to the classics but indirectly have a connection to *A Hard God* and its tradition. Jim McNeil was familiar with *A Hard God* at the time of writing *How Does Your Garden Grow* and felt a strong connection to Kenna and his world. *How Does Your Garden Grow* is Jim McNeil's third play and his first full length one. He spent most of his adult life in prison and at the time was serving a 17-year term for shooting a policeman. He wrote the play as his seven-year non-parole period was coming to an end; acceptance by the Nimrod Theatre contributed to his being granted parole and he was released in time to attend the opening night. Between the completion of the play and his release, a riot by prisoners over conditions occurred at Bathurst which destroyed the prison.

Violence within prisons became the subject of public debate. The extent of homosexuality and rape was taken up by the popular press and the reformer Professor Tony Vinson, then head of the Department of Corrective Services, made an unsuccessful attempt to convert government to the view that violence breeds violence and another way was needed. In the light of this *How Does Your Garden Grow* appears a remarkably tame, even childlike, account of prison life by a man whose own life was marked by bouts of uncontrolled violence.

The manuscript was, of course, subject to censorship; and this provided a discipline which gives the play a rich subtext. But, like his earlier work, this play is not aiming to shock or proselytise, but simply to engage the audience with the idea that prisoners are ordinary people with ordinary domestic needs. Mick, Sam and Brenda are all absorbed in creating a surrogate reality; a place peopled by friendly faces, kind thoughts and laughter in which to live until the outside world is returned to them.

MICK: We're mad, yer know.
BRENDA: I know we are.
MICK: Right off.
BRENDA: Hnhn. No, not really.
MICK: Nah. Always carrying on as if we were, though. Wonder why we do?
BRENDA: So we don't *go* mad, of course.

Their lives are subject to even greater restrictions than those of the Cassidy family; and they are equally uncomprehending of them. But these are no willing players; on the contrary, their energy is derived from their ability to subvert. Their subversions include playing at domesticity; inventing company and social life; bullying and accommodating; sharing private dreams and scavenging small comforts—and above all by simple humour. There is no mention of assaults, drug-taking or suicide. Warders' officiousness is treated with verbal sparring and fair-mindedness receives silent recognition. Nevertheless, the walls of the prison, though never mentioned in the text, are vividly present for the audience, a monument to the limitations imposed by society.

This is a world as old-fashioned as the Cassidys' and moves as slowly. McNeil is especially skilful at recreating the slow passage of time, drawing out with an engaging humour each subject of conversation lest, once dropped, no other can be found to replace it. Mick's encounter with his 'liberated' wife is the most obvious example of the way that time has passed them by; he very quickly discards his childish imaginings when the real becomes tangible. Brenda, the man/woman forced by life and by nature to live forever in that imagined world, is the realist of the three; and accepts the compromise because he can do no other.

In 1973 Robert Merritt was a young Koori who had befriended McNeil and knew him as a playwright. The idea of dramatic performance as a platform for the civil rights debate was in its infancy when Merritt began work on a play about the Cowra (NSW) mission on which he was raised. His motives were much the same as McNeil's—to demonstrate to outsiders, to involve the emotions of the outside world, in the sufferings, the aspirations, the universally human needs, of his own deprived society. With sly irony and simple morality he shows us a society as ridden by mindless authoritarianism as that of the world of prison; and to this he adds an amalgam of Catholicism, folk lore and the first dramatic representation of Aboriginal double-consciousness. The form is deceptively simple—a dramatised Dickensian fable. It is a form invented by someone who knew nothing about the theatre but understood the communicative power of emotion. Ruby and Sweet William speak tellingly of the great gap between dreams and achievement for those at the bottom of society.

In 1975 published writing by Aboriginals was still relatively rare but the time was right for performance. The 1967 referendum in favour of Commonwealth responsibility for Aboriginal welfare; the related civil rights movement with its freedom rides, its Aboriginal Embassy and street theatre; had raised the issues of Aboriginal health and civil rights to a national level. Merritt's manuscript was quickly taken up by a group creating a Black theatre in Sydney's Redfern; and moved on to further production. Merritt became the first Aboriginal playwright to enter the professional theatre.

The white bosses are caricatures with much the same purpose as the unwritten prison walls in *How Does Your Garden Grow*—to remind us there is no way out. But the Aboriginal characters are vividly alive and in the simple act of bathing the baby's eyes there is a revelation of hidden destitution which creates ripples through the whole of Australian society.

The issues of the play are now the subject of daily debate and so it can no longer draw the surprise that it did in 1975. Conditions on country missions are much more familiar to general audiences than they were then; and new writers are dealing with the deeper issues of broken families, spiritual deprivation and deaths in custody. But *The Cake Man*'s characters still have considerable emotional power; and Sweet William's final monologue, the story of the eurie woman, penetrates to the enduring need at the heart of the Mabo decision and the Wik debate; and remains one of the most compelling scenes written for the Australian theatre.

So in these four plays the authors continue the exploration of Australian society. A movement which began in the 60s by satirising and celebrating the more gaudy aspects of our language and our manners, in the years 1973–75 began to seek out the origins of our diversity—and the mood of the writers is essentially one of exploration of the past and present; a balancing act in which recognition of change and the need for change is accompanied by a warning of loss if too much is swept away too quickly. It was a rich period, and included John Romeril's *The Floating World* (1974), which examined the moral conflict faced by many ex-servicemen about trade relations with Japan; David Williamson's *What If You Died Tomorrow* (1973) which deals most overtly with the domestic impact of social change; and *The Department* (1974) about changing academic politics; and Dorothy Hewett's *The Tatty Hollow Story* (1973), a critique of the kind of male construction of women against which Coralie rebels. Unfairly, it is the nature of publication to be a more lasting record of theatre than performance can be; and this selection is only a small reflection of this exciting period. But the themes of Irish immigration, Aboriginal despair, prison culture and the rise of feminism, make not a bad small snapshot of how Australians were looking at themselves in the first half of the 1970s.

A Hard God

Peter Kenna

Peter Kenna (1930–87) was one of thirteen children brought up in an Irish Catholic family in the working-class Sydney suburb of Balmain. A radio and stage actor, he first attracted national attention as a writer in 1959 when *The Slaughter of St Teresa's Day* won a General Motors-Holden National Playwriting Competition. He moved to London in the 60s where he wrote *Talk to the Moon* and *Muriel's Virtues*. He returned to live in Sydney in 1971 debilitated by a chronic illness. Nevertheless the 70s proved to be his most fruitful decade during which he wrote *Listen Closely, Mates, Trespassers Will Be Prosecuted* and *The Cassidy Album* trilogy—*A Hard God, Furtive Love* and *An Eager Hope.*

Gloria Dawn as Aggie and Graham Rouse as Dan in the 1973 Nimrod Theatre production of A Hard God.

FIRST PERFORMANCE

A Hard God was first performed at the Nimrod Street Theatre, Sydney, on 17 August 1973 with the following cast:

DAN CASSIDY	Graham Rouse
AGGIE CASSIDY	Gloria Dawn
JACK SHANNON	Andrew Sharp
JOE CASSIDY	Tony Sheldon
MARTIN CASSIDY	Gerry Duggan
PADDY CASSIDY	Frank Gallacher
MONICA CASSIDY	Kay Eklund

Directed by John Bell
Setting designed by Larry Eastwood

For my mother and Gerald Sheedy

CHARACTERS

DAN CASSIDY
JOE CASSIDY
AGGIE CASSIDY
JACK SHANNON
MARTIN CASSIDY
PADDY CASSIDY
MONICA CASSIDY

The voice of SOPHIE CASSIDY, Paddy's wife, is heard offstage.

Note: The three brothers in the play speak with light Irish accents. This is the result of being isolated with Irish-born parents during their childhood.

SETTING

The action of the play takes place in the living room of the Cassidy home in the western suburbs of Sydney, and in various locations around the area, as well as at Woy Woy, New South Wales.

The time is 1946.

The play is performed on two stages. The larger stage represents the Cassidys' living room. The other area is used exclusively by the boys in the play and represents various locations indicated in the dialogue.

The Cassidys are working-class people and their furniture and decorations are all mass-manufactured objects, yet chosen with an eye for harmony and restraint. The room is comfortable but not too tidy. People are passing through the house all the time. There is a practical window in one of the walls and a Kosi stove, which is alight in some scenes of the play. A sideboard, dining table with chairs, a lounge: the usual appointments to be found in such a setting. There is a shaded electric light hanging over the dining table.

ACT ONE

The lights rise on the living room. DAN CASSIDY *is discovered sitting in a chair on top of the dining table. He has placed part of a newspaper under the legs of the chair so that it will not mark the table. He reads the rest of the paper through a magnifying glass, holding it as close to the overhead light as possible. He whispers what he is reading as if to be doubly sure of its meaning.* DAN *is in his late fifties, a gentle, courteous man. Voices are heard offstage.* JOE CASSIDY *is saying goodnight to his mother. He enters dressed in an overcoat and looks about for his scarf. He sees it on the lounge and moves to take it up.*

JOE: Goodnight, Dadda.

DAN: [*not looking up from his paper*] Where are you going, Joe?

JOE: The Catholic Youth Organisation.

DAN: Don't be too late.

JOE: No.

He moves off. AGGIE CASSIDY *enters and stands regarding* DAN *for a moment with amused puzzlement. She is a few years younger than her husband, a sharp-tempered woman, highly sceptical of other people's motives. She worships* DAN *and obeys his commands unquestioningly.*

AGGIE: What in God's name are you doing up there, Dan?

DAN: It's this bloody eye, Aggie. I think I must be losing the sight of it.

AGGIE: You'd better get yourself off to the doctor, then.

DAN: I had to climb up here to be able to read the paper. Is this the strongest bulb you can buy?

AGGIE: It's sixty watt, same as we always get.

DAN *gets down from the table and removes the chair.*

DAN: Not even sitting up here is satisfactory.

AGGIE: I ought to go out and buy you one of those table lamps. Do you think that would help?

DAN: It might. It's like a veil in front of me. I want to keep brushing it aside.

AGGIE: I hope it's not a cataract. [*Pushing his head back and examining his eye*] I can't see anything. Take a Bex. I'll get you one.

AGGIE *moves from the room.* DAN *continues to read.*

DAN: Huh! Typhoon Lad! That bloody thing. It hasn't finished the course from last Saturday's races yet.

AGGIE *returns with a Bex APC powder and a glass of water.*

AGGIE: Here you are.

DAN: [*taking the Bex*] Thanks. I don't want the water.

> *He pours the Bex powder onto his tongue and swallows it, then throws the paper wrapping into the top of the Kosi.*

Cyril Angles tips Typhoon Lad for tomorrow.

AGGIE: That thing! It hasn't finished the course from last Saturday's races yet.

DAN: That's what I said.

AGGIE: Who to?

DAN: Myself. I was talking to myself.

AGGIE: How's your eye now?

DAN: The sight hasn't improved.

AGGIE: [*taking the paper from him*] No, and I don't suppose it will while you go on using it. You go through that paper from back to front twice a day.

DAN: I like to know what's going on.

AGGIE: Well, ask Martin when he gets here. Will he be coming from Wollongong or Warragamba?

DAN: Warragamba.

AGGIE: Yes, why should he go home to Monica when he can get three square meals and a sympathetic ear here!

DAN: I don't begrudge him either, Aggie. There isn't much for him down there in Wollongong with Monica.

AGGIE: That's hardly your fault. And anyway, from all I hear, she's never at home herself. Mass every morning, benediction at midday and the rosary at night! She'd set up house in a confessional if they'd let her.

DAN: Well, it's an unhappy state of affairs and that's a fact. She should never have married him in the first place. She had her heart set on going into the convent and she'd have been happier there.

AGGIE: The nuns ought to be grateful to Martin. Monica'd drive even them mad with her religion. Still, he ought to be in his own home. Labouring up there on Warragamba Dam. At his age!

DAN: He's as fit as a fiddle. He's flat out in his spare time too, getting that newspaper out. It sells like hot cakes, he tells me.

AGGIE: Go on! And three quarters of them up there would be reffos without a word of English between them. I'll say this for Martin: he's a first-class con man. He could sell boomerangs to the blacks.

DAN: This is all above board, Aggie.

AGGIE: [*aware she is treading on delicate ground*] Not like that property business he had in Surry Hills during the Depression.

DAN: [*hastily*] Oh, then he just got carried away with his own salesmanship.

AGGIE: That isn't how the judge put it.

DAN: [*sharply*] Let's drop the subject.

AGGIE: [*placatingly*] He was all right. They gave him that job in the prison library and he sat around writing poetry all day. He was still reading it to us six months after he got out. It was a bit like serving his sentence with him.

DAN: [*firmly*] My brother Martin is a very clever man, and I'm proud of him. You be nice to him when he gets here.

AGGIE: When have I ever been rude to him?

DAN: Well, it's more what you don't say.

AGGIE: I can't help that.

DAN: You must learn to forgive people, Aggie. Poor Martin's had a hard time of it these last few years.

AGGIE: Huh! If hard times were a recommendation, Dan, we'd be covered in medals ourselves.

DAN: We're all right now.

AGGIE: Oh yes, now we're all right. It was a marvellous war for us. You haven't been out of work a single day. I was remembering those terrible times before the war when Martin had money to burn and Paddy was coining it in that bootmaking business. They saw you walking about practically barefoot and me and the kids near starvation. Oh, every time I think of those terrible days!

DAN: It's the past, Aggie.

AGGIE: Not for me, it isn't. Not while I have to look either of them in the face and smile and put a meal on the table in front of them. I can't forget the desperation of wondering what I was going to put into our mouths each night. You know, I've never told you this, one day I went to visit Paddy's Sophie. I went at lunchtime, thinking she'd be sure to offer me something to eat. I knew that even if she did, I wouldn't enjoy it because you'd had to go off looking for work without any breakfast and I'd sent the kids to school on damper and dripping. But I needn't have worried. She ate her meal right there in front of me and never offered me a morsel. She had salmon. A big tin of Captain brand salmon. Red, not pink. She put it out on a plate and chopped up a whole white onion over it and then added vinegar. I had to sit there swallowing the saliva that kept rushing into my mouth from the smell of it. When I got out into the street again I just sat down in the gutter and cried. I thought I'd die with longing for a plate of salmon.

DAN: God! Why didn't you tell me?

AGGIE: What was the use? Could you have bought me a tin of salmon? We couldn't afford sardines.

DAN: I'd have gone out and stolen you a tin.

AGGIE: No, you wouldn't have. You're too good a Catholic. Well, now it's us that's on easy street. Martin's Monica's never out of church and Paddy's Sophie's gambled away every penny he's ever earned. You know, Dan, on some of those days during the Depression, I used to doubt that God was there. Well, I don't any more. Not when I see how their chickens have come home to roost.

DAN: You mustn't crow, Aggie.

AGGIE: I'm not crowing, Dan. I swear I haven't got a crow left in me. Those days will never be far enough away for me to feel safe from them.

DAN: We came through, that's the main thing. [*Placing his arm about her*] And, you know what, you're still a fine looking woman!

AGGIE: Oh, get away with you. Now my hair's lost all its life and the colour's gone out of my eyes. But I was pretty once. You've only got to look at our girls to see that.

DAN: [*kissing her on the cheek*] Now, remember what I asked you. Be nice to Martin when he gets here.

AGGIE: Oh, all right, I'll be nice to him. But it won't stop me boiling inside.

DAN: Boil all you like—inside.

> *They are now sitting on the sofa and fall to silence as the lights dim.*
>
> *The lights rise on the boys' area.* JACK SHANNON *enters. He walks slowly, muffled up in an overcoat, just audibly weeping.* JOE CASSIDY *enters at a brisker pace. As he passes* JACK *he glances at him, pauses, then returns.*

JOE: Hello, Jack.

> JACK *turns away quickly to hide his tears.*

Are you Jack Shannon?

> JACK *takes a handkerchief from his pocket and blows his nose.* JOE *now sees he is upset and steps away from him.*

Oh, I'm sorry.

> *Now* JACK *turns.*

JACK: What do you want?

JOE: Nothing. I'm Joe Cassidy.

JACK: [*recognising him*] Oh, yes.

JOE: I didn't mean to interrupt you.

JACK: That's all right.

JOE: I've just come from the club. We had this debate: 'The age of chivalry is not dead'. Our team won.

JACK: That's good. I had to go somewhere else tonight.

JOE: Oh.

They stand looking at each other, uncertain of what to say next. JOE CASSIDY *is sixteen, slight and rather feminine in his appearance. He is intense and desperate to be liked.* JACK SHANNON *is the same age, stockier in build and remarkably handsome. His is a brooding nature, given to sudden outbursts of extrovert behaviour.* JOE *begins to move off.*

Well... I might see you there next week.

JACK: Yeah. [*Stepping after* JOE] Do you live over that way?

JOE: Yes, we're in Denison Road.

JACK: I live round the corner with my aunt. My mother's dead.

JOE: Oh. I'm sorry.

JACK: I've been living there about three months ever since we closed our house at Parramatta. That's where I had to go tonight—to show some people around who are interested in buying it. I haven't been back there since. Well, that's why I was so upset when you came along.

JOE: I wouldn't have spoken to you if I'd known.

JACK: That's okay. I'm all right now. Now I feel like talking to someone.

They gaze at each other for another moment and then both sit as if by common consent. JOE *shivers.*

You're not cold, are you?

JOE: No.

There is a pause and then JACK *bursts into speech with the relief of uttering thoughts suppressed.*

JACK: The day my mother died she was out in the front garden planting some stocks. I was helping her. She hadn't been ill or anything, just worried. My father came back from the war shell-shocked and, boy, he really hit the bottle. Well, this day when we were out planting the stocks, she just collapsed. I managed to get her into the house and she seemed to recover. She went round writing something on bits of paper. The same thing over and over again: 'Everything for the children'. I guess it was like a will. Then she collapsed again and by the time the doctor got there she was dead. Tonight, when I went back there, those stocks she'd planted were out in bloom. I could smell them as I came round the corner of our street. That's what upset me.

There is a pause. JOE *considers.*

JOE: And... is your father all right now?

JACK: He's in a sort of military home. A few weeks after my mother died he sent us all off to the pictures and he took a blanket out into the backyard with a penknife and he cut his wrists. One of the neighbours saw him do it and she called the police. When we got home from the pictures the house was all lit up and there was an ambulance there. We had nobody to look after us after that, so they sent us off to the relatives. You won't tell anybody I told you all this, will you?

JOE: No.

JACK: My aunt won't let us talk about it. She says it's a closed book. How old are you?

JOE: Sixteen.

JACK: So am I. They've apprenticed me to a pastrycook, but I'd like to be on the land, growing things.

JOE: I want to be a writer.

JACK: Hell! You won't write down any of what I've just told you, will you?

JOE: Not if you don't want me to.

JACK: Would you like to come round to my aunt's house some time? There's nothing to do, but we could hang around.

JOE: Yes, I'd like that.

JACK: We've got a big backyard with some huge trees all round it. Or we could go over to the park.

JOE: I'm easy. When will I come?

JACK: How about tomorrow night?

JOE: Okay. What number's your house?

JACK: Twenty-three.

> There is a pause. The encounter is over but JOE would like to force more out of it, so he remains seated. JACK rises and then JOE does. JOE shakes hands with him.

JOE: Well, it's been nice meeting you again, Jack.

JACK: Sure. And listen, I won't tell anybody I told you what I did.

JOE: Neither will I.

JACK: Spit your death and cross your heart?

JOE: Spit my death and cross my heart. Ta-ta, Jack.

JACK: Ta-ta.

> They move off in opposite directions.

> The lights dim on the boys' area and rise in the living room. DAN and AGGIE are still seated. A hat flies into the room and MARTIN CASSIDY's voice is heard outside.

MARTIN: God bless this house!

> DAN indicates to AGGIE that it is she who should answer the greeting.

AGGIE: [calling] Yes, come in, Martin.

> MARTIN CASSIDY enters carrying a bulging chaff bag over his shoulder. He is the eldest of the three brothers we will meet, an expansive man, given to expressing himself in a highly original

manner. Now and again a personal devil affrights him and he shudders, moans and exclaims prayer in order to drive it away. He is without an overcoat.

MARTIN: Hello there, Missus. Hello, Dan.

DAN: Hello, Martin. I'm glad to see you.

The brothers kiss each other on the cheek.

Did you have a good trip down?

MARTIN: Listen to this, Dan.

He assumes a declamatory pose.

> The light that from the engine glows
> Splits the darkness, comes and goes.
> So do we. We're here, then gone.
> A spark! A flash! And life moves on.

[*Breaking his pose*] I composed that on the way here.

DAN: It's very true, Martin.

MARTIN: My mind's working all the time, you see. It's a dynamo. I think I've discovered perpetual motion.

DAN: It's very true, isn't it, Aggie?

AGGIE: Oh, don't ask me, Dan. I know as much about poetry as poetry knows about me. What have you got in that chaff bag, Martin?

MARTIN: It's a favour I want to ask you, Missus. I've a few papers I want to go over and I haven't the room to lay them out in my tent. I thought I might sort them here and then ask you to store them for me.

AGGIE: I suppose we can. Papers you say! There looks to be enough jumble there to fill a library.

MARTIN: It's true, I've lived a full life. Your eyes were playing up on you the last time I was down, Dan.

DAN: And they're a little worse now, Martin.

MARTIN: Parsley and carrots. I told you. Parsley and carrots. That chaff bag, Missus, holds my entire literary output. Every poem I've ever written. Every thought I've considered worthy of setting down. Copies of all my letters to the papers.

DAN: We'll guard it as though it were our own. There'll be a great deal of valuable material in that bag, Aggie.

MARTIN: Well, time will tell. Time will tell.

DAN: It's cold out tonight, Martin. Come and sit by the fire.

MARTIN: [*sitting at the table*] No, Dan, I'll be more comfortable over here. I prefer the cold. It activates the brain. I see all these people standing round with their backs to the fire. What are they doing? They're melting the fat on their kidneys!

AGGIE: [*snorting*] Melting the fat on their kidneys!

MARTIN: It's a fact, Missus. A medical fact. [*He shudders, groans, and utters his prayer.*] Oh, God forgive us our sins!

> DAN *is used to this demonstration of* MARTIN's *interior agony. He is firm with him.*

DAN: Come on now, Martin. Pull yourself together. None of that.

MARTIN: [*sighing deeply*] It's only a prayer, Dan. Pay no heed to it.

AGGIE: Have you had anything to eat, Martin?

MARTIN: Oh yes, I had something on the train.

AGGIE: Well, would you like a cup of tea?

MARTIN: I would. If it isn't too much trouble.

AGGIE: [*rising reluctantly*] No, it isn't *too* much trouble.

> DAN *glances at her, indicating caution. She exits quickly.* MARTIN *moves to a chair closer to the fire.*

MARTIN: Well, I might toast my toes for a minute, Dan. Though it's the worst thing you can do to them. The chill blains breed like rabbits.

DAN: Make yourself comfortable. How are things at the camp?

MARTIN: Hotting up somewhat, Dan. There was an attempt made to burn down my tent last week.

DAN: Get away with you!

MARTIN: Oh yes. The comrades! I'm getting a bit too troublesome, it seems. They're not having it all their own way at the union meetings any more. The other men are starting to ask questions.

DAN: Have you informed the police?

MARTIN: They know, Dan, they know. But it's difficult to prove anything unless you actually catch them at it. But, don't worry, I'll beat the bastards.

DAN: You be careful.

MARTIN: God's with me, Dan. It's his fight I'm fighting.

DAN: Then he *will* bless you.

MARTIN: [*with a sigh*] And have mercy on me. [*He shudders, groans, and utters his prayer.*] Oh, God forgive us our sins! [*Then quickly, to cover it*] Did you know they have free love in Russia, Dan?

DAN: The dirty sods! What's free love, Martin?

MARTIN: Well, it's cohabiting outside marriage.

DAN: God forgive us, I hear we've got some of that out here as well.

MARTIN: Ah, but not as a rule of law. That's the difference.

DAN: Well, you're cleverer than I am, Martin. I'll take your word for it.

MARTIN: You're very wise. I do know a legal point when I see it.

DAN: Have you been home recently?

MARTIN: No, not recently. Between you and I, it's no home for me there any more. Monica and I have had many differences of opinion and remembrance is like a disease with her. And then, since the little fellow was taken...

DAN: [*quickly*] Yes, a tragedy, Martin. A tragedy. But we won't dwell on it.

MARTIN *fishes for his wallet and removes a yellowed newspaper clipping from it.*

MARTIN: No, but I just want to show you. I keep a clipping of the details of it in my wallet always.

DAN: Why do you want to do that? That's only upsetting yourself.

MARTIN: I know it doesn't help. It's just that, sometimes, I doubt it happened; then I've got it before me in black and white. Then I'm sure.

DAN: Put it away, Martin. Put it away.

MARTIN: [*reading*] Child struck by lightning in local baths. [*He shudders, groans, and utters his prayer.*] Oh, God forgive us our sins. They found him floating there, black and broken at the bottom of the pool. Apparently, when the storm came, there was a general scramble to get out of the water and the lightning must have caught the buckle on his bathing suit. When the storm was over, one of the children diving off the high board saw him down there and gave the alarm. I don't know. Nobody knows for sure how it happened. And I could never bring myself to look at him like that. Not even after the nuns had laid him out, and the others said he seemed just like a smiling little angel, overjoyed to be free of this puzzling world. The loss of him only hit me when I saw them lowering him into the ground. Then, they tell me, I fought like a lunatic to keep him out of the hole. I don't remember any of it myself. You see, that's the reason why I have to keep this clipping. It's a blank to me otherwise. [*With a sigh*] Oh, he's a hard God, Dan. He's a hard God.

DAN: There's probably a pattern to it somewhere, Martin, if only we could see.

MARTIN: That is his hardness, Dan. He doesn't allow us to. We just have to stumble on blindly, with his mercy raining down on us like thunderbolts. [*He shudders, groans and utters his prayer.*] Oh, God forgive us our sins! [*He yawns and sinks back in his chair exhausted.*] Oh well, it will all end some day. The sun will finally set on our endeavours... some day.

He drifts off to sleep, sighing heavily. AGGIE *comes back into the room, carrying a cup of tea.*

AGGIE: [*to* MARTIN] And you weren't going to sit by the fire!

DAN: Shh! Aggie. He's asleep. He's got the miseries on him, brooding over little Christopher.

AGGIE: The poor old bugger. That was one of the chickens I mentioned.

DAN: God couldn't have meant that to happen.

AGGIE: You're forever telling me it's all God's doing.

DAN: Not that. I don't know who was responsible for that.

AGGIE: Here. Do you want his tea?

DAN: I might as well. Oh dear, Aggie, now he's given me the miseries too. They're my brothers and I love them.

AGGIE: [*kissing him on the cheek curtly*] You're a silly old fool. Drink your tea.

> *She leaves the room again.*

> *The lights dim on the living room and rise on the boys' area. Deep green shadows lie over it.* JACK *and* JOE *enter and sit close together.* JACK *looks upwards.*

JACK: It's dark back here. Those trees are so high you can't see the tops of them.

JOE: It's real private.

JACK: Listen. You can't hear anything. Have you had a good time?

JOE: Oh, sure.

JACK: [*lifting his hand again for silence*] Listen now. That same bird comes here every evening. I wish I knew what kind it was. I've enjoyed myself too. I like talking to you. I'd like to tell you a whole lot of things I never get the chance to say to anyone else.

JOE: [*delighted*] Would you?

JACK: I sure would. And, believe me, there's plenty of things. Have you ever gone all the way with a girl?

> JOE *is so surprised at the question he isn't sure he has heard correctly.*

JOE: I beg your pardon?

JACK: You know what I mean. Have you ever had a real root?

JOE: [*indignantly*] No. That's an awful way to talk, Jack.

JACK: [*laughing*] Well, I'll make an act of contrition before I go to sleep tonight. I enjoy saying things like that, but I never get the chance to. I can't say things like that to my aunt.

JOE: You shouldn't want to talk like that to anybody.

JACK: Why not?

JOE: Because it's wrong. You know it is.

JACK: [*laughing again and placing his arm about* JOE] Oh, aren't you a little saint!

JOE: [*shaking his arm off*] If you keep on saying things like that I'll have to go home.

JACK: Calm down. I was only trying to get you going.

JOE: What for?

JACK: I don't know, when I get to like somebody I enjoy teasing them.

JOE: Well, I'm glad you weren't serious.

JACK: Oh, yes I was. I went all the way with this girl in the bush at Parramatta.

JOE: Then you ought to be ashamed of yourself.

JACK: Well, it was mostly her fault, if that will make you feel any better.

JOE: It's got nothing to do with me.

JACK: I was just walking along the road and she came out from behind a tree. She went to the same school as I did. She lifted up her dress and she didn't have any bloomers on. Then she walked back into the bush and I followed her. Oh boy!

JOE: I don't want to hear about it. You shouldn't be telling me.

JACK: You didn't mind me telling you about my mother dying.

JOE: That was different.

JACK: Go on, I'll bet you would have enjoyed it as much as I did.

JOE: I would not. I hate that sort of thing.

JACK: Why? Aren't you interested in girls?

JOE: No. Yes. I mean, not like that.

JACK: It doesn't surprise me. If you ask me you're a bit of a girl yourself. You toss your head and get all huffy.

JOE: [*rising*] Now I *am* going home.

> JACK *laughs and drags him back to the ground.*

JACK: I'm sorry. I'm sorry. I didn't mean it.

JOE: You did. I bet I've taken out more girls than you.

JACK: And did you kiss them goodnight?

JOE: Of course I did. There's nothing wrong in that.

JACK: And you never wanted to do anything else?

JOE: No. I don't think that's necessary.

JACK: Well, you're going to have to do it some day.

JOE: When I'm married it'll be different.

JACK: How?

JOE: Well... it will be. You're not supposed to do that to people until you *are* married.

JACK: Then there must be something terribly wrong with me. Most of the time I want to go all the way with every girl I look at. To tell you the truth, I've got a horn on right now.

JOE: Jack! I asked you not to talk like that.

JACK: [*placing his arm about him again*] Oh, come on, let me. I enjoy sitting here with you talking about going all the way. It's almost as good as the real thing.

He places his other arm about JOE *and holds him fast. He kisses him sloppily on the cheek.*

Umm! Wow!

JOE: Don't be a fool.

JOE *struggles to be free.*

JACK: But I like you. It's no use struggling. I'm much stronger than you are.

JOE: You're just making fun of me. I'm sorry I came here and I won't come here ever again.

JACK: [*squeezing him tighter*] Yes you will. Say you will.

JOE: No. You're going to have to confess, saying things like you said tonight. I'll have to confess for listening to you.

JACK: Okay. We'll both confess together.

JOE: You've got to be truly sorry for your sins.

JACK: Well, I will be… then.

JOE: Let me go, Jack. Please.

JACK: I will if you'll take back what you said about not coming here any more.

JOE: Okay. I'll take it back. I'll come again.

JACK: And you've got to admit something else.

JOE: What?

JACK: You've got to admit you like me.

JOE: I've already told you I like you, haven't I?

JACK: Then you've got to tell me you think I'm good-looking.

JOE: I don't notice whether other boys are good-looking.

JACK: I think you're good-looking. Would I be sitting here with my arms around you if I didn't think you were? Now you tell me I'm good-looking.

JOE: No.

JACK: Go on. I'll give you a wrist burn if you don't.

JOE: No.

JACK: All right. You asked for it.

He grips JOE's *wrist and applies a wrist burn: pressure applied by the hands squeezing in opposite directions.*

JOE: No, Jack, don't! Ouch!

JACK: Come on. All you've got to admit is that I'm good-looking and I'll let you go.

JOE: No. Oww! You're hurting. All right! I'll admit it. You are.

JACK: Are what?

JOE: Good-looking.

JACK *releases him.* JOE *rubs his wrist.*

JACK: You see, it wasn't so difficult to say, was it?

JOE: It doesn't count. I'd have said anything to stop you hurting me.

JACK: [*menacingly*] You mean you don't think I'm good-looking?

JOE: Yes! Yes! I said it, didn't I?

JACK: Then let's have another big hug.

He squeezes JOE *again.* JOE *struggles to be free.*

JOE: Jack, suppose someone came out of the house. What would they think if they saw us?

JACK: They'd think we liked each other. And we do, don't we?

JOE *is silent.* JACK *squeezes him tighter.*

Don't we?

JOE: Oww! Yes! Yes!

JOE *stops struggling and resigns himself to* JACK*'s attentions.*

JACK: It's nice and warm together like this. I can hear your heart beating. Can you hear my heart?

JOE: Yes.

JACK: That other time, when I went all the way with that girl at Parramatta, it was like we'd quarrelled and were taking it out on each other. It wasn't quiet like this. I think I like this better.

JOE: Well, I don't.

JACK: How do you know? You told me you'd never done the other thing. [*Squeezing him again*] Or have you been lying to me?

JOE: No! No! Oh, Jack, I'm scared someone's going to come out of the house.

JACK *releases him and turns away sullenly.*

JACK: Oh, okay. You're a real spoilsport. You don't seem to enjoy anything much.

JOE: I do.

JACK: I'm telling you, you don't.

JOE: Now don't you get huffy. [*As* JACK *continues to sulk*] Listen, you're not threatening to give me a wrist burn now, are you? I'll tell you, I do think you're good-looking.

JACK: Arr, now I don't know whether to believe you or not. You might be only trying to humour me.

JOE: No, I'm not. Honestly. I've had a real good time tonight and I don't blame you even if you did try to push me around.

JACK: I didn't push you around. Getting you to like me isn't trying to push you around, is it?

JOE: No.

JACK: Well then!

JOE: [*rising reluctantly*] Listen, Jack, I really do have to go now. When am I going to see you again?

JACK: I don't know. I'm going up to Woy Woy in a couple of weeks' time.

JOE: Not for good?

JACK: Just a holiday. My aunt says I'm acting a bit strange because of what I've been through and that I need a change.

JOE: Are you going by yourself?

JACK: Sure. You think I can't take care of myself?

JOE: I didn't mean that.

JACK: We used to go up to Woy Woy every holidays when my mother was with us and my father was okay. Hey! Why don't you come up there with me?

JOE: Gee, I'd like that, Jack. But I don't know whether I could get off work.

JACK: You could say you were sick, couldn't you?

JOE: I don't know. That wouldn't be honest.

JACK: Well, if you don't want to come.

JOE: Look, I would like to. I'll try.

JACK: I'm going to hire a boat. We could go right into Gosford in it.

JOE: It sounds terrific.

JACK: You mean it? You really would like to come?

JOE: Yes! Yes! How many times do I have to tell you?

JACK: Well, I believe you now.

> *He rises and moves to embrace* JOE *again.* JOE *steps back.*

JOE: No, Jack, no. I do have to go. Walk across the park with me.

JACK: Okay.

> *He quickly crooks his arm through* JOE's *arm, holding him tightly.*

And if anybody asks me what I think I'm doing, I'll tell them you're my steady.

> JACK *endeavours to move off, but* JOE *will not budge.*

JOE: Oh, Jack, don't. You'll make a show of me.

JACK: [*tugging him*] Come on. You wanted to walk across the park with me, didn't you?

JOE: Not if you're going to make a fool of me.

JACK: I wouldn't make a fool of you. You're my steady. You've told me I'm good-looking.

JOE: But—

JACK: You don't know what you want from one minute to the next. You're scared of everything.

JOE: I'm not.

JACK: [*tugging him forward*] Then come on.

JOE: Jack!

They exit.

The lights die on their area and rise in the living room. MARTIN *is still asleep,* DAN *still in his chair.* DAN *rises and, as quietly as possible, pours coke into the Kosi from a scuttle.* PADDY CASSIDY *appears in the doorway. He is a small, sharp man. His eyes dance about in anticipation of a threat. He is argumentative and a coward. At the moment he is in a dishevelled condition and is also without an overcoat. He calls across to* DAN *in a whisper.*

PADDY: Hey! Ssst! Dan!

DAN: Oh, hello, Paddy.

PADDY: [*motioning him to be quiet*] Sophie hasn't been here, has she?

DAN: You know very well she never comes here.

PADDY: [*relaxing into a state of desperation*] Holy Jesus, today she could be anywhere. She's turned on me again, Dan. I've been running in fear of my life all afternoon, skulking from one place to another till I'm exhausted.

DAN: [*shaking his head sorrowfully*] Oh, Paddy!

PADDY: [*seeing* MARTIN *and jolting to attention again*] Who's that? Martin?

DAN: Yes. He's just got in from Warragamba. Talk quietly so we don't wake him. What started Sophie off this time?

PADDY: I don't know. It comes over her like a fever. She'll go to bed as meek as a mouse and get up the next morning a gambling devil, raging for the booze.

DAN: Oh dear, oh dear! Poor Sophie!

PADDY: Never mind about poor bloody Sophie! What about me? I'm at my wits' end. I've done all I can to content her. I signed over control of everything I own to her because she said I didn't trust her and it made her unhappy. She promised me then she'd never throw another dice or turn another card. Oh God! The shop! All that valuable bootmaking equipment! Even the house! It's all hers and it'll all go.

DAN: It was a silly thing to do, knowing there was even a chance she might break out again. I told you at the time not to do it.

PADDY: Yes, Dan, yes. I know how stupid it was. But how could I help it? I love her.

DAN: For Heaven's sake, what's that got to do with it?

PADDY: I can't resist her. She winds those tiny hands through my hair and buries her head in my shoulder... I'd give her the world if I owned it. I'm mad on her and she's mad on gambling.

DAN: You've got to put your foot down. Give her a good belting.

PADDY: No, I'd never lay a finger on her. I'd as soon strike myself.

DAN: Then things are never going to be any different.

PADDY: I thought there was something funny about her when we got up this morning. She was dragging herself round with a kind of angry weariness. Slapping at the taps in the bathroom, kicking the floor mats out of her path. She perked up a bit when the boys came down to breakfast. You can say what you like about her, Dan. She loves those boys! Well, they went off to school and then her mood changed again. She was like... furtive. Looking at me out of the corner of her eye and humming to herself quietly. All I could do was cross my fingers and hope for the best. I opened up the shop and began to work. She usually calls me for a cup of tea about ten, but this morning, not a peep out of her. I started to get worried so I went back into the house and fft! She was gone. My next stop was the old tea caddy where she keeps the money for the household accounts. Fft! That was gone too. I knew then the worst had happened and there was nothing else for it but to shut up the shop and go looking for her. Well, I tramped here and I tramped there. Ryan's in Neville Street, The Stockman's Rest down by the Strand. She wasn't in any of her old haunts. Then, as luck would have it, I ran into a bloke who'd just finished playing cards with her in a poker game down at this Col Morgan's place. He told me she was losing heavily and playing on IOU's, so I rushed round to where he told me the place was. And there she is sitting at a big table surrounded by men, a cigarette in the corner of her mouth and no two cards even remotely alike in her hand. I moved in behind her and whispered very gentle like: 'Sophie, dear, I think you've had enough now. I think it's time you came home.' Well! She turned to me and I could see she'd been drinking as well as losing. Her eyes were puffed up and her teeth were crooked in her mouth. 'Who are you?' she snarls, making out she'd never seen me before. 'You know very well who I am, Sophie,' I replies. 'Come along now, you've had enough.' 'I'll say I have,' she says. 'Enough of you and the same bloody things day in and day out. And tell me something else, where's my girlhood gone?' Where's her girlhood gone! What a question to ask me. She goes through twenty dresses a year and expects her girlhood to be in its place when she turns around to look for it. Then she gave me a dressing down that would have done credit to a wharf labourer. The obscenity was breathtaking. And all the trollops and the bludgers there were cackling like cracked bells in a slow hurricane. I didn't care about the consequences by then, I just had to get out of it. And when I got back to the house I was all in. I fell down on my bed and went to sleep. I suppose I woke up about two hours later, and as I opened my eyes, I could hear this ripping sound. And that's what it was. Sophie was standing in front of the wardrobe, with a cut-throat razor in her hand, slashing all my clothes to shreds. I jumped up to take it from her and she turned on me with it. I tell you, Dan, if she'd connected just once, I'd be lying there on the floor now, bloodless and lifeless. Fortunately she was still a bit drunk and unsteady on her feet. At one swish I ducked under her arm, down the stairs and out into the street. And her after me. I ran for my life but never seemed to lose her. You'd have thought she was attached to me by a string. When I looked back I could see the sun glinting on that razor and, I tell you, I broke every track record until I lost her. Since then I've been moving on regardless, until I dared come here.

AGGIE *enters.* PADDY *has his back to her.*

AGGIE: Hello, Paddy.

PADDY: [*leaping with alarm*] Jesus, Mary and Joseph!

DAN: Quiet now, you'll wake Martin.

PADDY: It was you creeping up on me like that, Aggie. I'm moving in terror of my life.

DAN: It's Sophie, Aggie. She's broken out again.

AGGIE: Oh. I'd break her out again if I was in charge of her.

PADDY: Dan, what if she goes back to the card game with the proof she owns everything and they start accepting more IOU's?

DAN: Well, all you can do is go down there again and tell them not to accept them.

PADDY: And have my throat cut! What use will my property be to me then?

DAN: You've got to do something.

PADDY: How can I ever go home again! I'd be afraid to close my eyes for fear I'd open them only to see the razor descending on me.

AGGIE: She threatened you with a razor?

PADDY: She chased me all over the streets with it. It was like a dangerous comic strip.

AGGIE: Go to the police. Ask them to bring her under control.

PADDY: The police! Do you think I want everyone to know? I'm ashamed enough as it is. If I brought charges against her it'd be in all the papers. What would the Christian Brothers say where the boys go to school?

AGGIE: If she kills you, she'll hang. Then what will the Christian Brothers say?

PADDY: I couldn't! I couldn't turn her in like that.

MARTIN *stirs in his sleep. They all pause.*

DAN: Quiet, Paddy! Listen, when Martin does wake, don't tell him anything about this. He's got troubles of his own.

PADDY: No, I don't want Martin to know. Aggie, do you think... would you mind if I stayed here tonight? I'm not worried about where I sleep. I'll doss down by the fire.

AGGIE: What about the boys? Who's going to take care of them if you stay here and Sophie's out gambling?

PADDY: Oh, she'll arrange something about that. She's a good mother, Aggie, you can say what you like about her as a wife.

AGGIE: I don't trust myself to say anything.

DAN: Aggie! That's enough now.

AGGIE: All right, Paddy, you can stay the night. Just as you like.

    MARTIN *stirs again.*

DAN: Sshh!

    MARTIN *opens his eyes and looks about.*

MARTIN: Oh, hello, Paddy. You're here.

PADDY: I'm sorry if our talking woke you up, Martin.

MARTIN: No, no, I wasn't asleep. Just deep in thought. Are you keeping well?

PADDY: Oh yes, fine.

MARTIN: And your pretty little Sophie?

PADDY: In full flower, Martin.

MARTIN: Ah, God be praised. We don't see enough of each other. You're still keeping to the Mass, I hope?

PADDY: We never miss a Sunday. Or a holy day of obligation. The priests remark on it.

MARTIN: Good, good. Our religion is a great inheritance, boys. Our poor old Dad and Mother didn't have much to pass on to us, but that was the most precious of their gifts.

DAN: Indeed it was, Martin.

MARTIN: And they regarded it as such. Will you ever forget those evening rosaries in the old homestead?

PADDY: I'll never forget them. [*To* AGGIE] Father used to make us kneel as straight as ramrods on the hard stone floor. One sag at the knees and you'd catch it across the shoulders with the buggy-whip he held in the hand that wasn't dangling the beads. How he could watch us and concentrate on the Hail Marys was always a wonder to me.

MARTIN: It was discipline, Paddy. Discipline. And it didn't do us any harm. Think how we could work in the fields from our earliest years. We were proud in our vigour.

PADDY: Yes. Until that drought cut us down to size.

MARTIN: Oh God! We'd have been there yet, lords of the land and rich, if it hadn't been for that drought.

DAN: Two long years!

PADDY: And it lasted another year and a half after we went. We could never have seen it through.

MARTIN: Funny, it's just occurred to me, I was thinking about the drought and Dad and Mother while I was sitting here—meditating. I must have had like a dream. It was confused but part of it made sense. We were all back on the property, but not young men like we were then. Middle-aged as we are now. We had to leave again because of the drought but this time we were forced to take everything with us. Not only the bit of stock that was left and the timber that made up the houses and sheds, but even the shrubs and vegetables we'd tried to grow. Not a trace of us was to remain on that land. It was to be as if we'd never turned a furrow. Oh, the misery of it! Mother was giving instructions for the move. Walking about swatting the flies away with that little cane fan she always carried.

DAN: Oh, I'd forgotten that fan!

MARTIN: The main thing she was concerned about was that Father would remember to dig up her coffin and take it with us. She was dead but alive again, if you know what I mean. Well, that faded and then I was standing on a hill overlooking the desolation all about us. Awestruck by its beauty. The cracked earth and the sand blowing in among the withered trees! It was the same feeling I always had when I looked over the land in the good years, when the well was pumping and the grass green and thick underfoot; and the blacks bringing in wild honey to exchange for flour. Ah! Dreams are peculiar things!

DAN: I often regret the loss of the old place. I don't mind admitting my eyes fill with tears when I consider it. But I never dream about it.

PADDY: Maybe we could have held on through the drought—but when Mother died! We all seemed to lose heart after that.

DAN: God love the little lady, she *was* our heart.

MARTIN: I remember thinking at the time we left we should have been taking her body with us. It was dreadful having to leave it there in unconsecrated ground. Perhaps that's what my dream was about.

AGGIE: [*to* MARTIN] Did you go *straight* up north after you left the property?

MARTIN: Yes. Paddy and Father and me. We left him with Kate in Brisbane.

DAN: I headed east. Shearing, droving, fencing... [*Considering* AGGIE *fondly*] Until I came to Narrabri.

He takes her hand. She returns his loving gaze.

AGGIE: Yes.

MARTIN: We struck things plushy up among the bananas and the mangoes didn't we, Paddy? In a few years we'd made all the money we needed to give ourselves a start when we got down here.

DAN: Things became worse where we were. We *had* to come to the city. There was at least the possibility of work here.

AGGIE: And didn't we hate it! It seemed lonelier than the scrub. And then the Depression hit us.

MARTIN: [*expansively*] Oh, it wasn't so bad for Paddy and me. Businesses were going cheap then. It was just the time to buy in.

> PADDY *sees the change in* AGGIE'*s face and clears his throat loudly.* MARTIN *glances at him and sizes up the situation. His manner becomes suddenly doleful.*

Oh... even though we had to use every penny of our capital to do it.

PADDY: I know I ran myself into debt to get into that bootmaking shop.

MARTIN: Yes, they were difficult times. Difficult times for us all.

AGGIE: [*almost spitting the words*] I'm sure they were.

> DAN *looks at her startled. He now grasps the situation.*

DAN: Aggie, my eyes are starting to hurt again. Have you got another Bex in the house?

AGGIE: I'll see if I can find one.

> *She marches out of the room.* DAN *speaks to his brothers confidentially.*

DAN: Boys, I don't think it's wise to go on talking about the Depression while Aggie's here. It upsets her.

PADDY: I did think she sounded a bit sharpish just then, Dan.

DAN: Well, those times were terrible for everybody.

PADDY: I don't know how any of us came through.

MARTIN: Now, Paddy, I must say this. I'm the eldest and it's my duty. I did think at the time you might have given *some* assistance to Dan and the Missus. All the little children they had to feed and Dan making himself ill looking for work.

PADDY: That's very unfair of you, Martin. And you must know it. Didn't I show you my account books when you raised the matter with me then?

DAN: Don't let's go into all that again, boys. Leave it be.

PADDY: No, Dan, it's something that has to be cleared up. I showed Martin my books, accounting for every penny I owned. And it was all tied up.

MARTIN: Yes, with sending your oldest boys to the most expensive school in Sydney.

PADDY: And what about you? Monica had a maid in the house.

MARTIN: Of course she had a maid. She was a lady. How could she do without a maid? She'd never learned anything about cooking or cleaning.

PADDY: She seemed to pick it up quick enough when you was in gaol. Then she was on her beam ends.

MARTIN: Don't you dare bring Monica's beam ends into this conversation.

DAN: Please! Be quiet the both of you. Don't start a quarrel.

PADDY: Well, he's only trying to make things difficult between us, Dan. He was always trying to do that.

DAN: Look, I must say this. Aggie wouldn't have minded so much if either of you had asked us over for a meal occasionally. There were times we had to sit here and listen to the children crying with hunger.

PADDY: [*genuinely sorry*] Oh, terrible! Terrible.

MARTIN *has been brooding. Now he turns on* PADDY *again.*

MARTIN: It's like your bloody cheek to go slinging that miscarriage of justice up at me.

PADDY: I didn't say you was guilty of it, did I? I just said that Monica didn't have to have a maid.

MARTIN: How would you know what Monica needed or didn't need? You haven't the slightest idea of what a lady is.

DAN: It's of no consequence any more.

PADDY: Oh, no? And what do you think I'm married to then?

MARTIN: Sophie Rigby? Oh, she's a nice enough little girl, Paddy. I'm not degrading her. But you could hardly call Sophie Rigby a lady.

PADDY: She is indeed. You bloody well take that back.

DAN: Boys! Boys!

MARTIN: Don't be ridiculous.

PADDY: She's every bit as fine a lady as your Monica. Her manners is something beautiful. To see her eat is like watching a play on the stage.

MARTIN: Yes. A comedy.

PADDY: What! I'm warning you to watch your tongue, Martin Cassidy, or you'll find reason to wish you had.

MARTIN: Oh, really now?

PADDY: Yes, really! Another word from you about my Sophie and I'll—

DAN: Stop it. Stop this!

MARTIN: You'll what?

AGGIE *re-enters. They all pause.*

AGGIE: What's going on in here?

MARTIN *and* PADDY *become shamefaced.*

DAN: Nothing, Aggie, nothing. Just a little difference of opinion. Have you got the Bex?

AGGIE: It's a bit old but it's the only one I could find.

PADDY: [*with exaggerated concern*] Have you got a headache, Dan?

AGGIE: [*sharply*] It's his eyes playing up again.

DAN: I'll be all right.

He shakes the Bex onto his tongue and swallows it.

MARTIN: Poor Dan! You was never a strong fellow.

AGGIE: He's had to be strong. Nothing's ever come easy to Dan.

DAN: That'll fix me.

AGGIE: [*to* PADDY] I thought you weren't going to say anything to Martin about Sophie.

PADDY: [*quickly*] We weren't talking about that, Aggie.

MARTIN: Talking about what?

DAN: Leave it be, Martin. You've no need to concern yourself.

MARTIN: Well, if it's something I ought to know about!

DAN: Paddy had a bit of a disagreement with Sophie, that's all.

AGGIE: [*to* PADDY] I'm sorry. I thought that's what you was talking about when I came in.

MARTIN: Well, she always did have a bit of a temper, didn't she, Paddy? If I remember rightly she was fighting tooth and nail with you at the wedding reception.

PADDY: That was nothing. Nothing at all. A bit of a misunderstanding over where her people were to sit.

MARTIN: She was shouting at the top of her voice about it. She smashed a plate, she brought down a fork on it so hard.

PADDY: That never happened at all. Or if it did, it was an accident. They tell me Monica never went near you while you was in gaol.

DAN: Paddy! Martin!

MARTIN: Because I told her not to. So now you know the truth about that. If Monica's name passes your lips once more—

PADDY: Then you lay off Sophie.

MARTIN: I wouldn't go near her!

PADDY: [*moving toward the door*] Come on, outside then! Let's settle this outside.

MARTIN: [*stepping towards* PADDY] Right!

DAN: [*between them*] Sit down, the both of you. You're not going anywhere. This is my house and you'll behave yourself in it.

PADDY: Don't try and stop me, Dan. I can teach this fella something. Nothing's ever as good as the thing he's got.

MARTIN: Monica—a thing!

> MARTIN *nudges* PADDY *further toward the door.* AGGIE *keeps a straight face but her eyes express a kind of pleasure at their falling out.*

Well, I suppose I *will* have to teach you a bit of respect. Into the backyard!

DAN: Martin! Paddy! Don't be stupid.

PADDY: [*beginning to remove his coat*] I don't know whether I can wait to get into the backyard.

> *The strident voice of a woman is heard calling offstage. This is* SOPHIE CASSIDY *and she is drunk.*

SOPHIE: [*off*] Paddy Cassidy! Are you in there?

PADDY: [*turning to* AGGIE *imploringly*] Holy Jesus, Aggie, it's Sophie! Where can I hide?

AGGIE: You stay right where you are.

PADDY: But she might still have that razor with her.

MARTIN: Oh, so it was a bit of a disagreement with a razor, was it? Personally speaking, I never allow Monica to carry one.

PADDY: Oh, don't mock me now, Martin. This is serious.

SOPHIE: [*off*] Paddy Cassidy! Are you coming out here or do I have to come in there and get you?

AGGIE: [*moving to the window*] I'll settle that lady down.

PADDY: Oh, don't say anything that might make her worse, Aggie. She'll only take it out on me later.

DAN: Yes. There's Paddy to consider, Aggie.

AGGIE: Paddy's got nothing to do with it. She's in front of my house now. [*Throwing open the window and calling to* SOPHIE] Sophie Cassidy! You go along about your business or I'll come out there and send you along.

SOPHIE: [*off*] I want to speak to the organ grinder not his monkey. Who asked you to poke your nose into this?

AGGIE: [*calling*] If there's a bad smell outside my door I've got every right to poke my nose into it.

PADDY: [*whimpering*] Oh, God! She'll be as black as thunder after that salvo.

DAN: Aggie! No more of that now.

SOPHIE: [*off*] I want to talk to my husband.

AGGIE: [*calling*] Well, he doesn't want to talk to you.

PADDY: Don't let her know I'm here!

AGGIE: [*calling*] Always supposing he's here, which I'm not saying he is.

SOPHIE: [*off*] Ha! Where else would he run to when he wants to hide behind a woman's skirts?

AGGIE: [*calling*] Certainly not to his wife! Now, get away from here and leave us decent people alone.

SOPHIE: [*off*] Decent people! You know what you can do with your decency. You can shove it right up your arses.

PADDY: Oh God! Oh God! I'm going to die of humiliation.

MARTIN: Well, she mightn't be a lady, but she certainly knows how to curse.

DAN: It's appalling!

AGGIE: [*calling*] If you're not careful I'll have the police onto you and you can play cards in the cells all night.

SOPHIE: [*off*] Thanks all the same, I've got a card game to go to.

AGGIE: [*calling*] Yes, and buttons to play with, I suppose.

SOPHIE: [*off*] Does this look like buttons?

AGGIE: [*quietly*] Good God! Look at that.

PADDY: What is it?

AGGIE: She's shaking a wad of notes at me bigger than a Sunday second collection.

PADDY: Where'd she get it? Ask her where she got it.

AGGIE: [*calling again*] A fool and her money are soon parted.

SOPHIE: [*off*] Not this time, dearie. This is just what I won when I went back to the game this afternoon. I'm out to double it tonight, so you tell that husband of mine to go home and see to our boys. Tell him to expect me when he sees me. Oh, and if he dares set foot in that place again to jinx me, tell him I won't go for his throat this time... I'll go for his balls!

PADDY: [*falling to his knees and imploring Heaven*] Oh, St Anthony of Padua!

MARTIN: Get up off the floor, Paddy. It's not *his* balls you have to worry about.

DAN: Shut the window, Aggie.

AGGIE: [*shutting the window*] She's gone anyway. You're going to have to end up having her certified, Paddy.

PADDY: How much did it look like she had in her hand, Aggie?

AGGIE: Oh, there were fivers and tenners! I didn't see a green one or a ten bob in the whole bunch.

PADDY: And you can be sure she'll lose it all again. Anyway, I'll be able to go home to my own bed after all.

AGGIE: It's disgraceful when a man has to worry about whether he can go home to his own bed!

PADDY: Oh now, you mustn't think too badly of her, Aggie. She's not responsible for the way she behaves when the gambling fever gets a hold of her.

MARTIN: He's right, Missus. I've seen it often in the camps. I'm sorry for all those hard things I said to you, Paddy.

DAN: God bless you, Martin! And Paddy's sorry too. Aren't you, Paddy?

PADDY: I am, Martin. Truly sorry.

DAN: That's it, boys. Kiss and make up.

> PADDY *and* MARTIN *kiss each other on the cheek.* DAN *joins them and they all hold each other for a moment.*

For after all, no matter what happens, we must all stick together.

PADDY: If I had any idea of what's happened to change her! That ugly woman, ranting and screaming outside the window, has got nothing to do with the sweet little creature I married, who'd blush and hide her face if anyone so much as said 'damn' in her company.

MARTIN: It's a puzzle all right, Paddy. My own personal opinion is that it's got something to do with time.

PADDY: Time, Martin?

MARTIN: Yes. It's a big thing to consider.

PADDY: All I know about time is that it comes and goes too quickly.

MARTIN: I believe it's like a germ we're breathing in continually. Like the 'flu. Except that everybody catches it. And some catch it worse than others. And it affects them in different ways.

PADDY: Yes, yes. That could be it. Sophie's suffering from a bad attack of time.

AGGIE: Time! You do talk a lot of nonsense, Martin.

DAN: Now, Aggie, don't you dismiss what Martin says. He's a very clever man. He ought to know about such things.

AGGIE: People change, that's all. And Sophie Cassidy's changed for the worst.

MARTIN: The Missus is entitled to her point of view as well, Dan. We've got to grant her that.

DAN *presses his eyes.*

AGGIE: Are your eyes still hurting, Dan?

DAN: It'll pass, Aggie.

PADDY: And then again, it could be coming to the city that's changed Sophie. Certainly the city changed all our lives. None of us are the same people we were in the bush.

DAN: That's true too, Paddy. Things were much simpler there. There weren't as many decisions to be made. If you had a crop to sow there was a time to do it and that was the only time. It either rained or it didn't. And when the crop ripened you harvested it. When Aggie and I came to Sydney, I quickly learned you had to walk cautiously. A man could turn you down for a job because he didn't like the way you talked or on a whim that didn't mean anything. You had to be cunning if you wanted to survive. And you had to survive. That's how the city altered us all.

PADDY: The bloody city!

MARTIN: Oh yes, the bush! When the crop was harvested, do you remember those Saturday night dances, boys? The word went out and it was understood everybody was to be there. If you played an instrument you brought it with you and, if you didn't, you collected a few gum leaves on the way. And when everybody danced, the dust rose up off the floor and they had to open the windows. And then all the insects of the night swarmed into the light. And the girls cried because they'd spent the entire day starching their petticoats and ironing the ruffles on their dresses. And we'd been at it for hours as well, scrubbing our toes and plastering our hair down. But another reel came up and the dust and the insects were forgotten.

PADDY: We were the most popular boys in the district, Aggie. Dan played the piano by ear and Martin sang like a lyrebird.

DAN: And what about your jig, Paddy? They'd clear the floor for you and clap their hands until you fell exhausted.

> MARTIN *begins humming and tapping his foot. Gradually* PADDY *falls into a jig. It isn't rowdy: a quiet little dance of memory, almost inside the head. It fades to nothing.*

MARTIN: Oh, those days!

PADDY: And if it hadn't been for that drought we'd be there still. Lords of the land!

DAN: The bloody drought!

MARTIN: Well... maybe we would have left anyway.

PADDY: Never!

MARTIN: That's another of the effects of time. You breathe in time and it gives you the wanderlust.

AGGIE: I always hoped I'd never have to leave Narrabri. Every person I knew in the world lived there. But Dan had to go where the work was. We couldn't sit and starve. So we came to Sydney and went into that residential. A pokey little room in Surry Hills with the use of a kitchen! Oh, it was awful. The kids weren't allowed to do this and you weren't allowed to go there. We'd all been used to running free and now we were harnessed. And lonely! Dan seemed to be away from earliest morning until late at night, either looking for a job or labouring at one. Like I said, I didn't know a soul and not a soul seemed to want to know me. I remember one day I couldn't bear it any more. I decided to go for a long walk. Bernard was the eldest. I left him in charge of the others and I made up my mind to go straight and not turn any corners so that there wouldn't be a chance of my getting lost. Well, I suppose I got gawking at the people in cabs and the things in shop windows, and unbeknown to myself I wandered into Oxford Street. Suddenly I didn't have any idea of where I was. It was as if I'd been picked up and dumped down in some other country. I was sure I'd never see Dan and the kids again. I was too frightened to ask the people passing by where I was. All the men looked like brutes and the women had rouge on their cheeks. Finally I came to the Sacred Heart and I went inside. But the only sign of a priest was a light over a confessional. So I went in there. The poor fella got such a shock. After I'd blessed myself and said that bit about, 'Forgive me, Father, for I have sinned,' I burst into tears and sobbed: 'Can you tell me the way back to Crown Street?' Oh, but he was very nice about it. He came right out of the box and called to one of the boys in the schoolyard and got him to take me all the way home to my door. Of course it was a long time after that before I went out by myself again.

PADDY: Yes, there was fear in the city all right. And confusion too. In a way, all these years, it's been like an exile.

MARTIN: Oh, they were grand days when we were young before...

He pauses. They all lose themselves in reverie for a moment. PADDY *breaks the spell.*

PADDY: Well, I suppose it's time I was going home. I must see to the boys and I'm dead tired. [*Kissing his brothers*] Goodnight, Dan. Goodnight, Martin.

MARTIN: Goodnight, Dan. Goodnight, Missus.

AGGIE: Goodnight, Martin.

AGGIE *and* DAN *leave the room.* AGGIE *turns the light out as she goes.* MARTIN *settles down in his chair.*

MARTIN: Ah, time! Time! Time!

DAN: Goodnight, Paddy.

MARTIN: If I said anything unkind...

PADDY: It's forgotten. It's forgotten. Goodbye, Aggie.

AGGIE: Goodbye, Paddy.

PADDY *exits.*

[*To* DAN] We'd better be off to bed too.

DAN: Martin, let Aggie make you up a bed?

MARTIN: No, Dan, no. I prefer to sit up. I haven't been horizontal for years.

DAN: But you must lie down sometimes.

MARTIN: I just can't bring myself to. I don't think my limbs would ever allow me to get up again.

DAN: But that's foolish.

AGGIE: Come on, Dan. He'll have his own way, you know he will.

DAN *kisses* MARTIN.

The lights rise on the boys' area with flashes of lightning and thunder. JACK *and* JOE *run on, dressed in bathing suits. They are exhausted and fling themselves to the ground to regain their breath.*

JOE: Are you sure you tied the boat up securely?

JACK: It'll be okay.

JOE: Did you ever see such a storm!

JACK: I was a damn fool. I could see it building up against the horizon. We should have stayed in Gosford until it had passed over. You should never try to beat the weather.

JOE: I was so scared.

JACK: Forget it now. It's all over.

JOE: [*anxiously*] If the boat had turned over it would have been the end of me. I can hardly swim at all.

JACK: [*to calm him*] It's all right. We're home now.

> *They pause to collect themselves. The light of a red sunset begins to bathe the area.* JACK *looks off.*

Look. All of a sudden the storm's passed over. There isn't a wave on the bay now.

JOE: Isn't that strange? It came out of nowhere and it's cleared up in a moment.

JACK: [*troubled*] You don't think it was like... a warning, do you?

JOE: What for?

JACK: Like a punishment.

> JOE *is still silent.*

[*Quietly*] For what happened last night, stupid. [*Turning away, seeing that he has hurt* JOE] You know what I'm talking about.

JOE: There was nothing wrong in that. We have to sleep together.

JACK: I could have made myself up a bed on the floor.

JOE: It was just like the first time I visited you and we sat together under the trees.

JACK: That was different. It was a game then.

JOE: And it was the same last night.

JACK: [*angrily*] How do you know how I felt?

JOE: I don't, but... I didn't want to do anything else. I was happy just as things were. It was comfortable being so near you. I don't think I've ever been so happy in my life.

JACK: Well, we're different, then. All that stuff may seem all right to you but it isn't all right to me.

JOE: What do you want to say things like that for? Are you telling me I should have felt like we were doing something wrong?

JACK: I'm not saying anything except I'm sleeping by myself tonight.

JOE: Oh, Jack! Don't do that.

JACK: Yes. We're going to stay away from each other from now on. I might have started it all but now I'm knocking it off. I'm not going to turn into anything I don't want to be.

JOE: Well, I don't see anything wrong with it. And I think I'm a better Catholic than you are. At least I've never done anything wrong with a girl.

JACK: That's just what I'm saying.

JOE *lowers his head and turns away. After a moment he looks off.*

JOE: Look. The sun's setting and everything's red. The sky and the water. All the windows in those weekenders on the point. It looks like the world's on fire. And yet it's peaceful. Maybe that's a sign too, Jack.

JACK: Of what?

JOE: That we didn't do anything wrong. That everything's all right and you haven't any reason to feel bad.

JACK: I learned my lesson from the storm.

JACK *turns away again.* JOE *edges closer to him and speaks quietly.*

JOE: Listen, Jack, I've never had a good friend like you before. I was always on my own because other kids didn't seem to like the same things I did. I used to fill in the time by going to the pictures maybe two or three times a week. And that was okay because pictures was one of the things I was interested in. I read up all about the movie stars and they became like friends to me. But I thought I ought to get to know more real people and that's why I joined the Catholic Youth Organisation. Well, that didn't work out so well either. It was all right while something was going on. A dance or a debate or drama night. But when it came time for everybody to go their own way, the others would drift off in groups and I always ended up walking home by myself. It was the same old thing. And then you joined the club and you asked me around to your place and we hit it off right from the start. I had something to look forward to at last, Jack. I really do look forward to being with you. And you must enjoy my company or you wouldn't have asked me to come on this holiday with you. Isn't that right? Oh, Jack, don't dump me. You're not going to dump me, are you? I haven't done anything to hurt you. And I never would. Oh, don't dump me, Jack. Then I'd have nothing to do but go back to the pictures. And they're just stars on the screen, Jack. They're not real like you. Please. Don't dump me, Jack.

JACK *rises, uncertain of how to respond to* JOE*'s appeal.*

JACK: I'll see that the boat *is* tied up properly.

JOE *rises to follow him.* JACK *indicates he does not wish him to come.*

I won't be long. [*He becomes angry at* JOE*'s disappointment.*] I want to be by myself for a while. [*He moves off a little and then turns back, still angry.*] Well, we don't have to go everywhere together, do we?

JACK *exits.* JOE *sits again and lowers his head.*

In the living room, MARTIN *stirs in his sleep. Suddenly he jolts into wakefulness. He shudders, groans and utters his prayer.*

MARTIN: Oh, God have mercy on our souls!

END OF ACT ONE

ACT TWO

The lights rise on the living room. AGGIE *is clearing the crockery from a meal. The Kosi is alight and* MARTIN'*s chaff bag of papers is on the floor.* PADDY *appears in the doorway carrying a suitcase. He places it out of sight before* AGGIE *sees him.*

PADDY: [*dolefully*] Hello, Aggie.

AGGIE: [*curtly*] Oh. Hello, Paddy.

PADDY: Dan not back yet?

AGGIE: No. I suppose the train's late getting in.

PADDY: Where's Monica?

AGGIE: [*critically*] Lying down. [*Pointing to* MARTIN'*s bag of papers*] She promised me she'd sort through all that before she goes home today.

PADDY: What is it?

AGGIE: A lot of stuff Martin left with us. His writing and the like. He was going to sort it himself but he never got the chance, poor fella.

PADDY: How's Monica bearing up?

AGGIE: Getting corns on her knees praying for Martin's soul, of course.

PADDY: I've been saying a prayer or two myself.

AGGIE: [*defensively*] So have I!

PADDY: You seem a bit put out, Aggie.

AGGIE: I am. It's Dan having to go all the way up to Warragamba to collect Martin's things. You know how sick he is. That eye's worse than ever.

PADDY: Yes, yes. It's terrible.

AGGIE: If you ask me the doctors just don't know what's wrong with it. They keep asking him to come back for examinations and there's different specialists there each time. The day before yesterday they took a lot of muck out of it. My own idea is that he's picked up something off one of those boats at Garden Island. You know, they come in from the East and God knows what infections they're carrying.

PADDY: Has Dan mentioned to them he repairs the boats?

AGGIE: He's told them everything over and over again. But, if it's a germ they've never heard of...!

PADDY: I'm sorry it was Dan had to go to Warragamba, Aggie. I'd have gone myself but Sophie wasn't home and the boys—

AGGIE: Oh yes, Paddy, I know all about Sophie and the boys! The boys are nearly men now. Surely they can take care of themselves.

PADDY: Well, it looks like they're going to have to from now on.

AGGIE: Oh, don't tell me you've had another row with her!

PADDY: No, not exactly. But... she's brought somebody else home to live.

AGGIE: Who?

PADDY: I don't know. I didn't ask to be introduced. He's just... this fella. A young man too. He was there with her when I got up this morning. He'd moved in.

AGGIE: Well, why don't you move him out again?

PADDY: Sophie said she wanted him to stay. She said it was her house and she was entitled to ask who she liked to stop there. In a way I suppose she's right. I came downstairs and there they were. They'd made themselves up a bed on the divan.

AGGIE: Paddy! You're her husband. You've got rights.

PADDY: I know, I know. And I pointed that out to her, Aggie. I said: 'You might at least sleep with me occasionally.'

AGGIE: And how did your precious boys take all this? Did they walk in on them too?

PADDY: Oh no, Aggie, I'm sure it was her intention to be up and around before the boys were out of bed. You can say what you like about her, Aggie, she's very careful with the boys.

AGGIE: Well, what *are* you going to do about it?

PADDY: I don't know. I've been trying to work that out on my way over here.

AGGIE: You know you could divorce her for what she's done?

PADDY: Aggie, we're Catholics! I wouldn't dream of disgracing the family with a divorce.

AGGIE: Oh, and I don't suppose Sophie's disgraced it by bringing men home and going to bed with them right under your nose.

PADDY: That's a different thing altogether, Aggie. That was in the privacy of our own home.

AGGIE: Well, if you say so!

PADDY: But, all the same, how can I go back there again?

AGGIE: No, I don't suppose even Sophie'd expect you to do that.

PADDY: And how can I leave? Where else is there to go? I don't know which way to turn. Oh well, I'll talk about it with Dan when he gets here. He'll know what to do.

AGGIE: You mean you hope he'll say: 'Stay here with us.'

PADDY: Oh no, Aggie. I know you're full up here.

AGGIE: Frankly, we are, Paddy. One of the girls had to get out of her bed because Monica wanted to stay. I couldn't have that as a permanent thing.

PADDY: No, no. Certainly not. Wait a minute! Monica's got a big place up there at Wollongong.

AGGIE: You wouldn't consider—

PADDY: Well, just for a few days until I could sort something else out.

AGGIE: She'd drive you mad, Paddy. Even if she'd have you. But I don't think she'd believe it was quite proper.

PADDY: Oh, her father's in the house with her, isn't he?

AGGIE: He's blind.

PADDY: He's not deaf.

AGGIE: Well, just as you like. I've got my own worries. Oh, I do hope Dan's going to be all right. I've got this awful feeling things are going to get worse before they get better.

PADDY: How could they get worse! Dan's eyes so bad, Martin falling off the dam and Sophie chucking me out. It's a litany of horror.

AGGIE: You'll know how much worse things can get if you go up to Wollongong. Monica'll work the insides out of you for a start. When they had money she had servants running around everywhere and when they didn't she picked up anyone she could find. She had this old lady with her once—Mrs English. She was so frail, Monica was supposed to be looking after her. But it wasn't long before she had her working by day and working by night. Dusting, polishing, washing and ironing. Finally the old lady collapsed. Well, Monica was so ignorant, one morning Mrs English wakes up and she's shivering. 'Oh, Monica, I'm so cold,' she says. 'Well, I'll fix that,' says Monica, 'I'll take you out and sit you in the sun.' And that's what she did. And the old lady hardly hit the air when she breathed her last. It was the death shivers she had, you see. And Monica had no idea.

PADDY: Well, of course, it takes a lot of thinking about. But she is a very holy woman.

AGGIE: Oh yes, she's that all right. You'd think she had a private telephone through to the Holy Ghost.

PADDY: Aggie, that's blasphemous!

AGGIE: It's worse than that. It's a damn nuisance.

> DAN *enters carrying two suitcases. He is exhausted.* AGGIE *moves to support him. He has a bandage patch over his bad eye.*

Oh Dan! Look at you, you're all in.

> *He drops the bags and falls into a chair.*

DAN: I am, Aggie. For God's sake, let me sit down.

AGGIE: You should never have gone up there. Can I get you anything?

DAN: Hello, Paddy. [*To* AGGIE] Get me a Bex, would you?

> AGGIE *moves quickly off.*

[*To* PADDY] I ran out of them on the train, but I was so anxious to get home I hopped into a cab at Central without stopping to buy any more. Oh, the pain, Paddy. It's been terrible. I haven't slept at all.

PADDY: What am I going to do, Dan? Sophie's thrown me out. She's brought this fella home. I came down and caught them sleeping together.

DAN: [*in sorrow*] Oh, Paddy!

> AGGIE *has come back and overheard* PADDY'*s last speech. She bears down on him, livid with anger.*

AGGIE: Will you be quiet! How dare you worry Dan with your own problems when you can see he's nearly mad with the pain in his eye.

DAN: Aggie, don't talk to—

AGGIE: I'll talk to him as I like. Here, take your Bex and be quiet.

> DAN *takes the Bex and swallows it.*

[*To* PADDY] It's always the same with you: Dan'll know what to do! Well, work it out yourself for a change.

DAN: Aggie, if you want to give me some peace—

AGGIE: All right, I'll be quiet. [*To* PADDY] And you be quiet too. [*To* DAN] Ever since I've known you, it's been cutting a piece off yourself for this one and cutting a piece off yourself for that one! Well, the time has come to call a halt to it. I'll knock down the next person who tries to take advantage of you.

DAN: Yes, yes, but don't quarrel. Don't be rude to my brother.

AGGIE: All right. [*To* PADDY, *through tight lips*] I'm sorry, Paddy. [*To* DAN] Is that better?

DAN: Yes, yes.

AGGIE: How many Bex is that you've had today, Dan?

DAN: I don't know. I've lost count.

AGGIE: Oh, dear! You can't go on taking them like that. They'll do you harm.

DAN: It's the pain, Aggie. The pain's terrible.

AGGIE: Worse than the day before yesterday?

DAN: Much worse.

AGGIE: Then that settles it. I'm taking you up to that hospital right now and we're not coming home again until I get some satisfaction out of them.

DAN: Yes, we will go, but I've simply got to put my head down first. I'd never make it up there without a rest.

AGGIE: I'll help you into bed, then.

DAN: Not until I've spoken to Paddy.

AGGIE: Paddy's problems can wait.

DAN: No, not about that. About Martin. I have to tell him about Martin.

AGGIE: Can't that wait too?

DAN: No. It's very important. Oh, the pain's easing a bit.

PADDY: What is it, Dan?

DAN: Well, when I got up to Warragamba I went straight to the foreman of the job to talk to him about how the accident happened. He was a very nice fella, found me a bed for the night and all. He even took me down to the exact spot where it happened, so that I'd be sure in my mind about the facts. Oh, it's a vast place that dam. And high! Apparently, as the foreman heard it—he wasn't there himself, mind you, and that's important—as he heard it, Martin was working near the edge of cliff, drilling some rock away. You know the power of those pneumatic drill things. It jolted out of his hands, threw him off balance and carried him over the edge. They both ended up in pieces at the bottom of the ravine.

PADDY: Poor Martin!

DAN: Anyway, that was it as *he* told it to me. But then, when I was having a cup of tea in this canteen place, another fella sidles up to me and gives me a different version of what happened. [*Quietly*] Where's Monica?

AGGIE: She's in bed.

DAN: Quietly, then. This fella claimed he saw Martin jump. On purpose, he said.

PADDY: No! Martin would never—

DAN: Well, perhaps not. But I don't want to rule it out entirely. I'm not saying he'd do it from thinking about it a lot. But, maybe, on the spur of the moment when his anxiety became too heavy a burden. He was... unpredictable. Well, that's another possibility. Then, that night when I was trying to find my tent in the dark, another man lunges out at me and drags me off behind a pile of timber to tell me *his* story. His name was O'Rourke and he's a member of the Holy Name Society. He wasn't actually on the spot either, but some others told him Martin was pushed over the edge by the Commos.

AGGIE: Oh, Dan!

PADDY: Pushed over the edge!

DAN: He said some of them stood in front of where Martin was working to hide what was going on while another lot let him have it.

PADDY: The bastards!

DAN: Martin told me himself they'd tried to burn down his tent. He was standing in the way of their controlling the unions, you see.

AGGIE: I said it was a funny sort of accident to have happened.

DAN: Well, my question is: What should I do about it? If it was an accident—then, of course, it's all over and done with. If it was suicide, ought I to tell Monica? And, if it was murder, I want to inform the police.

PADDY: It's a ticklish problem all right, since it seems that none of the people who told you what happened were there at the time.

DAN: The fella who said he jumped was.

PADDY: Oh, well, you wouldn't want to believe him!

DAN: I thought later on, he might have been a Communist himself, trying to throw me off the scent.

PADDY: That's possible. They're slippery customers those Commos. Suppose we did put them in and they came after us.

DAN: I'm not worried about that, Paddy. If they did kill Martin, I'll never rest until I see them hung.

PADDY: Oh, neither will I, Dan. Neither will I. But there's no use making a fuss if there's even a chance they didn't.

DAN: I don't know. What do you think, Aggie?

AGGIE: I say poor Martin's dead and nothing will bring him back. If there was an investigation it'd be this one's word against that one's. And what do we know about the law?

They pause and consider the puzzle of the law.

DAN: Well, what about the other matter, then? Should I tell Monica he might have committed suicide?

AGGIE: Oh, for Heaven's sake, no, Dan! She's just as likely to dig him up out of the earth and replant him in the Protestant section of the cemetery. [*Helping* DAN *out of his chair*] Come on into bed before you get any more ideas like that.

DAN: I really ought to decide.

AGGIE: How can you when you're so tired? The hospital will do something about the pain and then you can work out what's the best thing to do.

AGGIE *walks him to the door.*

DAN: Yes, yes. You're right as usual, Aggie. Don't go, Paddy. Stay until I get up.

PADDY: [*pathetically*] I've nowhere *to* go, Dan.

AGGIE *stops and glares at him.*

[*Quietly*] I'll be here when you get up.

AGGIE *and* DAN *leave the room.* PADDY *sits down for a moment, utterly dejected. Then he sees* MARTIN's *suitcases. He checks that no one is coming and then opens one of them. It is full of papers with just a few articles of clothing. He goes down on his knees to examine the papers more closely.*

Paper, paper and more paper! Martin would have dressed in paper if the idea had ever occurred to him.

MONICA CASSIDY *enters behind him. She is carrying a suitcase and a crucifix. She is a rather abstracted woman, except when talking about her faith, then she burns with a sincere devotion. She moves lazily and sighs a lot, as though on the edge of a trance. She sees* PADDY *and calls across to him in a whisper.*

MONICA: I've just come in, Paddy, but don't let me disturb your devotions.

PADDY *leaps to his feet and brushes down his trousers.*

PADDY: Oh hello, Monica. I was just finished. A prayer for poor old Martin.

MONICA: I've been offering them up every moment since it happened. Just think! He mightn't have had time for an act of contrition before he went over the edge!

PADDY: We can only hope he had time to say one on the way down.

MONICA: We certainly can't depend on it.

PADDY: Is that your bag packed?

MONICA: Yes. I thought I'd catch the afternoon tram. Sydney's all very well but I never feel at home away from my own parish church.

PADDY: I'm told it's beautiful there, Monica. Just like Paradise.

MONICA: It is. You know, sometimes I'm in there, occupied over my rosary, and it's all so quiet and still and peaceful, I might have passed over into the next world without even knowing it.

PADDY: Isn't that a remarkable thing!

MONICA: Are those Martin's bags open on the floor?

PADDY: Yes. Dan was looking through them when he brought them in a minute ago.

MONICA: Where are they both?

PADDY: Aggie's putting him to bed. He's got that dreadful pain in his eye again.

MONICA: Poor Dan! [*Tapping her suitcase*] I have a relic in here. A piece of the fingernail of St Maria Goretti. And Aggie won't let me put it near Dan's eyes.

PADDY: Well, she's a very strange woman, is Aggie.

MONICA: Of course, she's standing in the way of a possible miracle. [*She remembers the crucifix she is holding and takes it over to a wall.*] See if you can find me a nail, will you, Paddy? Or a straight pin might do.

PADDY *turns back the lapel of his coat and produces a pin.*

PADDY: Oh. I have a pin here.

MONICA: Thank you. Have you something I could hit it in with?

PADDY: Use the crucifix.

MONICA *lifts her eyebrows in dismay.* PADDY *quickly removes his shoe.*

Oh well, try my shoe.

MONICA: I found this cross in my bag. I'll leave it here as a present for Dan and Aggie. They have precious little in the way of religious ornaments. [*She attempts to hit the pin into the wall with the shoe.*] No, the shoe won't do. And now I've bent the pin.

    Suddenly PADDY *grips* MONICA*'s arm with fervour.*

PADDY: Monica, I have to admit something to you.

MONICA: [*startled*] Why? What have you done?

PADDY: I haven't been keeping up my religious duties these last few years. I was so ashamed I used to lie to Martin about it.

MONICA: You don't mean you haven't been going to your Sunday Mass, Paddy?

PADDY: Worse. I've been making boots when I should have been there.

MONICA: But that's... terrible!

PADDY: I know it is. And I'm telling you because you're a good woman and my sister-in-law. If there's anybody can help me, you can.

MONICA: Well, I can pray for you. Even put you down on my novena list. But, as for the rest of it, well, it must be up to yourself.

PADDY: But... I need an example, Monica.

MONICA: I see. [*Considering*] Then let me tell you about a dream St Teresa had. She dreamed she stood on the edge of hell and watched the lost souls fluttering into the abyss like millions of leaves fluttering off a dying tree.

PADDY: Oh God! It'd make you want to go down on your knees in the middle of Market Street. But what I mean is a *real* example. More like a person. More like you, Monica.

MONICA: Me?

PADDY: Yes. What I had in mind was to watch you working, as it were.

MONICA: But... I'm just about to leave.

    PADDY *falls on one knee and clutches her again.*

PADDY: Oh, Monica, can't I come with you?

MONICA: Paddy!

PADDY: Oh, I don't want you to get the wrong idea. This isn't a proposal.

MONICA: I should hope not... for Sophie's sake!

PADDY: Yes, yes. You see it's for Sophie's sake too I want to come with you. She hasn't been keeping up her religious duties either. In fact, she's the one who's turned me off mine. Mocking at it all the time! belittling the Church!

MONICA: Oh dear, oh dear!

PADDY: And I've simply got to break away from her for a while. Then, later on, I can come back and teach her better by the example you've given me.

MONICA: Well... when you put it like that—

PADDY: You'd be saving two souls, not just one, Monica. Two more jewels in your heavenly crown.

MONICA: I'm still rather confused, Paddy. You want to come to Wollongong to stay with me. For how long?

PADDY: Oh, just till I've sorted out the turmoil in my soul.

MONICA: I believe it took St Jerome a whole lifetime to do that.

PADDY: Well, religion's not as old fashioned as it used to be. Honestly, Monica, it'd be like a retreat.

MONICA: But, Paddy, there are so many things to be considered...

PADDY: Oh, we can do that on the train. I've got my own bag out there packed and ready. Oh, and I'd be grateful if you didn't mention our leaving together until just before we go. I think Dan and Aggie would like to have me here but, frankly, I can't see myself learning much holiness in this house.

MONICA: Well, I agree with you about that at least. But, I don't know, Paddy—

PADDY: Shh! Here's Aggie. Not a word.

> AGGIE *enters.*

AGGIE: Oh, you're up, Monica.

MONICA: Yes, Aggie. I thought I might catch the afternoon train home.

AGGIE: Oh well, if you feel you must go.

> AGGIE *looks down at the crucifix* MONICA *is still holding.*

MONICA: I was looking for a nail to hang this crucifix. I thought you might like to have it in here so you can see it as you eat.

AGGIE: Thanks all the same, Monica, but why don't you keep it and hang it on your own wall? I'd really rather not have it in here.

MONICA: But, Aggie, it's our blessed Lord crucified!

AGGIE: That's all right, I'd rather not have him crucified with my dinner, thank you very much.

PADDY: Aggie!

AGGIE: There's a place for everything, Paddy. And a dining room is no place for a crucifix, except in monasteries. And this isn't one of those.

MONICA: I'm sorry you feel that way about it, Aggie. I hope Our Lord doesn't say the same thing to you when you present yourself at the gates of Heaven. It would be a terrible thing if he decided that wasn't the place for you.

AGGIE: Well, I'll just have to depend on his idea of good taste, won't I? You're taking Martin's bags home with you, aren't you?

MONICA: No, I think they'll be too much for me to manage this time. Just put them away somewhere and I'll sort through them the next time I'm in Sydney.

AGGIE: Monica, you said you needed some papers Martin had. That was the only reason Dan went all the way up to Warragamba to get them for you.

MONICA: Well, now it doesn't seem as urgent as it did then. I simply haven't the time to sort through them now. If I miss the train I'll be late for benediction tonight and Martin's soul is more important than his papers.

AGGIE: [*angrily*] Yes, and my Dan's health is more important to me than both those things. Have you any idea how ill he is?

PADDY: Shh! Aggie. You don't want to wake Dan up. You know how upset he gets when you raise your voice.

AGGIE *glares at both of them and then moves to the chaff bag.*

AGGIE: And what about this chaff bag full of stuff? You were going to sort through that too before you left.

MONICA: Oh well, I suppose I've got time to look through some of that. [*Sitting and opening the chaff bag*] Open the top of the Kosi, Paddy. I'll burn what I don't want.

PADDY: But... Monica... All Martin's stories are in there. All his poems and articles.

MONICA: What use are they to me, Paddy... if it's the sort of stuff he used to scribble when he was at home?

PADDY: But... they're beautiful.

MONICA: [*taking out a paper and reading it*] Look at this. This is the first thing I pick up. 'Youth'. Look at this: [*pointing out words*] 'passion' and 'sap-hot blood'. [*Handing him the paper*] Put it in the Kosi.

PADDY: Oh no, Monica!

MONICA: [*quietly to him*] I can see you have let yourself go, Paddy.

Reluctantly, PADDY *throws the paper into the Kosi.* MONICA *continues to sort through the papers.*

AGGIE: Surely you could hang on to some of it, Monica? If only because it meant the world to Martin. Maybe when the children get older they'd like to have a look at it.

MONICA: Put this kind of literature in front of the children!

AGGIE: When they're a bit older.

MONICA: Age is no excuse for looseness, Aggie. If you ask me, a chaff bag is a good place for all this stuff. If Martin Cassidy had directed his mind to a higher purpose perhaps he'd have ended his life in a different manner. Certainly he couldn't have fallen off anything at home with me in Wollongong.

AGGIE: He's dead now, Monica. Forgive him his mistakes.

MONICA: Of course I forgive him. I always did. But it hasn't been easy, Aggie. It hasn't ever been easy.

AGGIE: He seemed to me the sort of man who had to go his own way.

MONICA: That's all very well but where would the world be if everybody practised that point of view?

MONICA has continued to pass papers to PADDY *for burning.* AGGIE *stays her hand.*

AGGIE: Don't burn any more, Monica. Please. If you don't think they're suitable for the children, leave them here for Dan.

MONICA: Aggie, you're making it very difficult for me.

AGGIE: Dan would have read them all before. Martin used to read him everything he wrote. You don't think they've done any harm to Dan do you?

MONICA: If I had time to look through them, decide what it was safe to leave—Aggie, I'll be frank with you. I'm not a woman of the world, but I know enough to be sure that if Martin didn't get the inspiration for these things from me, and he certainly didn't, then he must have got it from someone else. I'm not so innocent that I don't know what men are like.

AGGIE: As far as I know, Martin Cassidy never looked at another woman.

MONICA: Well, you'll forgive me, he'd hardly tell you about it if he had.

AGGIE: That's right. He was too decent to bring up a subject like that in my company.

MONICA becomes angry and passes more papers to PADDY *for burning.*

MONICA: Put this in the Kosi, Paddy. And this. And—

She passes PADDY *a letter in an envelope and then takes it back again.*

No, not that. That looks like—it's my own handwriting. And look at the date! I must have written this to Martin when we were courting. [*She takes the letter out of the envelope and reads it, half to herself.*] 'And in the evening when dinner is over and we sit in the parlour with the windows open to catch a breeze off the river, taking turns to read from Thomas à Kempis or St Augustine, the words of these great scholars are lost on the breeze that blows in the windows and blows out the door. My thoughts are all of you, of your arms about me, and I believe that thoughts of holiness are well lost in the thoughts of your embrace.'

MONICA lowers the letter and sighs deeply.

AGGIE: Into the Kosi with that too, Monica?

MONICA: [*regretfully*] No, Aggie. I'll keep this to remind me. [*She reaches into the chaff bag again and withdraws a bundle of letters tied in a blue ribbon.*] But these aren't mine.

AGGIE: What a pretty blue ribbon.

MONICA takes a letter from an envelope and looks at the signature.

MONICA: They're from someone called Lola. Lola Carmichael.

PADDY: [*thoughtfully*] Lola Carmichael. Lola... Oh yes. When we were lads in Queensland. Martin used to write her often even though she only lived on the other side of town. And she'd reply to his letters too. Poor Martin was very much the young swain. Sleeping on the ground in sight of her window, mooning about half the day, tugging at gum leaves absently! But her father was a strict old man and a Methodist. All of a sudden she returned his letters, they're probably in there too, and a couple of weeks later we heard she'd become engaged to one of the lads in her own circle. First love! Martin was heartbroken. I had to take him away from there. We rode on, far away to another place where the name of that town wasn't even mentioned in the conversation.

MONICA moves to the Kosi and throws the letters into it.

MONICA: [*bitterly*] He told me I was his first love. [*Taking up her suitcase, wearily*] Well, do what you like with the rest of it, Aggie. Keep it or burn it. I buried one Martin last week, I've had to bury another one just now. God knows how many others are in that chaff bag. Come on, Paddy. We're going.

PADDY: Oh... yes. [*To* AGGIE] Monica's asked me to stay with her for a while. If Sophie inquires after me, best keep mum about where I am.

AGGIE: All right, Paddy.

MONICA: Tell Dan I didn't want to wake him. I'll write from Wollongong.

She moves forward to kiss AGGIE. AGGIE *moves away from her.*

AGGIE: Goodbye, Monica.

MONICA is disappointed. She takes a step back herself.

MONICA: Goodbye, Aggie.

PADDY: Goodbye, Aggie.

AGGIE: Goodbye, Paddy.

PADDY *and* MONICA *exit.* PADDY *collects his suitcase on the way out.* AGGIE *sits and idly sorts through the chaff bag herself. She takes up a page torn from a book and reads it, uncertain of its meaning.*

Ah, Love! Could thou and I with fate conspire
To grasp this sorry scheme of things entire,
Would not we shatter it to bits—and then
Re-mould it nearer to the heart's desire.

DAN *enters. He holds a bloodstained towel over his eye.*

DAN: Aggie! My eye! It feels like it's burst in my head.

AGGIE: [*rising and moving to him quickly*] *Dan!*

> *Blackout.*

> *The lights rise on the boys' area. Again, deep green shadows lie over it.* JACK SHANNON *is discovered, waiting. After a while* JOE *enters, leisurely. He has taken a deal of trouble over his appearance. The boys are curt with each other.*

JACK: Oh. I didn't think you were coming.

JOE: I had a few other things to do first.

JACK: *Yeah!* I'll bet you've been hanging around waiting, just so I'd *think* you weren't going to arrive.

JOE: What did you want to see me about?

JACK: I didn't say I wanted to see you about anything, did I?

JOE: Well, you haven't asked me around here since we came home from Woy Woy. You practically ignore me when we meet at the club. I supposed you must want to talk to me about something.

JACK: Well, I don't. I've been busy since we came back from Woy Woy.

JOE: Doing what?

JACK: Oh, you'd be surprised. For one thing I've been writing letters.

JOE: Who to?

JACK: People.

JOE: Where abouts?

JACK: Places. Up north. Coffs Harbour.

JOE: Who do you know there?

JACK: Nobody… yet.

JOE: Well… what have you been writing letters about?

JACK: A job, maybe.

JOE: You're not thinking of going all the way up to Coffs Harbour to work, are you?

JACK: Nothing's settled as yet.

JOE: When might you go?

JACK: I told you, nothing's settled as yet. But it might be sooner than you think. [*Glancing above*] Listen! That same old bird.

JOE: I suppose it's been coming here every evening even though we haven't. Your aunt isn't making you go to Coffs Harbour, is she?

JACK: No. I'd be on the land. That's the sort of job I've always wanted.

JOE: But you wouldn't have any friends up there. I'll guarantee they haven't got a Catholic Youth Organization at Coffs Harbour.

JACK: I'll manage.

JOE: I hope you don't go away, Jack. *I* don't want you to go.

JACK: Go on, you can't give me that. You don't care one way or the other.

JOE: I do.

JACK: You don't.

JOE: I've been as miserable as anything because you've been ignoring me. You're right, I didn't have anything else to do today. I just hung around so that you'd *think* I wasn't coming.

JACK: There you are! Now why didn't you admit that in the first place?

JOE: Because I didn't want you to see how hurt I was.

JACK: You *should* have told me.

JOE: Okay, I should have.

JACK: Then say you're sorry.

JOE: I'm sorry.

JACK: That's better.

JOE: You were only joking about going away, weren't you, Jack?

JACK: Oh, no. But nothing's *definitely* decided yet.

JOE: [*hopefully*] Oh?

JACK: [*teasing him*] Though some of the arrangements are very advanced.

> JOE *looks miserable again.* JACK *bursts out laughing, delighted to have touched him so deeply.* JOE *moves towards him lovingly.*

JOE: Oh, Jack!

JACK: [*moving away quickly*] No, none of that. Stay away from me.

JOE: I wasn't going to do anything.

JACK: Yes, you were. Is that the way you go on with the new bloke I've seen you hanging round with at the club?

JOE: Who? Neville Jackson? No. He's just this boy who's moved in down the street from us. He doesn't know anybody and I've been introducing him around.

JACK: Introducing him around! Every time I've seen you together you've been clinging onto him like a leech.

JOE: I haven't, Jack.

JACK: You have. Everybody's talking about it.

JOE: Talking about what? What are they saying?

JACK: They're saying somebody ought to tell him about you.

JOE: Tell him about me!

JACK: You know what I'm talking about.

JOE: You're absolutely rotten saying things like that.

JACK: I'm not saying them. I told you. It's everybody else.

JOE: Then you shouldn't let them say it. You know it's not true.

JACK: How do I know what you get up to behind my back?

JOE: You know I wouldn't. Please, don't torment me, Jack.

JACK: Then admit you're only walking round with that fella just to make me wild.

JOE: I'm not. He spoke to me first. You haven't been around. I've got to talk to somebody, haven't I?

JACK: Not him.

JOE: Well... what do you want me to do? Say I'll dump him?

JACK: Yes.

JOE: Okay. I will.

JACK: I bet you won't.

JOE: I'll give you my word.

JACK: See you keep it then.

JACK *turns away, feigning casualness. He whistles to himself.*

JOE: You're the only friend I want, Jack. Can't we be friends the same as we were before?

JACK: I'd like to... but I can't.

JOE: Why not?

JACK: I just can't. We'll see each other. I'll be going to the club for as long as I'm still here.

JOE: Stop talking about going away, will you! And when you say you'll see me at the club I know what that means. You'll turn your head away whenever I speak to you. You'll make jokes about me whenever you're talking to someone else. And I don't know why you behave like that. I don't know why we can't go on being friends.

JACK: You do know why. Stop pretending to be stupid.

JOE: Is it because of what happened at Woy Woy?

JACK: You know it is. You've been trying to make *me* say it, haven't you?

JOE: Yes. I wanted you to say it so I could tell you how stupid *you* are.

JACK *slaps his face.*

JACK: Don't you tell me I'm stupid. Don't you say that to me again. You understand?

JOE *lowers his head, accepting the blow.*

Obviously you haven't been to confession since we got back.

JOE: I have. I've been twice.

JACK: Well... what did the priest say to *you*?

JOE: I can't tell you that. It's a secret.

JACK: He's the one who's got to keep the secret. You can tell who you like.

JOE: Well, he didn't say anything to me because I didn't tell him about Woy Woy.

JACK: You didn't tell him! But that's a bad confession. Phew! I wouldn't like to be in your shoes.

JOE: There was no sin to confess. All that happened was that I was happy. And that's not a sin.

JACK: [*half to himself*] When I told him what I felt that night, I thought he was going to jump out of the confessional. He said I wasn't ever to go near you again. That I was to positively avoid you. Next time I suppose I'll have to confess that I've asked you over here today.

JOE: He told you not to come near me again! But, Jack, he doesn't know me. I'm a Catholic too. He can't speak about me like I was some sort of terrible bad influence.

JACK: Well, he did.

JOE: [*angrily*] But he can't. I'm not a bad influence. If there's anybody a bad influence it's you. You're a bad influence on yourself.

JACK: [*pushing him*] I told you not to talk to me like that. Now, go on, piss off before I have to hit you again.

JOE: I won't go. I don't care if you do hit me. I'm not leaving until you say we'll be friends just like we were before.

JACK: What do you want from me? Do you want me to lose my soul?

JOE: I'm not afraid of losing my soul. One of us has to be wrong.

JACK: This isn't just something between you and me. I've got to take notice of the priest or I can't get absolution. Come on, you're so clever, you tell me what I'm supposed to do about that.

JOE: [*lowering his head again*] I don't know.

JACK: Yes. A big help you are!

JOE: All right, but if you won't go on being my friend, then I'll just have to find someone who will. Neville Jackson's got a film developing outfit. He's suggested I buy a camera and we go out taking pictures together. Then we could develop them at his house. I might do that. Maybe I could have a lot of fun with Neville Jackson.

> JACK *throws himself on* JOE, *livid with anger.*

Jack! Don't!

> JACK *rains down blows on him until* JOE *is forced to his knees. He pushes him flat then sits astride him, rubbing his face into the ground.*

JACK: You think I haven't wanted to see you again! You think I haven't wanted to...

> *He pushes* JOE *away from him.* JOE *scrambles to his feet, weeping.*

Oh, Christ! Get out of here. Go away. But, let me tell you this: if I see you with that Neville Jackson again I swear I'll strike you down in the street. Now, go on, get out!

> JOE *stumbles off. Blackout.*

The lights rise in the living room. DAN *sits before the unlit Kosi. One eye of his glasses is set with frosted glass and there are a few patches on his neck covering boils. He sits stiffly as though in slight pain.* AGGIE *sits in another chair reading the* Daily Telegraph. *The window is open and both characters wear light clothes.*

AGGIE: You know, Dan, they say here there's still Japs hiding in New Guinea who don't know the war's over. Huh! Thank God I don't have to be the one to try and convince them.

He smiles at her.

Do you want anything?

DAN: No.

AGGIE: You're not in any pain, are you?

DAN: Only a little.

AGGIE: I could give you another one of those tablets. It's time.

DAN: They make me groggy. I like my mind clear.

AGGIE: Yes, I know. You want to think. [*Sitting beside him and taking his hand*] You was always a thinking man.

DAN: Did the doctor tell you why he wanted me in hospital again?

AGGIE: He just said… tests.

DAN: That's all he'd tell me.

AGGIE: Tests! You've had so many tests already it's a wonder they don't keep you in a cage in the lab.

DAN: I suppose they must find out what's wrong with me eventually.

AGGIE: Of course they will. You've always been a reasonably healthy man.

DAN: I've had a time of it all right. Sometimes I feel like Job in the Bible.

AGGIE: He was a rich man, wasn't he? [*Laughing*] That's the difference between you and Job, Dan.

DAN: Well, God can take my health away from me as long as he leaves you where you are.

AGGIE: I'm not going anywhere. And if God wants to decide otherwise, I'm telling you, he'll have a fight on his hands.

DAN: I've never asked you before, Aggie. Not in all the years we've been married. What do you think about God? Honestly.

AGGIE: Honestly! I don't think I think much about him at all, Dan. I believe I've always been a good Catholic, doing everything I was told I should. I've never had much of a chance to do the things I was told I shouldn't. I was always too busy having kids and then bringing them up. Just… surviving. Do you know what, Dan? I think you've been my religion. I've loved you above everything else in my whole life. Above myself and the kids and comfort and… Well, I don't suppose that makes me a very good Catholic after all. What do you think, Dan?

DAN: I've always supposed I was a good Catholic too. But, lately I begin to doubt it. I don't mean I think our religion is a bad thing. I was born into the Church and I'll die in it... gratefully. It's just that I don't think it's the only thing any more. Working on those ships I've watched the Buddhists and the Mohammedans and the Hindus at their worship and I can't believe they're praying to an empty space. But, whoever it is, whatever it is outside ourselves, it's not telling anybody. Martin was right. He's a hard God, and our total ignorance of what he's about is what finally drives us to distraction. It would be unbearable if I wasn't sure he loved me. And I am sure of that.

PADDY *enters with a suitcase.*

AGGIE: Paddy!

DAN: Hello, Paddy.

PADDY: Holy hell, Aggie, I've just blown in like the wind from Wollongong. Monica's gone clean off her head. Hello, Dan.

He kisses DAN *and flops into a chair.*

AGGIE: Clean off her head! What do you mean?

PADDY: Let me get my breath first. Oh God, I'm glad to be here. Such a time I've had of it.

AGGIE: I told you you'd be swapping Sophie for something worse.

PADDY: Something worse! Aggie, if that woman ever hits Heaven, God the Father and everyone else below him will move right out. She'll clear the place.

DAN: I think you'd better get him a cup of tea, Aggie.

AGGIE: Not on your life. Not until he's told us what's happened.

PADDY: Well, for a few days after I arrived there everything was very comfortable. Mind you, it was up in the early morning when the frost was on the grass, crunching our way through it to the earliest possible Mass. Getting there before the priest even. Stamping our feet and rubbing our hands together waiting for him to open up the church. And, Holy Ghost, it was even colder when we got inside. Then it was benediction at midday and the rosary at night and any number of visits in between to pray for this one's soul and that one's special intention. But that was the easy part of it. I expected that. Then she began to find little things for me to do about the place, like grubbing out tree stumps or putting in a crop of potatoes. Oh! And I mustn't forget helping to look after the goats.

AGGIE: The goats?

PADDY: Yes. Monica keeps a few goats for milking. They hate the sight of her. They're forever butting her in the backside or sitting down and refusing to move. She carries her rosary with her everywhere. Getting in a decade on the hop, as she puts it. And you ought to see her with the beads in one hand and a goat in the other, pulling and praying until you wouldn't know whether it was a prayer she was offering up or a curse.

They all laugh.

DAN: Oh, poor Monica!

AGGIE: Go on, what happened then?

PADDY: Well, then the jobs she asked me to do got more extraordinary. One day she pushed me up through a manhole in the ceiling to clear the cobwebs from the top of the house. And, another time, she made me move all the rose bushes around the garden! Well, then, this particular morning, I was clipping the hedge out the front and she grips me by the arm and points to the sky. 'Look, Paddy,' she says, 'Angels!' Well! I nearly put my neck out I jerked it up so suddenly. I'm inclined to believe anything people tell me, you know. But there was nothing there at all. Not even clouds. We were looking into a clear blue sky and Monica was seeing angels everywhere. She went down on her knees and dragged me down beside her. Naturally I pretended to go along with her. I don't know what the people passing by must have thought. There we were kneeling on the grass exchanging observations over the anatomical details of heavenly creatures that weren't even there.

AGGIE: They must have thought you was as mad as she was.

PADDY: I did hope they'd be so used to seeing us on our knees they wouldn't consider it unusual at all. Anyway, one slate off and it became a landslide. She went to pieces utterly. We called a doctor to the house and he had her carted off to the hospital.

AGGIE: Who's looking after the children then? And the old man?

PADDY: Some of the neighbours are helping out. And, considering the hard time she gave them too, it proves there's still a lot of Christian charity left in the world.

AGGIE: You know, I've always suspected Monica would go like that. I knew someone who knew her sister Eva. And Eva used to get up in the cold frosty mornings, go down to the orchard in her nightdress and swing on the apple trees singing hymns to herself. Of course, eventually she caught pneumonia and died.

PADDY: Well, there was no sense in my staying any longer after Monica had gone. I packed my bag and made a break for it.

AGGIE: What are you going to do now?

PADDY: I'm back again where I started, I suppose.

DAN: Never mind, Paddy. We'll be able to fix you up with something here.

PADDY: Oh no, Dan. I know you're full up here.

AGGIE: Don't make him persuade you, Paddy. He's too ill to play games.

DAN: Aggie!

PADDY: No, Dan, she's right. I have relied on other people too much. But this time I'm honestly going to try to stand on my own two feet. I mean there's nothing else for it, is there? I'm not an old man. I've still a lot of life left in me. I'll strike out on my own.

DAN: Where will you go?

PADDY: I'll have a look around. The city's full of rooms.

AGGIE: Oh, Paddy! One of those terrible rooms!

PADDY: They were good enough for us when we first arrived from the bush. I'll look around until I find a nice one.

AGGIE: You're in for a long search.

PADDY: It'll keep me moving. The quicker the better. The only chance life has of defeating you is if you stand still long enough for it to catch up with you. I'm sorry you've been so ill, Dan. How is it with you now?

AGGIE: He's going to be all right.

DAN: I've got to go into the hospital again next week, Paddy. They want to take some more tests. They're still not sure what's causing all the trouble.

PADDY: Well, I hope to God they find out. I do indeed. For you're the best of us all, Dan. There's no doubt about that.

    AGGIE *begins to leave the room.*

AGGIE: I'll get you that cup of tea, Paddy.

PADDY: No, Aggie, no. I'd like to stay and talk but I mustn't allow myself to. The sooner I find myself a room the sooner I can settle myself into it. I'll get a *Herald* at the corner and mark off the likely prospects on my way into town on the tram. I'll come back for my bag when I do get a place.

AGGIE: Have you heard anything from Sophie?

PADDY: Never a word. Has she been around here?

AGGIE: Not a sign of her.

PADDY: Well, there's no reason why she should come looking for me, is there? She's already had everything there was to get out of me. [*Regretfully*] Oh, dear! [*Then brightly*] Well, I musn't look back. That's the motto for today. [*Kissing DAN on the cheek*] See you later, Dan.

    Suddenly DAN *clutches him in desperation and clings to him tightly.*

DAN: Paddy!

PADDY: Oh, Dan! Dan! What's the matter now?

DAN: I'm glad you're back, Paddy. In case—

AGGIE: [*moving in to comfort* DAN] Nothing's going to happen to you, Dan. I wouldn't allow it to.

DAN: [*regaining control and releasing* PADDY] Well, anyway, I'm glad you're back.

PADDY: [*kissing* AGGIE] See you later, Aggie. You know, there's a kind of excitement about setting out on your own again, even at my age. I'm not as afraid of as many things as I used to be. More puzzled you understand, but not as afraid. And I want to find happiness again. I must. After all, you're a long time looking at the lid. Cheerio!

> PADDY *exits.* AGGIE *takes up the paper again and tries to read, but in a moment she turns her attention to* DAN. *Slow fade to blackout.*
>
> *The lights rise on the boys' area. A large bell is heard tolling the angelus.* JACK SHANNON *waits. In a moment* JOE *enters. Both boys are dressed in light clothes.* JOE *tries to move past* JACK *and avoid an encounter, but* JACK *speaks and he pauses, lowering his head.*

JACK: Joe?

JOE: Yes?

JACK: I saw you in church. I was waiting for you to come out.

JOE: Oh?

JACK: Because... this is the last visit I'll be making here.

JOE: You're going to Coffs Harbour.

JACK: Yes. Had you heard?

JOE: No. I thought you might have forgotten all about that.

JACK: Well, the letters were written and the arrangements made. I had to go through with it.

JOE: Even if you didn't want to?

JACK: I think it's best to go.

JOE: How long are you going for?

JACK: I don't know. Nobody's said anything about my coming back.

JOE: Surely that's up to you.

JACK: Maybe, after a time passes, maybe it won't be any use. Maybe everyone will have forgotten me.

JOE: I won't forget you, Jack.

JACK: And I'll tell you something. I'm not going to look for another friend like you up in Coffs Harbour. That was something special between us and I'm not ever going to let it happen to me again.

JOE: Oh, don't go, Jack.

JACK: I must.

JOE: Then let me come with you.

JACK: No. That's silly.

JOE: It isn't. If you can go there, so can I. I could find work in Coffs Harbour too. I wouldn't care what I did.

JACK: Joe, I'm leaving tonight by the eight o'clock train.

JOE: I could go home right now and put some things in a bag. Let me come with you, Jack.

JACK: No. What would your mother and father say?

JOE: I won't tell them. I've got enough for my fare. I would write them a letter from Coffs Harbour telling them where I was.

JACK: They'd only bring you back again.

JOE: Then I wouldn't tell them where I was.

JACK: It's impossible.

JOE: Then suppose you go first and I follow you later. I know I could persuade my mother and father to agree to my going up there to work.

JACK: You can't come now and you can't follow me later. Now, that's all there is to it.

JOE: Why not?

JACK: Because you know the real reason I'm leaving is to get away from you.

JOE: Well, you won't! After all, I don't need your permission to go anywhere. I can go to Coffs Harbour any time I feel like it and you can't stop me.

JACK: For God's sake, Joe, let go. Can't you just let go?

JOE: No. I care too much.

JACK: I've got to go now.

> JACK *moves to go but* JOE *detains him.*

JOE: Just wait a bit, Jack. Listen, I want to tell you something. If you do go away without me I'm finished with the Church.

JACK: You wouldn't do such a thing.

JOE: I swear I would. Because it was the Church that said we shouldn't see each other again. [*Desperately*] Jack, I've just thought of a way out of that. If I did come to Coffs Harbour without your saying I could, then you couldn't help that, could you? You'd have done everything in your power to be separated from me.

JACK: It's not only that.

JOE: But I thought it was.

JACK: It's the whole thing. The whole idea of it. I've got to go, Joe.

> *He endeavours to move off again and again* JOE *detains him.*

JOE: Well, I will leave the Church. I promise I will. When you're at Mass this Sunday just remember I won't be there. Let your conscience live with that. And I won't go to confession either. And I'll leave the Catholic Youth Organisation. Jack, isn't there anything I can say?

JACK: [*extending his hand*] Say goodbye, Joe.

JOE: I can't. I just can't.

JACK: Then I must.

> JACK *begins to move off.* JOE *follows him.*

JOE: And I'll tell you what else I'll do if you leave me here. I'll go with other men. You'll be responsible for that too.

JACK: It's your soul, Joe.

>JACK *exits.* JOE *calls after him.*

JOE: Oh, no it's not, because you're taking it away from me. You're responsible for it now. You hear me! And I hope you suffer because of it.

>*As the lights die on the boys' area* JOE *exits.*

>*The lights rise on the empty living room. In a moment* JOE *enters. He sits on the lounge and begins to cry. The grief comes from his stomach and he holds himself there as if he had pain. Then* AGGIE *enters, wearing a hat and carrying a purse. She seems dazed and only gradually notices* JOE, *though when she does she moves to him with concern.*

AGGIE: Joe! Joe!

JOE: [*making an effort to control himself*] Oh. Mumma.

AGGIE: Why ever are you crying like that, Joe?

JOE: I was just feeling miserable. No reason in particular.

AGGIE: [*taking him in her arms*] Come here to me. A big boy like you crying like that! A working man! Tell me what happened.

JOE: Nothing. I told you, I was just feeling miserable.

AGGIE: You're not lying to me, are you?

JOE: No.

AGGIE: Well, you're growing up. I don't suppose anything's easy for you growing up. Are you better now?

JOE: Yes. Have you been to the hospital to see Dadda?

AGGIE: [*resuming her state of abstraction*] Yes.

JOE: Is he all right?

AGGIE: I don't know. He seemed all right. But, while I was there, one of the doctors asked to see me and I went into the hall and we sat down on this sofa thing together and he told me that the tests they took proved your father has a cancer.

JOE: That's serious, isn't it?

AGGIE: He said it was hopeless.

JOE: Oh. And did he say...?

AGGIE: I didn't wait to find out any more. Telling me a thing like that in a hospital corridor on an ordinary sofa. I just got up and walked away from him. I didn't even go back to see your father. I came straight home here.

JOE: Maybe you should have waited to get more details from him.

AGGIE: I don't believe it! I don't believe any of it! How *could* I believe such a thing? Why, I might just as well believe the ground was going to open up and swallow me.

JOE: You might have to believe it.

AGGIE: I won't! I won't! At least not yet. I suppose… eventually… but, not yet, dear God. Not yet! [*To* JOE] Don't you tell the others, will you?

JOE: No. Is there anything I can do, Mumma?

AGGIE *has withdrawn into herself and does not hear him.*

Mumma?

AGGIE: What? Oh, no. There's nothing. Though, later on, you'll stay close to me, won't you?

JOE: Yes, Mumma.

She rises and makes an attempt to pull herself together.

AGGIE: Well, I'm going to forget about it for the time being.

JOE: Do you want me to stay home with you tonight?

AGGIE: No. I'll listen to the wireless. There'll be something on the wireless. You go out and enjoy yourself. And, listen, don't ever let me catch you crying like that again. A big boy like you!

JOE: No, Mumma.

AGGIE: It's Saturday. You go to confession and then the dance at the club, don't you?

JOE: I don't feel like doing that tonight.

AGGIE: What *are* you going to do, then?

JOE: I think I'll go to the pictures.

JOE *exits. Again* AGGIE *withdraws into herself. She sits, but as the thoughts come crowding in on her, she rises again quickly as if to rebuff them.*

AGGIE: Not yet, dear God. Not yet!

She takes a few deep breaths to control her fluttering heart and sits again, slowly. She presses her hand to her eyes and recites the first part of the Hail Mary.

> Hail Mary, full of grace,
> The Lord is with thee,
> Blessed art thou among women…

The prayer fades off to a mumble and rises again for the second part.

> Holy Mary, Mother of God,
> Pray for us sinners now…
> and at the hour of…

She pauses. Her lips cannot frame the words 'our death'. With a great effort she mouths them silently as the lights die.

THE END

Coralie Lansdowne
Says No

Alex Buzo

Alex Buzo was born in Sydney and educated at the University of NSW. In the late 60s his early plays, *Norm and Ahmed, Rooted* and *The Front Room Boys*, pioneered a revival of Australian theatre. *Macquarie* (1971) and, recently, other historical plays such as *Big River* and *Pacific Union*, have helped to popularise the themes of individual and national maturity in the past and its influence on the present. Alex Buzo's books, *Tautology, The Longest Game, The Young Person's Guide to the Theatre* and *A Dictionary of the Almost Obvious*, confirm his reputation as a recorder of modern idiom.

Jude Kuring as Coralie in the 1974 Nimrod Theatre production of
CORALIE LANSDWONE SAYS NO. *(Photo: Warren Scott)*

FIRST PERFORMANCE

Coralie Lansdowne Says No was first performed by the Nimrod Street Theatre Company at Theatre 62, Adelaide, on 9 March 1974, with the following cast:

PETER YORK	Robert Newman
CORALIE LANSDOWNE	Jude Kuring
JILL LANSDOWNE	Donna Akersten
STUART MORGAN	Kevin Howard
PAUL COLEMAN	John Orcsik
ANNE COLEMAN	Berys Marsh
DR SALMON	Lloyd Casey

Directed by Ken Horler
Setting designed by Kevin Brooks

The manuscript of *Coralie Lansdowne Says No* is held by the National Library of Australia, Canberra.

For Merelyn

CHARACTERS

PETER YORK, forty-four, a solicitor. Urbane, handsome, good-natured. Black eye patch over one eye.

CORALIE LANSDOWNE, twenty-nine, former art teacher. Tall, with a dominating manner and a loud, coarse laugh. She moves quickly and lithely, and is attractive on her own terms.

JILL LANSDOWNE, twenty-four, government administrator, Coralie's sister. Plain, reserved, determined.

STUART MORGAN, twenty-eight, poet and public servant. Small, unhurried, naive, purposeful. Influential in manner. At least three inches shorter than Coralie.

PAUL COLEMAN, thirty-two, businessman. Good looking, strongly built, gregarious.

ANNE COLEMAN, thirty, housewife. Pretty, ragged, frail, English.

DR SALMON, middle-aged doctor with one artificial leg.

TIME

The action takes place in the living-room/sunroom of a large modern house, high above the sea in the Bilgola-Palm Beach area north of Sydney. Centre stage is a large tree which grows up through the ceiling. Towards the front there are a rounded sofa and chairs; at the right, a transparent staircase going up to a landing. There are two doors facing front on the landing. The kitchen is off, up left. Glass doors lead off right and left to banana groves and a path going steeply down to the beach. The only blemish in otherwise beautiful surroundings is a bar, down right.

It is summer.

SCENE ONE

Monday evening, about 8.30 p.m. Very gloomy twilight. Silence. PETER YORK *enters left through the glass door.*

PETER: Coralie? [*Pause.*] Coralie?

> *He turns on the light and goes towards the staircase. He stops and examines something on the floor.* CORALIE LANSDOWNE *comes out of the upstairs door right, wearing jeans and a blouse. She yawns and stretches.*

CORALIE: Hello, Peter.

PETER: What a mess.

CORALIE: Thank you.

PETER: On the floor. Just look at it. The remains of my crab.

CORALIE: That bloody dog. No class. Once a scavenger…

> PETER *gets newspaper, sponge and a broom and cleans up the mess.* CORALIE *comes slowly down the stairs.*

PETER: It was a beautiful concoction—boiled crab on a field of risotto with pineapple couchant round the perimeter. Crossed pincers and a Latin motto in parsley. What a creation! I had my children visiting for the day. I bought the crab at the markets on Friday and cooked it myself. Daddy the chef.

CORALIE: They probably wouldn't have liked it.

PETER: Probably not. Anyway, how are you?

CORALIE: Sleepy. There's only one thing to do with the stormy Monday blues and that's sleep 'em off.

PETER: I saw the lights on upstairs. I thought you were going to a seance at that clairvoyant's place this evening.

CORALIE: It was cancelled because of unforeseen circumstances.

PETER: Coralie!

CORALIE: [*grinning*] Sorry. No, actually, I've given it up. I've been sleeping for, oh, for hours. Just sleeping. [*Seeing herself in the mirror*] Yuk! What's that?

PETER: You look all right to me.

> *He takes the newspapers, etc. out to the kitchen.*

CORALIE: I'm looking at a piece of flotsam with a skin condition. Who are you talking about? God, it's hot. Would you like a drink?

PETER: [*off*] I'll have a scotch, thanks.

CORALIE: All I've got is Southern Comfort.

> PETER *comes back from the kitchen.*

PETER: Doesn't that belong to your American friend?

CORALIE: He bequeathed it to me, along with the house.

PETER: So you've said, but did he mean you could drain the lot?

CORALIE: Carte blanche. Now do you want some Comfort or not?

PETER: Thanks.

> CORALIE *mixes drinks at the bar.*

CORALIE: You know, there must be more to whoredom than a mansion with ocean views and a cellarful of Southern Comfort.

PETER: Sounds like beginner's luck.

CORALIE: I'd never had an affair with anyone like him. All my friends, i.e. the dog, were horrified. A square, middle-aged American businessman— undoubtedly a CIA agent or at the very least an IT&T spy.

PETER: Did you enjoy the affair? Was it exciting?

CORALIE: It wasn't unpleasant. I was about to break it off when he said he was going back to America and would I look after the house. Would I! I was unemployed, doing nothing, which still beats teaching art to recalcitrant yobs. The Renaissance. Who wants to know about it at Marrickville Girls' High? Contraception and how to make a pound of mince last a week'd be more to the point. Because it's in a working class area no one in the Government or the Education Department gives a bugger. It took me over a year to get a kiln for the art room and I was supposed to be teaching them pottery. How's your Southern Comfort?

PETER: Delightful. You certainly fell on your feet. I'll have to look around for a well-heeled American divorcée. She'd have to be about seventy, I suppose, for the chemistry to work.

CORALIE: What chemistry?

PETER: Sugar daddies and mummies have to be older than you. [*Quickly*] Not that age differences mean a great deal.

CORALIE: As long as they've got the loot, who cares how old they are? There, now I sound more like a whore.

PETER: You've done very well.

CORALIE: [*looking around*] It's not a bad place.

PETER: The tree is of course fabulous. And the view.

CORALIE: Yes, I can see the Pacific Ocean, and the sand, and the banana trees, and those porcine developers gouging bloody great welts out of the landscape and throwing up those horrendous erectile tunnels.

PETER: Indignation's an amazing quality. Amazing. [*Pause.*] I also like the silence. Which is of course the same next door. Particularly as I'm on my own. Which you are, too.

CORALIE: Yes, it's quiet, except for the boom and drawl of the surf and the cars on the main road and also this humming sound I hear from time to time. Do you ever hear it?

PETER: No.

CORALIE: Oh. Well, maybe I'm up myself. By the way, this arrived for you today while you were at work. The delivery man left it with me.

She hands him a package. He unwraps it.

PETER: Oh yes. [*Holding up a wooden board*] I ordered this to mount a silver plate. Thanks. You're a good neighbour.

CORALIE: My pleasure.

PETER: Coralie, I thought I might—we are alone in the house?

CORALIE: Of course we're alone.

PETER: I saw a girl on your terrace this morning.

CORALIE: That's my sister Jill. She's down from Canberra for a few days. If you've ever lived in Canberra you'd know why. What a dull town. Full of boring tarantulas and their barracuda wives.

PETER: Oh. Well, anyway, I wanted to ask you if, you see, I'm a member of the Australia Party, and they're having a bit of a do over in Castlecrag and I wondered if—it's on Saturday week—and, would you like to come with mc?

CORALIE: Well, uh, thanks, I don't know.

PETER: It should be quite interesting.

CORALIE: I'll think it over.

PETER: Okay.

Pause.

CORALIE: This bloody heat. I'm going to put a bit more Comfort in my ice. Like some?

PETER: I'll get them. [*He goes to the bar and mixes the drinks. Smiling*] I like the bar.

CORALIE: Isn't it a shocker? But I love the rest of the house—for what it is.

PETER: It's beautiful. But the bar is a giveaway. Love these vinyl sausages.

CORALIE: Yes, presumably they're meant to soften the fall of pissed midgets.

PETER: Millionaires think of everything.

They laugh.

CORALIE: He's not a bad bloke. Really.

PETER: I'm sure he's very sensitive.

CORALIE: Don't be a bastard.

PETER: Where's Jill?

CORALIE: Down at the beach.

PETER: Is that wise? You can get some unsavoury types down there at night. Shall I—

CORALIE: I'd back Jill against any mere 'unsavoury type'.

PETER: I can't imagine you with a family. Are your parents alive?

CORALIE: Only my mother. I saw her yesterday, actually. We had a terrible blue. She said—I believe the topic of conversation was thrift—she said: 'A paper bag is a paper bag'; and I muttered something about self-evident truths and she belted me one, expostulating all the while about some kind of come-uppance I'm apparently soon to receive. What a harridan! The full Jannali fishwife. I don't know how I coped.

PETER: She was probably trying to give you some advice.

CORALIE: Yes, but it's always the same. When I was nineteen she'd say: 'Why don't you wear a dress, Coralie, you'd look so much nicer.' Now I'm twenty-nine and she says: 'You're always in jeans, for Christ's sake buy a dress before it's too late.' She's immutable. In this transient age of flux and oscillation my mother stays exactly the same in her own little cobwebbed harbour.

PETER: You don't listen to advice.

CORALIE: Nope.

PETER: That's something about you young people that—

CORALIE: Young? What do you mean, young? I'm twenty-nine. In a few months my youth will be at an end.

PETER: Thirty? Is that old?

CORALIE: Thirty is death. I want to spend my thirtieth birthday in Bali on a beach surrounded by black candles.

PETER: You lot fascinate me. You drift through life, aimless, rootless,

CORALIE: That I have never been.

PETER: Flippant, smart-arsed,

CORALIE: I'm sorry.

PETER: Apologetic,

CORALIE: Oh shut up.

> She laughs.

PETER: [*smiling*] But you see what I mean.

CORALIE: Yes, I suppose to your legal mind I do seem a drifter. A vagrant. A kept de facto or whatever.

PETER: A bum living a transient life.

CORALIE: I thrive on transience. The shortest book in the world, shorter even than *Italian War Heroes* or *What's On In Canberra* is a slim volume entitled *The Prospects for Coralie Lansdowne*.

PETER: Maybe when you turn thirty you'll renounce this life of aimless leisure.

CORALIE: Oh, it's not that I'm idle. I have my interests—I cultivate bananas on the front slope, I collect and play old Lesley Gore and Brenda Lee forty-fives—'You Don't Own Me' is a personal favourite—I spend every morning on the beach, I read in the afternoon, I sleep—alone—at night. As far as I'm concerned, everything is sunshine, lollipops and rainbows—comparatively.

PETER: Transience, by definition, can't last forever.

CORALIE: You want to bet.

PETER: This is an atypical period in your life. You've been awarded a six-month respite, half of which is gone.

CORALIE: What do you mean, six months? I've had a twenty-nine-year respite.

PETER: Look, about this party…

CORALIE: Don't tell me you want to 'date' me.

PETER: Well…

CORALIE: You want to be my 'escort', is that it?

PETER: Do I detect a 'back off' tone in your voice?

CORALIE: More of a 'don't rush it', I would say.

PETER: You think I'm pushing you?

CORALIE: Yes, just let things develop in their own time.

PETER: Things don't just develop. They have to be nudged along.

CORALIE: You're starting to sound almost urgent. A mountain brook should not contain scarlet water.

PETER: You broke first. You came round that night and sobbed your heart out. I couldn't get rid of you.

CORALIE: Yes, but I slept on your sofa and wanted nothing else.

PETER: That doesn't matter.

CORALIE: It still doesn't. [*Pause.*] Relax, Peter, and wait for it.

> *The phone rings.* CORALIE *answers it.*

The Lansdowne residence. Yes. Who? Paul? Oh. Oh, fine. Uh… how are you? Great. Oh, are you? Yes, of course. Just the two of you. [*Flatly*] Terrific. Yes, there's lots of room. We put up twenty CIA agents here last week. Never mind. Okay, come any time. The address is 18 Jacka Avenue. Jacka. The Aboriginal for bourgeois. You go along Palm Beach Road, through Bilgola, turn right into Sunnyside Crescent, then left into Jacka. Yeah. All right. Goodbye Paul.

> *She hangs up and pauses, deep in thought.*

PETER: What is it?

CORALIE: Oh, nothing. Just some old friends. A bloke I used to live with and his wife. They're up from Melbourne, they're coming to stay here.

PETER: How long is it since you lived with him?

CORALIE: Five years.

PETER: Well, that's all right then, isn't it?

CORALIE: Yes.

PETER: Was it messy when you split up?

CORALIE: Very clean. I have the right to demand perfection from a relationship. No less. I have that right.

PETER: Of course. Let me know when you've thought over my offer.

CORALIE: Look, what is this? What's so important about this party? Why are you asking me?

PETER: I thought it would be fun if we had a... date.

CORALIE: Fun for whom?

PETER: Mutual pleasure.

> CORALIE *looks at him. She laughs.* PETER *smiles.* JILL LANSDOWNE *enters, through the side door, right. She carries a basket.*

CORALIE: Well, look what crawled out of the sea.

JILL: Oh. Sorry. I didn't know you were working tonight. I'll come back later.

CORALIE: All right, I deserved that, and more. There's a worm in my brain. Peter York from next door, my sister Jill.

JILL: Hi.

PETER: Can I get you a drink?

JILL: Thanks.

> PETER *prepares her a drink at the bar.*

It was beautiful down by the beach. Not much wind, the air was like a cloak, and the patterns in the water were out of this world. It was great. I'm so glad I came down. I'm living fully again.

PETER: Why do you live in Canberra?

JILL: For my job.

CORALIE: For her ambitions.

JILL: I'm in the Public Service, administering the House of Representatives. Nothing special.

CORALIE: Stepping stones never are.

JILL: What she means is there's a possibility I may become secretary to a Minister—I mean, a real secretary, not a crypto-bunnygirl. I came down here for a few days to think over the offer. What's doing, ma'am? Are you going out? Have you eaten?

CORALIE: Sort of. I won't be going anywhere tonight. A couple of acquaintances of mine are coming to stay.

JILL: Oh. Will there be room?

CORALIE: Of course there'll be room. This is a mansion. What do you mean, will there be room?

JILL: Oh, just wondered. Who's coming?

CORALIE: Paul Coleman.

JILL: Who?

CORALIE: You met him. One of my mistakes.

JILL: Oh yes, I remember him. A vaguely cunnilingual turd with big thick lips. Yuk!

CORALIE: His lips are not thick. They're thin.

JILL: Sort of mean and evil.

CORALIE: Well defined. Attractive.

PETER: I'm getting a mental picture of him already.

JILL: Who else?

CORALIE: Look, what are you, the maitre d?

JILL: Just interested.

CORALIE: His wife Anne.

PETER: A short tall girl, clean shaven.

CORALIE: That's enough. Actually, I know Anne. Well, I met her once or twice, briefly. She's English, a gaminesque harridan from some provincial ghetto called Finsburystead-upon-Harrowfordgate or something. Two swans and a marmalade factory—it's very picturesque. Doesn't stop her from being slightly on the smarmy side, though. She's a film buff—always rushing off to see *Man's Favourite Sport* or discussing guilt in Fritz Lang. Am I being unkind?

JILL: Very. But don't let that stop you. Anyway, you're jealous of Anne, that's why you don't like her.

CORALIE: If we could disregard that pubescent diagnosis for the while, we could possibly recognise that I dislike pretension, purely and simply.

JILL: You're against her because she married Paul.

CORALIE: Jesus! Jill darling, there are many things I'm against—capital punishment, racism, Morris West, pollution, but dear little Anne? No sir. I don't begrudge her Paul. When I met her I didn't see red, I saw vermilion, and I understand that's how it's turned out for them.

JILL: Ma'am, that is bullshit.

CORALIE: My sister. Yunnow, I've tried, I've really tried to do everything for this girl. What a story! Father dead, mother a fuckwit, grew up in Jannali with pimples and a concave chest, a tomboy at three, left at the post at twelve, latterly a failed political groupie... what am I hoeing into you for? Jill, I'm sorry. I mean, oh shit!

JILL: Coralie's being gracious.

CORALIE: I'm sorry, Jill, I'm so cruel sometimes.

JILL: I knew it couldn't last.

CORALIE: What?

JILL: You didn't talk about yourself for all of two minutes.

CORALIE: Jill, please, I'm sorry.

   Much grimacing and wincing from CORALIE.

JILL: Okay, ma'am. [*To* PETER] Nothing like a bit of mild familial bloodletting.

PETER: Oh, don't mind me. I'll just sit around and suck ice cubes.

CORALIE: Don't be silly, Peter. Help yourself.

> PETER *goes to the bar.*

JILL: If you two want to... well, I might go for a drive.

PETER: Not at all.

CORALIE: Peter just dropped in to ask me to an Australia Party party. I haven't handed down my decision yet.

JILL: You're a politician?

PETER: A lawyer with an interest in sanity.

JILL: And the Australia Party fulfils your needs?

PETER: Oh, on all levels. If peace of mind can be defined as the ability to relax in the company of mediocrities, then I've achieved a state of beatitude with the Australia Party. The poor buggers are so chronically progressive.

JILL: Good for them.

PETER: [*looking at her, then turning to* CORALIE] Well, I'm glad to see the Lansdowne family boasts at least one *bona fide* radical.

CORALIE: Don't you believe it. My little sister is heavily into the success ethic. She'll bury us all.

JILL: Just because I don't sit around all day on my big fat arse.

CORALIE: Anyway, you can't blame the poor girl. It's only a form of compensation.

JILL: Compensation for what?

CORALIE: [*to the stairs*] I'm going up to wash my face.

JILL: Compensation for what?

CORALIE: Back in a minute. If Paul and that elfin charmer he married should happen upon us, then give me a yell.

> CORALIE *goes up the stairs.*

JILL: Going up to change, are you ma'am? Going to make yourself look presentable?

CORALIE: [*leaning on the bannister*] No, actually, I thought I'd be tactful and leave you and Peter alone. So you can discuss politico-economic realities. Have fun, kids.

> CORALIE *exits upstairs, right.* JILL *pours herself another drink.*

JILL: Bloody bitch. You like Coralie, don't you?

PETER: Well, she's...

JILL: Coralie's a cream puff. Don't let all that aggression get you down.

PETER: I've seen worse. I wouldn't have picked you two as sisters.

JILL: We're a diverse lot. Mum, bless her soul, is a fuckwit. Dad was everything. The family. He held things together and brought us up. He was a very great man. Coralie and I worshipped him.

PETER: What did he do?

JILL: Oh, he was a kind of businessman. We had a roof over our head, which is the best place for it. Can I get you something to eat?

PETER: No thanks. I had a snack. A bit of left-over pineapple and risotto.

JILL: Have you got a family?

PETER: I'm divorced.

JILL: Oh.

PETER: I've got the house next door on my own. Tell me, do you and Coralie fight all the time?

JILL: Oh, I suppose we argue quite a bit. And seeing as Coralie's involved it's always on a completely irrational basis. She tends to lash out just for the hell of it. She's unfulfilled because nothing is ever good enough for her. Coralie used to hold us spellbound at the breakfast table with her plans for the day and then conduct lengthy post mortems over dinner.

PETER: Was she ever engaged or almost married or anything like that?

JILL: Not really. There was Paul, but no, not really.

PETER: Would you say she was in any way sort of hostile to men?

JILL: That's the way it's turned out empirically. She won't compromise on any emotional issue. When she was younger, and let's face it, she's no teenager, she was the most incredible combination of romantic gooiness and perfectionism. If a bloke was ten minutes late he'd get the chopper. She imagines she has this gigantic sensibility which one day will be gratified and there'll be this great star-studded connection of two minds and two bodies meshing together and achieving life's high dharma amongst the peaks of ecstasy.

PETER: That's a tall order.

JILL: I'll say.

PETER: But she has changed, though, hasn't she?

JILL: Oh yes, I think so.

PETER: I do like her. You're right.

JILL: I've seen it before.

PETER: But it's no great hassle. I'll see how it goes.

JILL: If I were you, I'd—

The door bell rings

PETER: That'll be the mythic Paul, I suppose. Shall I get it?

JILL: No. No, it's all right.

She goes over and opens the front door. STUART MORGAN *is there, carrying a small suitcase.*

STUART: Hello, Jill.

JILL: Oh, hi. Come in.

>STUART *comes into the room. He puts down his suitcase.*

Put your suitcase over there, out of the way.

STUART: Oh. Righto.

>*He moves it.*

JILL: Um, Peter, this is, uh, Stuart Morgan, a friend of mine from Canberra.

PETER: And a very nice pair of lips you have, too.

STUART: [*startled*] Eh?

JILL: Private joke. This is Peter York, a neighbour.

PETER: And a human being, too, I hope. How do you do.

STUART: Hi.

JILL: Would you like a drink?

STUART: Are you sure it's all right? I mean, you know...

JILL: Everything's under control. Would you like a beer? I got some in for you.

STUART: Thanks.

JILL: Sit down.

STUART: I'm all right.

JILL: Okay. I won't be a minute.

>*She goes into the kitchen.*

STUART: I don't drink spirits. Only beer and wine.

PETER: Wise man.

>*Pause.*

STUART: Is Coralie around?

PETER: I noticed her about the place a little while ago. She can't have gone far.

>CORALIE *appears at the top of the stairs. She is nervous. She hasn't changed her clothes, but has a bit of make-up on her face. Her hair is brushed.*

CORALIE: Paul? Is that you?

STUART: Hello, Coralie.

>CORALIE *comes down the stairs.*

CORALIE: Who the hell are you?

STUART: Stuart. You know. Stuart Morgan, poet and public servant. From Canberra. You remember, when you were staying with Jill.

CORALIE: [*flatly*] Oh. Yes. You.

STUART: We had some good times. I've got fond memories of that Elgar recital at Bungendore. Anyway, how are you?

CORALIE: On top of the world. And you?

STUART: Not too bad. I just hitched down today.

CORALIE: Oh really. And how was it?

STUART: The last stretch was a bit frightening. I was nearly involved in a terrible accident.

CORALIE: What bad luck.

STUART: Yes. I hitched a ride with an oil tanker driver and he was worried about falling asleep. 'Talk to me,' he said. 'Tell me anything, tell me your life story, just keep me awake.' So I started to tell him my life story and he feel asleep. Nearly went over a cliff.

CORALIE: What a pity.

STUART: Yeah. [*Looking around*] I like your humpy. The tree is of course fabulous. Do you have much trouble with leaves in the gutter?

CORALIE: I can't tell you. I just can't tell you.

JILL *comes back with a glass of beer and a bottle for* STUART.

JILL: Here we are. Oh, Coralie.

CORALIE: Yes.

JILL: You know Stuart.

CORALIE: Yes.

JILL: I must have forgotten to ask you. It's okay if Stuart stays for a little while, isn't it?

CORALIE: Yes, well, my reply to your anxious enquiry before still stands. There's plenty of room. He can have the den under the stairs.

JILL: It's not very big.

CORALIE: Neither is he. No offence.

STUART: I'm easy. Sorry you haven't had any advance warning.

JILL: That's my fault. I'm sorry.

CORALIE: No trouble at all. You and your paramour can have the run of the house.

JILL: My what?

CORALIE: Paramour. Lover. I got it out of Shakespeare.

JILL: Then you'd better put it back. Stuart is a friend.

STUART: I've come down for an interview with the State Public Service. About a new job.

CORALIE: Of course. You're a public servant. How about that, Peter? We have two public servants amongst us. Half the complement of our little gathering.

PETER: That makes this living room a microcosm, statistically speaking. Not that I have anything against people who work for the government.

CORALIE: The pragmatists. You two deserve each other. Actually, this reminds me of *Heritage*, a Charles Chauvel film about the founding of the Country Party—it's a tragedy. After society has been liberated from economic equality, the film fades out on the young lovers embracing on the steps of Parliament House, affirming the virtues of youth, love and wool subsidy. Sigh.

JILL: Stuart and I are certainly young, considerably younger than you, in fact, but lovers, no. That's the end of it. [*To* STUART] You'll have to forgive her. She's more than a little uptight about a visitor she's expecting.

CORALIE: You're up yourself, ma'am.

JILL: She's waiting with a pumping heart.

CORALIE: Like bloody hell. I got over that bloke years ago. He was impossible to live with. It just didn't work. Paul used to blunder home around dawn, reeking of perfume, alcohol, and his paramour's snatch. So I broke it off with him and never felt better. I went from screwing a phantom to laying a ghost and didn't regret a thing. In fact, I feel deep sympathy and understanding for Anne, knowing what she must have to put up with.

JILL: Easy, stomach, easy.

CORALIE: Bugger you, Jill, it's the truth.

JILL: I'm sorry, ma'am, but I don't believe a word of that carefully prepared communiqué.

CORALIE: Jill darling, shut up.

> *Pause.*

PETER: Well, who'd like some more Southern Comfort?

> *The door bell rings.*

JILL: I'll get it.

> JILL *opens the door.* PAUL *and* ANNE COLEMAN *come in.* PAUL *carries two bags.*

PAUL: Hi... uh...

JILL: Jill.

PAUL: Coral's sister.

JILL: Yes.

> PAUL *puts down the bags and advances into the room, followed by* ANNE. ANNE *is in the last stages of a nervous and physical breakdown, but maintains a defiantly 'pleasant' manner.*

CORALIE: Hello, Paul.

PAUL: Good to see you, Coral.

> *He pauses, then kisses her on the cheek gruffly.*

You know Anne.

CORALIE: Yes.

> CORALIE *and* ANNE *smile briefly at each other.*

Paul and Anne Coleman, this is Peter York, a neighbour.

PETER: [*groaning*] Not again. How do you do.

CORALIE: And…

STUART: Stuart Morgan, poet and public servant.

PAUL: G'day.

CORALIE: Would you like a drink? We've got mainly bourbon.

PAUL: Thanks, Coral.

ANNE: Thank you.

> CORALIE *goes to the bar. Silence.*

PAUL: Well, don't mind us, go on with the orgy.

> *He laughs.*

CORALIE: [*smiling*] We were just arguing about something or other.

PAUL: What was the subject of the argument?

CORALIE: Oh… a film we saw on TV—*The Blue Angel.*

ANNE: Really? Andrew Sarris said it was definitive in retrospect. What did you think of it?

CORALIE: I thought it was *just stun*ning. The street. The light. And Dietrich.

ANNE: Yes, it's very evocative.

PAUL: You look a bit out of sync, Coral. Hope we didn't take you too much by surprise.

CORALIE: Oh, not at all. I didn't expect you so… on time.

PAUL: Mum always said: 'If you say you're going to be there, be there. And be there on time.' She'd tell me: 'I don't want to hear your excuses. You said you'd be there, so you be there.'

ANNE: But darling, you're the most hopelessly unpunctual man I've ever met.

PAUL: You got any more ice there, Coral? I wouldn't mind a bit more.

> CORALIE *puts some more ice in a glass of bourbon she is preparing and hands it to him.*

CORALIE: So. What've you been doing?

ANNE: Paul's got this tremendous job with American Express—Operations Manager for the Sydney office.

PAUL: It's just temporary. Nothing much. They're in a bit of a mess, and they've hired me to help them out.

CORALIE: But haven't you got your own travel business in Melbourne?

PAUL: Oh yeah. My partner's looking after it while I'm up here.

ANNE: One has one's fingers crossed. Still, it's a fantastic opportunity for Paul.

CORALIE: Yes, I'm glad to see him doing well. He's come a long way from Marist Brothers, Mosman.

PAUL: But I still polish my own shoes.

He laughs.

CORALIE: When I knew him he used to polish his own trouser seats. Anyway, you're welcome to stay for as long as you like. You can have the Fireman Suite up there on the mezzanine. You'll find everything laid on. Where are the kids?

ANNE: Paul's mother's looking after them, which is beaut. You've never seen them, have you?

CORALIE: No, I've never had the pleasure.

ANNE: I'll show you a photo.

CORALIE: Terrific.

> ANNE *gets a photograph out of her handbag and shows it to* CORALIE.

ANNE: There's Joanna, on Paul's knee, and that's Tamsin.

CORALIE: Who?

ANNE: Tamsin. From Thomas Hardy. It's a Dorset variation on Tomasina.

CORALIE: Old Dorset, eh?

ANNE: Do you like the photo?

CORALIE: Oh. Yeah. Terrific.

> *She hands it back.*

PAUL: Coral, we'll find a flat soon, don't worry.

CORALIE: Take your time. There's lots of room here.

ANNE: Yes, what a palace. And the tree is of course fabulous.

PAUL: We heard about your absentee American boyfriend and his bequest.

CORALIE: [*laughing*] All lies. But it was just what I needed. I've run to ground in my cliff-hanger hide-out.

ANNE: That staircase is just fantastic.

CORALIE: It gets me up and it gets me down.

ANNE: We just put in a new staircase at home. We've got this terrace house in Carlton and the old staircase was failing apart with dry rot and claret seepage, so we bought this spiral steel affair and put it up ourselves. It was quite a job—we rigged up a block and tackle on the front balcony, hauled this long steel pole into place in the stairwell, and then welded on the steps with an oxy torch a friend of Paul's lent us. It's a bluestone terrace, so the steel doesn't look too out of place. It gives us lots more room to move, which is beaut. [*Pause.*] I'm pregnant again.

CORALIE: Congratulations.

> *Pause.*

PAUL: What about you, Coral? How are you getting on?

CORALIE: Well, apart from my caretaking responsibilities, nothing much. Just lying fallow, drifting.

PAUL: Just like when I first met you. You were at East Sydney Tech. Amongst the Art School Push.

CORALIE: I never belonged to the Push.

ANNE: Why not?

CORALIE: I didn't have enough Pull! [*She laughs loudly. To* STUART] Here, noisy, let me give you another drink.

STUART: Um, no thanks.

CORALIE: Get it into you! [*She fills his glass with bourbon.*] Yes, I saw the amount of wheeling and dealing, the heavy political shit that was needed on that in-group treadmill and I thought bugger it, if you have to trade in your tits you might as well be paid for it. I went to the beach instead. I was poor but honest and had a suntan. [*Pause.*] Things haven't changed much.

PAUL: Aren't you teaching any more?

CORALIE: No, I'm out of work. I've had it.

> ANNE *considers this.*

ANNE: I find unemployment among teachers hard to understand. Surely if one is qualified one could find a suitably rewarding job.

CORALIE: What you say is very true. But sometimes some of us pedagogues feel the need to jack up.

PAUL: What do you do with your time?

CORALIE: Oh, this and that. I belong to a film group, actually. I've seen *The Five Samurai* seven times.

ANNE: You mean *The Seven Samurai.*

CORALIE: Yes. I've seen it five times.

> *Pause.*

ANNE: That view looks just fantastic. I love those banana trees and that darling little bridge over the gap.

> *She wanders out onto the terrace.* STUART *and* PETER *go to the bar,* STUART *to exchange his bourbon for beer, and* PETER *to stock up.*

JILL: [*to* PAUL, *heavily*] It really is a beautiful view from the terrace.

> PAUL *goes out to join* ANNE. JILL *and* CORALIE *talk quietly among themselves.* PETER *looks at* STUART*'s discarded bourbon.*

PETER: Waste of good liquor.

STUART: I don't drink spirits. Coralie will have to learn that.

PETER: Oh? Why should she?

STUART: Because I'm going to marry her.

PETER: You?

STUART: Yes.

PETER: Does Coralie know about this?

STUART: Not yet.

PETER: I see, and you're going to sort of propose to her, are you?

STUART: That's right.

> PETER *giggles. He is slightly drunk.*

PETER: Don't you think you might be biting off more than you can chew?

STUART: I'm not a lawyer. I don't bite people.

PETER: Forgive me, but I'm trying to picture it. I mean, Coralie's a... big girl.

STUART: Big tits.

PETER: Oh, absolutely, yes.

STUART: She doesn't faze me.

PETER: Well, if I hear an explosion that sounds like the end of the world I'll know you've put the hard word on La Lansdowne. Incidentally, good luck.

STUART: Thanks.

> PETER *giggles.* PAUL *comes over to fill his glass.*

PETER: Is she giving you a bad time?

PAUL: Coral? Oh, she's all right. I've seen her in worse moods than this. I still don't know if what she needs most is a lot of loving or a well-aimed live telegraph pole.

PETER: But she's probably changed since you knew her.

PAUL: Not a bit. It's as if I left yesterday.

STUART: But she will change. I'm sure of that.

PAUL: Whatever you reckon. Bloody good stuff, this.

PETER: Yes, marvellous. I'm getting quite pissed.

PAUL: You're a lawyer, aren't you?

PETER: Lawyer, neighbour, these are mere labels. This man, I believe, is a poet and public servant.

STUART: Nothing more, nothing less.

PAUL: You look like death warmed up to me, mate. [*To* PETER] You sort of helping Coral through a bad patch, are you?

PETER: I take a paternal interest in the girl's welfare. After all, we're neighbours. Two solitary souls perched high above the Pacific.

PAUL: What about you?

STUART: I'm a house guest.

PAUL: Nothing more?

STUART: And nothing less.

PAUL: Jesus! Surrounded by smart farts. Here, let's all get pissed.

PETER: An excellent idea.

STUART: You blokes have got a head start.

PAUL: What are you drinking beer for? Bloats you up like a stuck pig.

PETER: Never been weaned, that's his problem.

STUART: You'll see the light. Your brains'll turn to putty with that stuff.

PETER: I look forward to that.

PAUL: I've had a hell of a day, driving up to Pokolbin and back, stopping every five minutes so Madam can get out and have a piss or buy some dill cucumbers and chocolate ice cream.

PETER: You'll have to pander to your wife's cravings while she's pregnant.

PAUL: I pandered to my wife's cravings and that's how she got pregnant. Come on, where's your glass?

ANNE moves away from the door.

ANNE: Oh, I almost forgot, how silly of me! We brought you a present, Coralie. Paul darling, it's in my bag. Would you get it, please?

PAUL goes over to the bag.

We drove up to the Pokolbin vineyards today and bought some vintage port. One puts it down for a few years and that's how one builds up one's cellar. It's there in my bag, darling.

PAUL: Righto, righto.

He pulls out an iron with curling pins. They scatter.

ANNE: Paul, please be careful. Those curling pins cost money and it saves going to a hairdresser.

PAUL brings out a bottle of wine wrapped in paper. He goes to CORALIE and gives it to her.

PAUL: Here you are, Coral. This is for you.

CORALIE: Thanks, I'm overwhelmed. The first present I've ever had from you. I'll treasure it.

ANNE: It's from both of us. Now don't open it. You must put it down.

PAUL: Why? Tell me why.

ANNE: So it can mature.

PAUL: Why not buy drinkable wine now that we know is good. This stuff could be shithouse and we will have wasted all that storage space.

ANNE smiles graciously.

ANNE: You're difficult, aren't you? You're difficult to get on with. You ought to know, Coralie, you used to live with him. You ought to know that it's not easy.

CORALIE: It was like drinking Fanta through a live eel.

ANNE: Well, I think we should build up a cellar and this is a start.

PAUL: Okay.

ANNE: It's very pretty up there, round the vineyards. We drove around them all and it was heaven without the children. It wasn't too hot, which was beaut. The only sour note in the whole day was when I lost my toothbrush. We stopped at this revolting Ampol service station and I went to the toilet, which was ghastly. The floor was awash with petrol and urine and I dropped my toothbrush in it. Urgh! [*Pause. She sits down.*] Paul, will you ring your mother and see if the children are all right.

PAUL: Of course they're all right. Jesus, you wanted to get away from them and now you—

ANNE: Are you sure your mother knows how to look after them?

PAUL: My Mum not know how to... Jesus!

CORALIE: You put your foot in it there.

> ANNE *indicates a tall cylindrical metal vase on the bar.*

ANNE: Coralie, I don't want to sound difficult, but there's something about that vase that throws me completely. I wonder if we could do without it for the time being.

> CORALIE, *puzzled, puts the vase under the bar.*

Thank you.

> *Pause.*

PETER: I must be going. Thank you, Coralie. Good night, everyone.

> *General goodbyes.*

CORALIE: See you soon, Peter.

> *She goes to the door with him.*

PETER: What about my... offer?

CORALIE: I want to say yes and I want to say no.

PETER: I have a world view which encompasses indecision.

CORALIE: You would. All right, yes, it's a date.

PETER: Marvellous.

> *She turns to go.*

You do know the Roaring Twenties were followed—

CORALIE: —were followed by the Great Depression. Yes, I do.

PETER: Palm Beach would be a good place to sit it out.

CORALIE: Let's take it one offer at a time.

> PETER *exits.*

JILL: He's a funny bloke, Coralie. He seems to sort of just hang around, doesn't he?

CORALIE: Well, he's by himself. And he's good company, so why not? He sustains me. He's a very cool, together man. He oozes equilibrium and reason and sanity and all those qualities Jill lost and I never had. When I want a bit of solace I drop in on him. When he's had a hard day and wants a drink, a bit of suppressed titillation and a good listener he comes over here. End of biased account.

JILL: Footnote: He's got money.

CORALIE: [*glaring at* JILL] I believe he has, yes.

STUART: I think Coralie sees him as a father figure…

CORALIE: My father??? I see…?? [*Coolly*] There's no such thing as a 'father figure' outside of some Canberra coffee shop where you'd belong. My father was a giant.

PAUL: [*to* STUART] You put your foot in it there.

ANNE: Has he only one eye? Or is that patch an affectation?

CORALIE: He has only one eye. He lost the other in a skindiving accident.

ANNE: What a pity.

CORALIE: Oh, Peter's well off. Everyone around here is rich and deformed. It's freaky territory—lots of Mercedes and wheelchairs, expensively dressed cripples and crutches and elegant ladies with only one real tit. Millionaires with limps or one arm, that sort of thing. Peter's a refreshing contrast.

ANNE: I didn't notice any cripples. They all looked pretty healthy to me.

> CORALIE *looks at her. She stands.*

Where's the bathroom?

CORALIE: One goes up the stairs and then one takes the second door on one's right.

> ANNE *goes up the stairs.*

PAUL: Are you feeling all right, Anne?

ANNE: Yes, thank you.

> *She goes up the stairs and exits off the landing.*

JILL: You were very mean to that lady, ma'am.

CORALIE: It's my party and I'll cry if I want to.

STUART: Perhaps you misunderstood her intentions in giving you the present.

CORALIE: Listen, comedy relief, when I want your opinion I'll ask the dog.

JILL: Stuart, I'd better show you your room.

STUART: Oh. Righto.

JILL: Bring your bag.

> STUART *picks up his bag and follows her under the stairs left. She gestures him ahead of her and looks at* CORALIE *coldly.*

Vicious fuckin' bitch.

> *She follows* STUART *out.*

PAUL: So. All by yourself.

CORALIE: Except for shit-for-brains from the corridors of power. She's been staying here.

PAUL: But you're really all by yourself.

CORALIE: Yes.

PAUL: Surprised to see me?

CORALIE: A little, yes.

PAUL: I thought I might give you a bit of a thrill. I should have seen you long before this.

CORALIE: Oh, why? Surely Anne and Joanna and Sing Sing are a big enough handful.

PAUL: Tamsin.

CORALIE: Tamsin. Is she a rhythm baby?

PAUL: Don't be a pain, Coral.

CORALIE: Of course, Joanna wasn't, considering the unseemly haste of the posting of your wedding banns.

PAUL: We were going to get married anyway.

CORALIE: Oh, I know. The decision had already been made by your tyke matriarch of a mother and that Irish thug, Brother Brengun.

PAUL: Brendan. Listen, it was my decision to marry Anne. Now you live with it, okay?

CORALIE: Oooo. All right, then.

PAUL: Anyway, forget all that. I wanted to see you.

CORALIE: Terrific. Just name the dates and times. I'll be there.

PAUL: Coral, you don't know how good it is to see you.

CORALIE: [leading him on] I missed you, Paul.

PAUL: I move into a different gear with you. A part of me has always wanted you.

CORALIE: A part of you, eh? A part. Now let me guess, it's the part of you which responds to sunsets, rum-soaked tobacco and windscreens in the rain. The yearningly romantic side of a responsible-but-unfulfilled businessman, husband and father. That part of you whose sensitivity has been bludgeoned by an unfeeling relationship and seeks a modicum of solace elsewhere. Well, I'm not going to be the bunny, not at twenty-nine, so go and do your scavenging away from here.

PAUL *laughs.*

PAUL: Give it to me, Coral, get stuck into it. Actually, I meant the part of me that thinks you're a good sport and just wants to have a relaxing drink. Tell me, what are you going to do when Rockefeller comes back?

CORALIE: Don't know.

PAUL: Still prone to sulking, I see. Ooohh, look at that bottom lip thrusting out.

CORALIE: [smiling despite herself] Oh, shut up.

PAUL: Look, what I wanted to say to you was if you want to go overseas or just on a trip I can fix it up for you. Big discounts, you know?

CORALIE: You're the travel expert, now, are you?

PAUL: Yep. I've been everywhere. Even had a book published.

CORALIE: What book?

PAUL: It's about travel, various places around the Balkans and the East. It's not an official guide telling you how many pairs of underpants to take, or what the Armenian for gonorrhoea is, but it tries to give the reader an insight into the people of each area and how they live and what their customs are and so on. Plus a few personal observations.

CORALIE: You'd be good at that. You've always been able to talk to people. Have you got a copy with you?

PAUL: I'll give you one. [*He goes to his bag and gets out a book.*] There we are. Do you want me to autograph it?

CORALIE: No, I don't go in for that sort of thing. It's a handsome book. Terrible photo of you, though. Were you constipated?

PAUL: No, I was thinking of you.

> *They laugh.* ANNE *appears on the landing.*

ANNE: Paul, I'm going to bed. Bring up my bag, will you?

> PAUL *takes up her small bag and hands it to her.*

You won't be long, will you?

PAUL: No.

ANNE: Don't be long. Goodnight, Coralie.

> CORALIE *waves.* ANNE *goes into the left door on the landing.* PAUL *comes back down the stairs.* CORALIE *puts the metal vase back on the bar.*

PAUL: I'm having another drink. Like one?

CORALIE: No thanks.

> PAUL *prepares his drink.*

PAUL: We'll go if you want us to.

CORALIE: Don't be silly.

PAUL: Anne likes you. She admires your strength and self-sufficiency.

CORALIE: Terrific.

PAUL: So do I. You won't be messed around with, will you?

CORALIE: Not unless I want to be. I seem to want to be.

PAUL: The only thing that depresses me, Coral, is to see you alone. I think you need someone.

CORALIE: I've survived for twenty-nine years on my own. With the warmth of my own body.

PAUL: That's a cruel thing to say.

CORALIE: You were there some of the time. But you're right about the self-sufficiency. Now you are. I don't have to do desperate things like getting on a crowded bus just to feel contact with people any more. I can sit out on the front slope and look down at the beach at all the bodies, see all that flesh roasting in the sun, and not feel a thing. That is an achievement.

PAUL: Look, when we were together, I know I bungled... I know I could have...

CORALIE: Let's not go into that. Anyway, it was fun. We had a few laughs.

PAUL: It was good, overall.

CORALIE: Yes. I've managed to bash it into some kind of perspective, along with a couple of other basics. You can't walk on broken glass any more with nothing on your feet but mayonnaise. That's my current outlook, anyway. What are you grinning about?

PAUL: I was just thinking how very you you still are.

CORALIE: You, you, what am I, a sheep? Of course I'm still me. This is still my skin, I'm still in here inside it.

PAUL: I can hear you.

> JILL *enters*.

JILL: Stuart's fixed up.

CORALIE: Did you tuck him in?

JILL: No, ma'am, I didn't.

CORALIE: This bright young pair have arranged an assignation in my house. Can you believe it?

PAUL: Shocking.

JILL: Where's Anne? Is she all right?

CORALIE: She's gone to bed, which is beaut.

JILL: What are you two doing?

CORALIE: Nothing much.

JILL: I'll bet.

CORALIE: Don't be ridiculous. We were just reminiscing.

JILL: You mean about when you lived together?

PAUL: Yeah, the good old days.

JILL: Was it like being married?

CORALIE: Not quite.

PAUL: We had an arrangement.

CORALIE: Hey, do you remember the time when we decided bits on the side would be brought into the open?

PAUL: [*laughing*] Bloody chaos.

CORALIE: Paul had been working as a builder's labourer all summer and he'd come home all fit and sweaty with a deep tan. Yummy. I regretted our arrangement, I can tell you.

PAUL: It never worked, anyway.

CORALIE: That time you picked up that seventeen-year-old girl at that big dinner at the Mandarin. Remember that?

PAUL: Yeah. I gave you the word not to come back before twelve and took her home.

CORALIE: And I had to sit there for hours drinking Chinese tea with that randy cretin from the bush.

PAUL: But what about when you came home? I was working overtime.

CORALIE: I kept my side of the bargain.

PAUL: There I was. Chockers. The poor kid was so embarrassed.

They laugh.

CORALIE: Serves you right, you bastard. No sense of time, no decorum, no propriety.

PAUL: Must be my background.

CORALIE: No education, that's Paul's problem. All those Fascist Marist Mickheads dinned into their charges was the three Rs: Repression, Regression and Recession.

PAUL: What was the girl? Relaxation?

They laugh. JILL *stares at the floor.* CORALIE *jumps up.*

CORALIE: Well, I'm going to bed. Everyone else, depending on where their heads is at, can sort things out for themselves. Goodnight.

She goes up the stairs.

PAUL: Goodnight, Coral.

JILL: Night, ma'am. [*Pause.*] Would you like something to eat?

PAUL: No, I'm all right, thanks.

JILL: Do you think you'll stay long?

PAUL: A few days. I'd best look for a flat as soon as possible.

JILL: Won't American Express get one for you?

PAUL: They've got a lease on a few padded cells, but I couldn't live there, and it's no place for kids.

JILL: Why'd you come here?

PAUL: Oh, we always stay with friends in rotation when we come to Sydney.

JILL *looks at him.*

I thought it'd be good to see Coral again.

JILL: She's very unhappy.

PAUL: Yes.

JILL: Well, I'm going to bed. See you.

PAUL: Right.

JILL *goes up the stairs. She stops on the landing.*

JILL: Turn the lights out, will you?

PAUL: Okay.

> JILL *exits left.* PAUL *goes to the window and looks out at the view. He drains his glass and puts it back on the bar. Then he picks up his bag, turns off the living room lights and goes up the stairs. He stops on the landing, outside* CORALIE'*s door. He hesitates, then puts the bag down.*

Coral? Can I come in?

> *He goes into* CORALIE'*s room, pushing the door to. The ground floor lights go on and* STUART *crosses and goes into the kitchen. He wears pyjamas.* ANNE *comes out of the left bedroom door on the landing, wearing a nightdress. She sees* PAUL'*s bag and goes to the door to* CORALIE'*s bedroom. She pushes it slightly ajar and looks in. Then she pulls it to, goes downstairs to the bar and pours herself a drink.* STUART *comes out of the kitchen carrying a sandwich.*

ANNE: Oh!

STUART: Just having a snack. Did I startle you?

ANNE: No, it's all right. I couldn't sleep. It's so hot.

STUART: Can you hear the surf from your room?

ANNE: No. [*Pause. She sits.*] That service station. Where we stopped today. There was a tanker there and we couldn't get to the bowsers for ages. The man who was serving petrol didn't seem to care how long it took. He told Paul to put out his cigarette and I went to the toilet and lost my toothbrush. And when I came back the tanker was gone and the man serving petrol said: 'You have to watch how you go in there.' [*Laughing gaily*] I said: 'That's good advice but it's a bit late.' Imagine! I could have drowned or been asphyxiated and his advice was too late. What presence of mind!

STUART: They're a bit slow out in the country.

ANNE: Slow! 'You have to watch how you go in there.'

> *She laughs. Pause.*

STUART: Well, I'm going to retire. See you in the morning.

ANNE: Good night.

> STUART *goes out left.* ANNE *smiles, hesitates, then goes up to the bar. She takes off her watch, her rings and a small pendant and drops them in the vase. She opens the glass door right. A light breeze ruffles her nightdress. She breathes deeply, relaxing. Then she goes out the door. Fade out.*

INTERVAL

SCENE TWO

One-thirty the following Friday afternoon. A hot, sunny day. There is a stain on the tree trunk. CORALIE *enters through the glass door, right. She wears a bikini and carries a towel, a basket and a spray of leaves. She goes into the kitchen, fills a vase with water and re-enters. As she moves about she sings to herself. She is arranging the spray in the vase on the sideboard when* STUART *enters, puffing. He wears swimming trunks and a casual shirt.*

STUART: You beat me!

CORALIE: I took a short cut. Isn't this a beautiful spray? Flowers tend to leave me cold, especially when they're clustered in posies and bunches, but I love sprays of leaves, the way they lift a room.

> *She is leaning over, concentrating on the leaves.* STUART *admires her from behind.*

STUART: Yeah, they're great. I feel hot again.

CORALIE: Do you? I feel good. The water was lovely.

STUART: Yes, but the climb up the hill, that was murder.

CORALIE: You poor thing. I felt so sorry for you when that lady in the wheelchair ran over your sandcastle.

STUART: Well, what a bastard of an act.

CORALIE: [*laughing*] You should have seen the expression on your face!

STUART: I was upset, and rightly so. You build a structure from the foundations up, you plan, you extend, you decorate, and what happens? A rich bitch in a wheelchair runs all over it.

> CORALIE *giggles and ruffles his air.*

CORALIE: Oh, stop being so pretentious. Actually I was intrigued by those two angels of death in white coats who were helping her. I wonder if they're kept men? I've always wanted an occidental house-boy.

STUART: I'm a bit thirsty.

CORALIE: That bloody dog's pissed on my tree! [*She examines the stain on the tree trunk, and then rushes to the sideboard drawer and gets out a hair dryer.*] Jesus F. Christ! Turn your back for five minutes and what happens? Rack and ruin, buggeration all round. Things fall apart, the centre cannot hold. Oh, my tree, my tree, my beautiful tree, light of my life, my tree, my tree! [*She plugs in the hair dryer, turns it on and rushes to the tree. She aims the dryer at the stain, but to no avail. She turns it off.*] Bloody thing. It's so ugly.

STUART: Don't worry. It'll fade away.

She goes to the sideboard and gets a carving knife. She cuts off the bark with the stain and drops it in the waste paper basket.

CORALIE: There we are. I couldn't bear it.

STUART: You're not going to leave it like that, are you?

CORALIE: What do you mean?

STUART: The tree will die unless you bathe the wound.

CORALIE: What with?

STUART: Olive oil and egg whites should do it. Have you got any?

CORALIE: I hope so. I'll look.

She makes for the kitchen. STUART *laughs.*

What's so... oh, you bugger!

She throws a cushion at him.

STUART: Sorry. I couldn't resist.

CORALIE: You don't deserve it, but would you like some lunch? A salad?

STUART: Yes, thanks.

CORALIE: You set the table while I get things organised.

STUART *sets the table.* CORALIE *goes into the kitchen, humming to herself. She comes out with two plates for the table, singing.*

I was going to be a singer once, did I tell you?

STUART: No, you didn't. Sort of like Janis Joplin, eh?

CORALIE: I should say not. Frightening woman. The idea of being found dead in a hotel bathroom. Yuk! No, I was going to be just like my childhood heroine, Brenda Lee—well, a bit taller.

CORALIE *sings into an imaginary hand mike, with much flicking of the cord.*

Lonely... yesterday
Lonely... today
Lonely... tomorow.

She bows her head.

STUART: Great lyrics.

CORALIE: They express a great sentiment. And what about my idol, Lesley Gore.

She sings.

Sunshine... sunshine
Good morning sunshine...

Oh God, no. It's no use.

CORALIE *shudders.*

STUART: Are you all right?

CORALIE: I can feel night over my shoulder. We're here in the middle of the day and the sun is warm but I can feel night over my shoulder.

STUART: Come on, you'll be all right.

CORALIE: For four days now I've been seeing Anne's face in my mind's eye. And her body when they fished it out of the sea.

STUART: Yes, it was very sad, but let's try to—

CORALIE: That poor girl! That poor bloody girl! Paul was just sitting on my bed talking to me.

STUART: Now look, just try to keep calm.

CORALIE: Okay, okay. You're right. Calm.

STUART: Calm.

CORALIE: I remember when my father died I managed to shut out the pain for hours on end. Found all sorts of things to take my mind off the pain.

STUART: You're doing very well this time, too.

CORALIE: Oh, this is different. And besides, you've been rallying round.

STUART: I do what I can.

CORALIE: You've been marvellous. It's such a relief to be with someone who doesn't want to force me into anything. Peter and Paul are always laying heavy numbers on my head, and elsewhere. Always trying to make me play a role, and a supporting one at that. Brenda Lee would never have stood for it.

STUART: Well, you shouldn't let them bully you.

CORALIE: Oh, I have the odd horseshoe in my boxing glove. Anyway, it's not them I'm worried about, it's Anne. She's dead and I can't get her out of my mind. I can't.

STUART: Look, you heard what Paul said. She would have done it anyway. It wasn't anything to do with you. She had nowhere to go, she was dragged down.

CORALIE: I'm so cruel.

STUART: You're not cruel. Not at all.

> *He puts his arm around her. Pause. She notices.*

CORALIE: What are you doing?

STUART: Putting my arm around you.

CORALIE: Well, don't.

STUART: Why not?

CORALIE: Because I don't want you to.

STUART: That's no answer.

> *He kisses her and puts his hand on her breast. She pushes him away violently, and jumps up.*

CORALIE: [*angrily*] What the hell do you think you're doing?

STUART: Come on, Coralie. Come on.

CORALIE: I don't believe it. You've got the nerve to try and... and...

STUART: What's so unusual?

CORALIE: You... you... worm. You little bastard. How dare you! I let you stay here and bludge off me, I treat you like a friend, and what happens? How dare you!

STUART: Coralie, I love you.

CORALIE: What???

STUART: I want to marry you.

> CORALIE *gapes at him. She tries to laugh.*

I'm not joking. The main reason I came here was to see you again. I really do love you. And I think you need me.

CORALIE: I can't believe I'm hearing this.

STUART: I think you're beautiful and devastating and so honest and you feel so strongly about everything, and you're vulnerable and passionate, and you've got dignity and some kind of solar energy inside you and you're a magnificent bitch with such ideals and... I'm not expressing this very well.

CORALIE: Oh, on the contrary, I get your drift.

STUART: I'm asking you to marry me.

CORALIE: How ridiculous! How dare you speak to me like that!

STUART: Coralie—

CORALIE: Christ, what a fate! What an inglorious end! Ambushed by an insect.

STUART: Look, who are you? What makes you so grand? What have you achieved?

CORALIE: You want a list of bourgeois accomplishments? Go somewhere else.

STUART: I see. You're just naturally grand, is that it?

CORALIE: Standing beside you I am.

STUART: The fact that I'm a bit shorter than you...

CORALIE: A good deal shorter.

STUART: ... doesn't mean that I'm not worthy of you.

CORALIE: You're not worthy of anyone. Go and find a female worm and leave me be.

STUART: I'm asking you to marry me. What do you say?

CORALIE: No! No! I say no to the worm. I tell the worm to piss off out of it. No! Oh, I want to, I want to hit you!

STUART: Just as I thought.

CORALIE: No! Do you understand that, you treacherous little pipsqueak? You worm. I say no! [*Rushing to a window and yelling out*] I say no! No! I spurn the worm! I want out! I tell the worm to piss off!

STUART *looks out of the next window.*

STUART: Those people way down there on the beach. They're looking up at you.

CORALIE: [*shouting*] I'm Coralie Lansdowne and I say no!

STUART: They're waving. [*Waving*] G'day there! How are you?

CORALIE: [*turning on him*] You prick! Get your things and get out of here and don't ever come back. Ever!

STUART: Look, just take it easy.

CORALIE: Shut up! Shut up!

STUART: Look, Coralie...

He advances on her.

CORALIE: Don't come near me!

STUART: Let me make two points. One: you're aggressive and hostile towards men. Two: you've got an idealised relationship in mind which is impossible.

CORALIE: Let me make three points. One: you're a supine fuckwit. Two: I am aggressive towards you but not towards men. Three: get the hell out of here.

STUART: It won't do, Coralie. I've tracked you down. You haven't got a chance.

CORALIE: You can't track me down. I'm a big high-flying bird. I'm bigness. I'm greater than you.

STUART: Cut it out. You're just a twenty-nine-year-old unemployed teacher with big tits. You're also fatter round the hips and arse than you were a few months ago.

CORALIE: Get away from me. Get out of here.

STUART: You're a paper tiger, full of bullshit.

CORALIE: No!

STUART: I'll give you time to think it over, but I know what your answer will be.

CORALIE: I'm bursting, I'm bursting out of the top of my head.

She slumps on the stairs.

STUART: What are the alternatives? Where do you go from here, Coralie? Answer me.

CORALIE: Leave me alone.

STUART: Just look at yourself. What are your choices?

CORALIE: I'm a... I'm a... high-flying bird...

STUART: What a pathetic illusion. All you've done, all your life, is describe a small spiral inside a vacuum . A collection of tiny arcs. How much longer can you go on?

CORALIE: [*weakly*] No...

The door bell rings. STUART *goes to the door and opens it.* PAUL *comes in.*

STUART: Oh. Paul.

PAUL: G'day.

> CORALIE *heaves herself up and goes up the stairs as* PAUL *comes into the room.*

Coral?

CORALIE: [*muffled*] Back in a minute.

> *She goes into her bedroom.*

PAUL: Is she all right?

STUART: She's fine. What about you?

PAUL: I got the afternoon off. They've been very good. What are you doing here?

STUART: Oh, I'm still on leave, and Coralie said I could stay on for a little while. Is there anything I can do for you?

PAUL: No. [*Pause. He looks out the window.*] It's great up here. The drive was amazing. All those used car lots and sun-tanned birds and fish and chips and real estate offices. I never really noticed before. But now it was sticking into my eyeballs. And when you get up here it changes into trees and bananas and flowers and cripples. I love it up here. [*Pause.*] Mum's been so good. And my sister Gabriel. I couldn't tell the children. I had to leave the room. I went down to the back fence and cried for an hour. Jees I came close to... jees it was close.

STUART: Paul, if there's anything I can do. Is there anything you want done that you don't want to cope with at this stage?

PAUL: Thanks. I'll let you know.

> JILL *comes in the front door with a shopping bag.*

JILL: [*to* STUART] Hi. Paul, how are you?

PAUL: I'm okay, thanks love.

JILL: If you want a babysitter I'd be glad to help out.

PAUL: It's okay, thanks. Mum's taken charge.

JILL: Righto, but give me a yell, you know?

PAUL: Yeah. Thanks.

> JILL *takes a pot plant out of her shopping bag.*

JILL: Look what I got down at the shops.

STUART: What is it, a thistle?

JILL: It's a bonsai plant, stupid. A fully grown live pine tree in miniature. They cut back the roots. Isn't it beautiful? I'm going to take it home with me. [*She puts it on the bar. Pause.*] Well, I think it's beautiful.

She goes into the kitchen with her shopping bag. CORALIE *comes out of her bedroom and briskly down the stairs.*

PAUL: Coral, I got the afternoon off. I thought we could—
CORALIE: Let's go.
PAUL: Well, what do you—
CORALIE: Come on.

She goes out the front door. PAUL *looks at* STUART *and shrugs.*

PAUL: See you.
STUART: Right.

PAUL *goes out the front door.* STUART *reaches for the spray in the vase.* JILL *comes out of the kitchen.*

JILL: Where's Paul?
STUART: Gone out with Coralie.
JILL: I thought that'd be on again soon. Well, what are you doing today?
STUART: Nothing special.
JILL: Want to go to the beach?
STUART: No, thanks. I've just been.
JILL: We could go for a drive.
STUART: I think I'll stick around here.

Pause.

JILL: You know, I've never seen any of your poems. Why don't you let me have a look at some, or perhaps you could read a couple out loud.
STUART: I didn't bring them with me.
JILL: You don't know any off by heart?
STUART: No, I'm afraid not.
JILL: Oh. [*Pause.*] I started writing poetry when I was thirteen. I thought it'd be a bit superficial to rely solely on my looks so I thought I'd have this surprise element at work, where I'd be good at basketball, a genius at maths, but really very aesthetic when you got down to bedrock. You know what I mean?
STUART: Oh, absolutely.
JILL: My first effort was called *Mozzarella Odyssey*, in which the poet— that's me—envisages herself as a pizza floating down a stormwater channel the morning after cracker night when the acrid smell of cordite was upsetting the seagulls. I—the pizza—lose all my olives and anchovies and finally get emptied out into the sea.
STUART: What happened? Did you get eaten by an Italian shark?
JILL: No, the sea symbolised eternity and the poem ended in three dots.
STUART: It's an interesting device, three dots.
JILL: I suppose this must sound a bit naive to you.

STUART: Not at all. Adolescence is entirely valid. Well, I think I'll go and catch up on my correspondence.

JILL: There's a good film on TV.

STUART: Oh?

JILL: Yes, on Movie Matinee on Channel Ten. *The Deep Blue Sea*. Let's watch it, shall we? Sit down.

STUART sits down. JILL *turns on the TV set.*

It's real fifties British stuff but quite good. It started at one-thirty so it's been going for fifteen minutes, but I'll fill you in. Vivien Leigh's left her husband to live with this pilot who's a sort of the-skipper's-gone-for-a-Burton type and he's burst the sound barrier or something and he likes golf and she's sort of unfulfilled. They're in this grotty flat and she's tried to gas herself. Her husband's a judge. [*She sits on the sofa beside him, then jumps up.*] Not enough contrast.

She turns the knob and sits down again, a little closer to STUART. They watch. JILL *turns and looks at STUART. He stares at the screen.* JILL *folds her arms and looks out the window. Fade out.*

SCENE THREE

Nine o'clock on Saturday night. The bonsai plant has gone. The living room is empty. PETER, *in dinner jacket, comes in through the glass door left.*

PETER: Anyone home?

He goes to the bar to get himself a drink and moves the metal vase. It rattles. He glances inside it. He empties ANNE's *watch, rings and pendant onto the bar and studies them.* STUART *comes out of the kitchen carrying a sandwich and a beer.*

STUART: Hi. She's changing.

PETER: Oh. Good. [*He gets himself a drink.*] Nasty business about that girl.

STUART: Yes.

PETER: I was quite shocked. Still, she looked all in. [*He puts some ice in his drink and sips it.*] So Coralie's still single, eh?

STUART: Yes.

PETER: How do you rate your chances? Do you think she'll come round?

STUART: I think she will. It's a question of coming to terms, it's not a question of what you want to achieve in life, it's a question of settling for what's available and reconciling fulfilment to an appropriate deal.

PETER: What does Coralie have to say about all this?

STUART: Coralie's gone a bit funny. She slops around the house thinking up song titles. Her latest effort is 'If There Ain't No Light In Your Bathroom Then You Got To Shit In The Daytime'.

PETER: How catchy.

STUART: But she'll come round. She'll come to terms. It's a question of survival and I don't rule out happiness.

PETER: You're a bit frightening, you know. You're like an apparatchik of the emotions.

STUART: That's better than being a green-keeper.

> PETER *stares at him.* CORALIE *appears at the top of the stairs. She wears a worker's cap, a dicky front and cut-away jeans.*

CORALIE: [*in a little girl voice*] Has my date arrived? Is my escort here? Gosh, I hope I make a good impression.

PETER: What the bloody hell...?

CORALIE: I was thinking, how could I dress to please tonight's assemblage. I thought you'd need a piece of ultra-nubile radical muff to water the mouths of your progressive colleagues.

PETER: Oh, for Christ's sake Coralie, grow up, you stupid bitch.

CORALIE: I was only trying to please.

PETER: Of all the sophomoric, asinine displays I've ever seen from you, this is rock bottom. Okay, I'm going without you. It would have been nice to have a young, intelligent girl who could—oh, bugger you, I'm going.

CORALIE: Peter. Please. I'm sorry. I've hurt you. I'm sorry. It seemed funny at the time, but now I feel like a real idiot. Please forgive me.

> PETER *hesitates.*

I'll go and change. Will you wait for me? [*Pause.*] Peter, we have something, and I'm sorry I've jeopardised it.

PETER: Okay.

CORALIE: Am I forgiven?

PETER: Yes, you're forgiven.

CORALIE: Terrific. I won't be a minute. [*Starting to go*] Oh, I almost forgot. [*Tossing an envelope at* STUART] A present for you, Stuart. A plane ticket for the earliest morning flight to Canberra. Understand? Back in a sec.

> *She exits.*

PETER: One of these days I'm going to introduce that bitch to a machine gun named reality. It'll be a messy but long overdue event.

STUART: I didn't think she'd... a plane ticket? How could she? I thought I was getting along... I mean, she was coming round...

PETER: Bad luck.

STUART: I was seeping into her consciousness. She needs peace, solace, a state of dharma. She needs kindness. She was opening herself up to me. It wasn't a big connection, but I was drawing her out, annealing her, she was coming to me.

PETER: I'm sorry to see your plans in chaos.

STUART: Yes, I moved too quickly. That was a big mistake. A few more days of infiltration would have done it, and then I could have built from there. She'll be the loser.

PETER: Stuart, you're giving me the shits.

STUART: I'm sorry. It's a slap in the face. I don't know what to do. Can you imagine Coralie at thirty-five? She'll end up like Anne. Apart from the calculations, I just wanted to give her love.

PETER: You're really stymied, aren't you?

STUART: A plane ticket. Poor Coralie.

PETER: I'm looking forward to tonight. It's going to be good. I haven't felt this alive for ages.

> *He pours another drink.* CORALIE *appears at the top of the stairs in a simple, flowing dress.*

STUART: [*stunned*] Jees, I don't believe it. A dress!

PETER: That's more like it. Sweet sixteen, my teenage queen.

CORALIE: Y'se can all get fucked.

PETER: What a virginal charmer. I'm odds-on for a goodnight kiss here.

CORALIE: Don't get too confident. This dress is a concession on my part. We are now back on even keel.

PETER: Fair enough. We'd better be on time or the politicians'll pinch all the food.

CORALIE: I think I'll tank up with a Southern Comfort first.

PETER: I gather you're not looking forward to the party.

CORALIE: We're not going to romp across the moonlight beaches of Polynesia and have Gauguinesque orgasms under the trees, but I'll accommodate myself. I won't be inconvenient. You can steal mah chickens but you cain't make them lay.

PETER: Don't take that attitude. You'll enjoy yourself.

CORALIE: I'll enjoy myself. I'll enjoy myself.

PETER: All right, have it your way.

CORALIE: Oh Peter, don't be silly. I'm only joking. God, you're touchy tonight. Thank you for inviting me. It should be terrific. Better than hanging around here with old Moth Balls.

> *A car horn toots outside.*

[*Calling out*] Taxi, Jill! Pity she's going. I got used to having her around again.

JILL *comes out onto the landing and down the stairs. She carries a suitcase, a handbag, and a shopping bag. She looks very business-like.*

Want a quick one before you go?

JILL: No, thanks. I won't keep the taxi waiting.

PETER: I'm sad to hear you're leaving us.

JILL: Yes, it's been fun, but I start work on Monday.

CORALIE: She's going to be Secretary to a Minister. What do you think of that?

PETER: Congratulations.

JILL: Well, goodbye Coralie. Thanks for everything.

CORALIE: Oh, Jill!

They embrace and kiss.

JILL: You look after yourself, ma'am, won't you?

CORALIE: Yes, and you too. I'll come down and see you soon.

JILL: I'll come up again as soon as I've got the job under control. That's if you'll have me.

CORALIE: Oh, Jill, of course I'll have you. Now you write to me next week and tell me all the ministerial secrets.

JILL: There won't be any. I believe in open government.

They smile at each other.

CORALIE: I'm sure you'll be a big success.

The taxi toots again.

JILL: I'll have to go. Try to be good.

She kisses CORALIE.

Goodbye, Peter.

They shake hands.

PETER: Good luck.

He picks up her suitcase.

STUART: Goodbye, Jill.

JILL: [*briefly*] Bye.

CORALIE *goes to the door with her.* PETER *follows with the suitcase.* JILL *takes it off him.*

I can carry it myself, thanks.

CORALIE *kisses* JILL *and she goes out the door.* CORALIE *looks a bit lost.*

PETER: She's going to do very well.

CORALIE: Yes. Well, I suppose we'd better push off. How do I look? Are any more adjustments necessary?

PETER: You smudged your make-up.

> *He takes out a tissue and dabs her face with it.*

You don't know where you are, do you?

CORALIE: Not really, but...

PETER: I help?

CORALIE: Yes, you help.

> *She smiles at him.*

PETER: Well, let's go.

> *She puts the glasses back on the bar. The front door opens and* PAUL *comes in. He looks around at them. Pause.*

PAUL: Entertaining again.

CORALIE: Uh... yes.

PAUL: I was at a meeting down the road. My boss's beach house. It was all full of shit so I walked out. I wanted to see you.

CORALIE: Paul, I wasn't expecting you.

PAUL: What do you mean, expect? I wanted to see you. I came here. Let's do something.

CORALIE: I'm sorry, but I'm going out with Peter tonight.

PAUL: Him? What's he got to offer?

PETER: Uh... look, I like to avoid unpleasantness wherever possible, but in this case I feel some sort of prior—

PAUL: You're not serious.

CORALIE: Yes, I am, actually.

> STUART *holds up a deck of cards from the bar.*

STUART: Why don't you cut for it?

CORALIE: You. Out.

STUART: Now hang on, I was only—

CORALIE: Out!

> STUART *exits to his room.*

PAUL: I need you, Coral. I blew out of the meeting and came here because I've got to see you.

CORALIE: And I'm always on tap.

PAUL: Look, there's no schedule for things like this.

CORALIE: There never was with you.

PAUL: You're not exactly a robot yourself. I seem to remember—

CORALIE: That was five years ago, you moron.

PAUL: And now I walk in and you've got two blokes on your string.

CORALIE: Two friends. Well, one and a half.

PAUL: You're like a rabbit, hopping in and out of the cot with all and sundry. Don't talk to me about your well-ordered existence.

CORALIE: In actual fact I've spent days without end getting smashed with Wormy and the Pirate Man, neither of whom could be classified as giants in the field of erotica.

PETER: Now look here, Coralie—

CORALIE: Sorry. Sorry. Unconsidered. Top of my head.

PAUL: My car's outside. Let's go.

CORALIE: No! I'm not going to drop everything for the sake of your whims. There used to be something appealing about your unpredictability but now there's nothing to compensate.

PAUL: You're a truly nasty bitch. There used to be a bit of zing along with the malice, but not any more.

CORALIE: The way you treated me, the, the way you treated me...

PETER: I don't really feel any useful purpose can be—

PAUL: Shut up! Coral, let's get out of here. I want to be with you. We can work things out.

PETER: She's changed, Paul. She wants different things. She doesn't want to be knocked around any more.

CORALIE: What would you know about it?

PETER: I can see you. I understand.

CORALIE: You have no inkling of what I am or what I aspire to.

PETER: Look, I'm not totally insensitive. I can understand your aspirations. For example, you wanted to be an artist, paint magnificent, brilliant pictures and so on.

CORALIE: Art nothing! I wanted to be brilliant in life, do you understand that, brilliant in life! [*She turns her back for a moment and then faces them.*] We shall now address ourselves to a couple of realities. I am going out with Peter tonight and we are leaving now. I know you've had a rough time, and I am sorry to disappoint you, but this was arranged a week ago. Good evening.

> PAUL *is undecided. He leans on the bar, and then notices* ANNE*'s things. He picks them up.*

PETER: They were in the vase.

> PAUL *stuffs them in his pocket.*

PAUL: Coral...

CORALIE: Paul, will you go, will you go?

> PAUL *hesitates and then goes out slamming the front door. Pause.*

PETER: How do you feel?

CORALIE: I hope Paul will be all right. He drives too fast when he's in a mood like this. I should have let him—

PETER: He'll be fine.

STUART *comes out of his room.*

STUART: I heard a terrible noise out the front—

PETER: Everything's under control.

STUART: What happened?

CORALIE: Nothing. A hard rain's gonna fall on that long train runnin'.

STUART: Song titles again. That's a bad sign.

PETER: We were just going.

CORALIE: Yes. Love shouldn't linger, love shouldn't wait. Who needs forever?

STUART: I remember Astrid Gilberto singing that.

CORALIE: Right. A voice from the past. I like my past. I wasn't mad about it at the time, but I like it now. [*To* PETER] Come on.

CORALIE *goes out.*

PETER: At last! I got her out of here. See you.

STUART: Bye. Have a good time.

PETER *goes out.* STUART *finds a book and lies down on the sofa to read. Fade out.*

SCENE FOUR

Late that night. STUART *is asleep on the sofa, the book on his chest. Silence.* CORALIE *appears in the right doorway. She stands there very still. She carries her shoes in her hand. When she starts to speak,* STUART *wakes up and looks at her.*

CORALIE: Night makes it better, you know. The whole area seems reasonably beautiful, the whole palsied landscape seems tangible when you're down by the beach looking up and you walk through the shadows of the bananas and there aren't all that many lights. The freaks are asleep. All the moaning has stopped. It's silent, like a ship in the night. I've been down on the beach and among the bananas. I've been there for hours. I left the party, left all the creeps to drink and talk and line up screws for the night. I left my 'escort', he was far too charming, and he frightened me a bit because he really is serious and he does seem to want me for something I can't face at all. So I left and walked and walked and sat on the beach and looked at the outline, the rocks and gums, the cracked shells and clustered droppings with very few lights and the freaks within and I surged up inside because I wasn't really part of this design, this conspiracy. And the surging peaked and then sank inside and I lay on the sand and I thought of the party and him and what he wanted me to do and the more I thought and the deeper I got into the night the more blurred the landscape became and the hill seemed like floodlights through a skeleton and the humming got louder so I went for a paddle in the sea. And I tried to think and my thoughts were physically painful and I walked through the rocks and the trees, through the bananas and heard the odd snatch of freaky life as I hauled up the steps to the top, where the most frightening thing of all was that this house seemed almost comforting.

She is by now sitting on the sofa beside STUART. *They kiss.*

You'll have to treat me well. I must be treated well.

Fade out.

SCENE FIVE

Four o'clock the following Saturday night. PETER *drinks at the bar. He looks at his watch.* PAUL *comes in the glass door, right. He too has been drinking.*

PAUL: What are you doing here?

PETER: Oh, I want to see Coralie, actually. She's not home. I'm waiting for her.

PAUL: Where is she?

PETER: I don't know. I haven't seen her for a week. Not since she walked out on me at the party.

PAUL: I want to see her.

PETER: So do I. I'm keeping a bourbon vigil.

PAUL: I want to see Coralie.

PETER: Then both of us will have to wait until she comes home.

PAUL: Both of us, eh?

PETER: Yes, I think that would be the best arrangement.

PAUL: What's your interest now? Still paternal?

PETER: I like the girl, even if she did call me a pirate.

PAUL: Yeah, well you just stick to being a good neighbour.

PETER: I'll do just as I please. Would you like a drink?

PAUL *nods.* PETER *prepares one for him.*

PAUL: Have you been here all night?

PETER: Most of it. I went to see a film with some friends of mine, a couple we've, I've known for years. It was a good film, I suppose, but I didn't like it. Too harrowing. I really don't want to see anything too strong or too depressing any more. They don't tell me anything new, which would be the only compensation. So my friends said come back for a drink but I knew it would be the usual ritual so I said no and came here. No sense in going home. There's nothing there.

PAUL: You haven't seen Coralie lately?

PETER: No. Tell you who I have seen hanging around a lot. Stuart.

PAUL: That obnoxious little twat.

PETER: Yes, I thought his 'Federation' campaign had proved a failure, but he's still here.

PAUL: Who is this turdlet? He says he's a poet but have you seen his poems? Has anybody seen his poems?

PETER: I don't know who he is and I don't believe a word he says.

PAUL: I can't believe he exists. If he's a poet, where are his poems? The whole thing's got me beaten. Coralie, where are you?

PETER *hands him a letter.*

PETER: This was on the bar.

PAUL: [*reading to himself*] Dear Ms Lansdowne... what? She's going back to teaching?

PETER: It's not definite. Obviously she's just made a few vague inquiries.

PAUL: But even to think of it.

PETER: Yes, it's a reversal of form. I've often suggested to Coralie that she ought to reconcile herself to the modest aspirations of our society, but she's always interrupted me and complained of headache, dizziness and nausea.

PAUL: What was she like last time you saw her?

PETER: At the party? Oh, she was lively and charming to start with—a smash hit—but then she withdrew into a corner and played mah jong for hours with the host's nine-year-old son Tarquin. When I tried to dissuade her she'd just smile beatifically and say: 'Tarquin and I are at peace with the universe.'

PAUL *shakes his head. They drink.*

How's your business going?

PAUL: What business? From what I can work out, the nuns are at Katmandu, the speed freaks are in Lourdes, and the Narrabri CWA are demanding their money back at Nairobi airport. Old travel joke.

PETER: What about your partner? Wasn't he—

PAUL: Hopeless. He's hopeless. No, that's not very fair. He's an old mate of mine. I've got a highly individual way of working and he couldn't follow it when I left. The debts are enormous.

PETER: That's most unfortunate.

PAUL: I finish up with American Express in a couple of weeks and then I've got nowhere to go. I've got nothing. Except Coralie.

PETER: But you had her before.

PAUL: I've got a different set of values now. [*The phone rings.* PAUL *looks at his watch.*] That'll be for me. I booked a call to Germany. I knew I'd be here. [*He picks up the phone.*] Hello? Yes, Coleman speaking. Right. Hello, Walter? Paul Coleman. Yes, how are you? Good. Sun shining over there? Oh, well, good for skiing, eh? Listen, Walter, fact is I wanted to ask about that account you were going to give us. Yes. Well, fact is Walter, we'd appreciate it if you could push it through pretty smartly, you know. You what? Oh. Yes. Look, Walter, that's a bit disappointing. Yes. Oh, come on, Walter, be fair. I don't think that's being very constructive. Now hold on, Walter, hold on... are you there? [*Pause. He hangs up.*] Bastard of a kraut cunt.

PETER: What are you going to do?

PAUL: Oh, I don't know. Bankruptcy, I suppose. They'll take the house, but who cares? Coralie's all that matters now.

PETER: What about your children?

They drink. The front door opens and STUART *comes in, looking happy and preoccupied, laden with a pile of presents in coloured paper. He dumps them on the floor with a grunt. He is wearing a suit, and shoes which make him five inches taller. He goes out again without noticing* PETER *and* PAUL. PETER *and* PAUL *look at each other.* STUART *comes in again with another pile of presents, dumps them and goes out again. He reappears, staggering in carrying* CORALIE, *who wears a beautiful dress. She is laughing.*

STUART: I'll make it. You watch me. I'll make it.

CORALIE: Careful, I'm not insured.

They collapse on the floor with much laughter, giggling and embracing. Then they become aware of PETER *and* PAUL.

CORALIE: Oh, hi. What are you two doing here?

PETER: Waiting for you.

CORALIE: What, all night?

PETER: Most of it, yes. What's... what...

CORALIE: [*giggling*] I had a pressing engagement.

STUART: A date with... Destiny!

They collapse with laughter. PETER *and* PAUL *are stunned.*

CORALIE: Followed by a Black Banquet.

STUART: A Saturnine Supper.

Much laughter.

PAUL: What's going on? Where have you been?

STUART: We just got married.

CORALIE: And then we had a big reception with all the Morgan and Lansdowne hordes and whoever else we could muster at short notice. All the relatives would have preferred a church wedding, even my hypocritical agnostic uncle.

STUART: We got pissed on champagne.

CORALIE: But we're all right now. We drove back in Stuart's new car at twenty miles an hour.

STUART: And this is our loot. Piles of it. And there's more in the car. I'll go and get it.

CORALIE: Do you want a wheelbarrow?

STUART: She'll be right.

He gets to his feet.

CORALIE: No one believed I wasn't pregnant, did they?

STUART: No one on my side of the family.

They laugh.

CORALIE: Stop big-noting yourself. [*Hugging his leg*] And guess what? My mother likes Stuart. She thinks he's lovely.

STUART: Short, but lovely.

CORALIE: They all said: 'But Coralie, he's so much shorter than you.' As if that matters! Anyway, what am I, a giraffe? But after they got used to the idea, they decided that Stuart was wonderful.

STUART: They were pleased for you.

CORALIE: And relieved. Especially my mother. She's convinced I'm now only a skip and a jump from the middle class waxworks. Oh, and you know what we did between the wedding and the reception? We went out and bought Stuart a pair of shoes. Show them, Stuart.

STUART *pulls up his trouser legs to show* PETER *and* PAUL *his five-inch heels.*

STUART: They're bloody killers, I can tell you.

CORALIE: If I'd been in bare feet we would have been a perfect pair. But alas, with my heels I was still taller than him. Never mind.

STUART: I'll get the rest of the presents.

He goes out. Pause. CORALIE*'s smile fades and she looks away from* PAUL.

CORALIE: How are things with you, Paul?

PAUL: Coral...

CORALIE: Let's have a drink to celebrate my marriage.

PAUL *goes to the glass door, right. He shakes his head.*

Look, what's the matter with you? Are you going to get all...?

PAUL: Coral, you did it. You did it.

CORALIE: Yes.

> PAUL *looks at her and then goes out.* CORALIE *steels herself.*

I married the man of my choice. Do you have any objections?

> PETER *stares at her.*

PETER: You? And Stuart?

CORALIE: Yes, me and Stuart. What of it?

PETER: It's absurd... ridiculous... I have a world view which... [*Stumbling towards the glass door, left*] It's absurd... totally ridiculous.

> *He goes out.* CORALIE *is still for a moment, then she goes over to the presents and looks at them. She picks one up and opens it. It is a Sunbeam electric frying pan. She looks at it.* STUART *staggers in with another pile of presents and dumps them on the floor.*

STUART: That's the lot.

CORALIE: Come and sit down and we'll open them.

STUART: Righto. I'll just take these shoes off first. I want to see if the floor's still there. [*He sits on the sofa and takes off his shoes.*] Ahhhhhh.

CORALIE: Stuart.

STUART: Yes?

CORALIE: Come and give me a kiss.

> *He goes over and kisses her. She has to bend down to reach him. She smiles at him.*

I don't care how tall you are.

STUART: That's good, because I'm not going to grow any more.

CORALIE: Come on, let's open the presents. This was the first, a Sunbeam frying pan.

STUART: You start at that end.

> *They sit on the floor and start opening presents.*

CORALIE: I had a ball at the reception, actually. It was good fun.

STUART: Pink sheets with a curly design.

CORALIE: Yuk!

STUART: Yes, it was good, except for the food.

CORALIE: Oh God, yes. That lethal roast lamb. And the dessert! I can't think of anything more right-wing than Bombe Alaska.

STUART: A Sunbeam frying pan.

CORALIE: A set of barbecue cutlery.

STUART: I liked your mother.

CORALIE: Stop being diplomatic. We're home now.

STUART: No, I did. I really did.

CORALIE: Claggy harridan. What's that?

STUART: A car-washing gift pack with bio-degradable shampoo.

CORALIE: Look at this awful vase. Bet it's from Sandra. [*Checking the card*] Yes, I bet she got it for her wedding, the bitch.

STUART: You won't believe this.

CORALIE: What is it?

STUART: A Sunbeam frying pan.

CORALIE: Christ, what imagination. They all think you'll be cooking breakfast for me. I could see what they were thinking.

STUART: Everything turned out all right. We all got pissed towards the end.

CORALIE: Yes, when things got a bit lively I said to Betty—that middle-aged cousin of mine, I introduced you—the ovoid lady in the black hat. I said to her: 'Betty, this is a vulture's banquet.' And she said: 'Why is that, Coralie?' And I said: 'Because there's a lot of carrion on!' [*She laughs. Her laughter is softer and more musical than previously.*] Well, it didn't happen exactly like that, but you've got to laugh. What's that?

STUART: A toaster. You can get three slices in.

CORALIE: This feels like a record.

STUART: What is it?

CORALIE: Janis Joplin. That'll have to go.

    She tosses it away.

STUART: Give me a hand with this one, will you?

    They open a box.

CORALIE: A Sunbeam Mix-Master.

STUART: That'll be useful.

CORALIE: Speak for yourself.

STUART: Here's something simple. A cook book.

CORALIE: I just know what this is going to be.

    She unwraps a Sunbeam frying pan.

STUART: Let's have a fried egg party. We can feed the masses.

CORALIE: I want another kiss and a cuddle.

    STUART *kisses her. They roll among the presents, giggling.*

Ohh! My lungs have been crushed. [*Hugging him*] You're solid, aren't you? You're really solid. I bet you were good at football. Did you play football?

STUART: I used to play on the wing for University Rovers, actually.

CORALIE: I bet you were fast and good at tackling.

STUART: Well, I was fast.

CORALIE *giggles.*

CORALIE: Let's go to bed.

STUART: All right. But I'm not going to carry you up the stairs.

CORALIE: Then I'll carry you up. Come on.

STUART: No, absolutely not.

CORALIE *coughs.*

CORALIE: Oh come on, Stuart, don't be a bad sport. I can carry you.

She coughs again.

STUART: You'll have to catch me first.

He runs around the sofa and she chases him with shouts of glee.

CORALIE: Come back here, you little bastard.

STUART: I'm still fast. I was a flying winger.

He runs halfway up the stairs.

CORALIE: Now that's not fair.

She coughs.

STUART: Are you all right, Coralie?

CORALIE: [*coughing*] Just something…

She subsides on to the sofa, wheezing. STUART *runs back down and gets her a glass of water.*

STUART: Here, drink this.

She tries to drink it but splutters all over the place.

Coralie, what's the matter? Can't you speak?

She gags, shaking her head.

Did a bit of food go down the wrong way?

CORALIE *wheezes and moans painfully.* STUART *slaps her on the back, but it doesn't do any good.*

Jees, I'd better call a doctor. [*He gets the phone book.*] Have you got a regular doctor?

She manages to shake her head.

Hang on, there's one down in Sunnyside Crescent, at the bottom of the steps. What's his name? [*He flips through the Pink Pages phone book.*] What's his name? I've been past there a thousand times. I could run down… No, I'd better not leave you. Salmon! That's it. Here it is.

He dials a number on the phone. CORALIE *tosses on the sofa.*

Doctor Salmon? My name's Morgan and… my wife's in terrible pain. It's an emergency. She's coughing and gagging and she can't breathe properly. 18 Jacka Avenue. Look, we're just at the top of the steps if you go out the back. I can see your house from here. Ours is the one with the tree growing out the top. Good. Thanks a lot. Really appreciate it. [*He hangs up.*] He's coming right up. Can you hold on?

> CORALIE *is breathing only with great difficulty.* STUART *makes her comfortable.*

Are you warm enough? Are you too hot? [*He takes off her shoes.*] Are your clothes too tight? Can I loosen anything?

> *She manages to shake her head.*

I'll get you a cold washer.

> *He rushes out to the kitchen and returns with a wet washer. He sponges down her face and neck.*

What a thing to happen on our wedding night! You'll be all right, Coralie, you'll be all right. Is there anything I can get you? Have you had this before? Have you got any special pills?

> *She manages to shake her head.*

Coralie, I can't lose you now. Not after all… Coralie, you've got to be all right. Oh, hurry up, Doctor Salmon, hurry! [*He goes to the right door and looks out.*] Oh no! Oh jees! [*He comes back into the room.*] He's coming, but oh God! Still, how was I to know? I couldn't have known. He's a doctor, he must have done this before. Oh jees, what have I done? [*He comforts* CORALIE.] He's coming, Coralie, he's coming. Just hold on, darling. You'll be all right. You've got to be all right.

> *Noises are heard on the terrace outside.* STUART *rushes over and opens the door.*

Doctor Salmon, do come in. I'm terribly sorry.

> DR SALMON *limps into the room. He wears sunglasses, casual clothes, carries a black bag, has an artificial leg, and walks with the aid of a walking stick.*

DR SALMON: Mr Morgan?

STUART: Yes, and I'm sorry about, well, you know, the steps, and your, you know, coming up, with the, uh…

DR SALMON: She can't breathe, you say?

STUART: No, she's been coughing and wheezing. Can't talk. It's terrible.

> DR SALMON *eases himself into a chair beside* CORALIE.

I'll get a cushion for your leg.

DR SALMON: I haven't got a leg. It was amputated above the knee.

STUART: Oh.

DR SALMON: Breathe in, dear.

CORALIE *struggles to breathe.*

Uh-uh. Now breathe out.

She wheezes.

STUART: See what I mean, she can't breathe properly. Could be food inhalation. Maybe it's a blockage in the larynx or the oesophagus.

DR SALMON: Thank you for your help, Mr Morgan.

STUART *retires to the bar.*

Now, Mrs Morgan, I want you to sit up. Here we go. Come on, dear.

He hauls CORALIE *into a sitting position.*

That's it. Steady. [*He brings a torch out of his bag and examines her ears.*] All right now. I want you to say 'ah' loudly, breathing out.

CORALIE *gags.*

Come on, you can do it. Lean forward.

CORALIE: Ah.

DR SALMON: Again, and longer.

CORALIE: Aah.

He slaps her hard on the back.

DR SALMON: Again.

CORALIE: Aahh.

He slaps her hard on the back.

Aahhhh!

DR SALMON: Big one, big one.

He slaps her.

CORALIE: AAAHHHHH!!!

DR SALMON: That's it. Now see if you can breathe.

CORALIE *breathes more or less normally.*

That's good. You're all right now.

He writes out a prescription.

STUART: What was it? Her epiglottis? Did any blood come up?

DR SALMON *writes.*

That was a bit scary there for a while. I didn't know what to do. She couldn't breathe properly.

DR SALMON: Here's a prescription for some antibiotics. There's a bit of inflammation in her upper respiratory tract. She should rest for a couple of days.

STUART: All right. Thanks, doctor.

DR SALMON *looks at the presents.*

DR SALMON: Just married, eh?

STUART: Yeah. What a way to spend your wedding night. Not a very good start, eh?

DR SALMON: That's the least of your worries. Goodnight, or morning, rather.

He goes out.

STUART: Bloody doctors. They never tell you anything. Poor darling. [*Kissing* CORALIE *on the forehead*] You had me worried. But you're all right now. What a night!

He goes to the windows and doors and pulls back the curtains. Dawn light fills the room.

Looks like a beautiful day. A few board riders out already. We could have some breakfast outside, if you feel up to it. Or maybe you'd prefer to go to bed. [*Pause.*] I suppose I'd better go and look for a chemist and get this prescription filled. [*Pause.*] Poor darling. [*Pause.*] You won't be able to go surfing for a few days.

Pause. CORALIE *stands up, a bit gingerly at first. She walks a few paces and stops. She looks around the room slowly and calmly and then her eyes come to rest on* STUART. *They stand there, looking at each other. Silence.*

CORALIE: You'll do.

STUART *looks at her apprehensively. Silence. Fade out.*

THE END

How Does Your Garden Grow

Jim McNeil

Jim McNeil (1935–82) was born in Melbourne. As a teenager he entered
the world of Melbourne's racing gangs and from the age of 21 spent most
of his life in prison, graduating from petty to graver offences. He wrote *The
Chocolate Frog* (1971) and *The Old Familiar Juice* (1972) whilst in
Parramatta Gaol, serving a long sentence for armed robbery and shooting
a policeman. He wrote *How Does Your Garden Grow* in 1974, following a
transfer to Bathurst Gaol, and was released just before the play's premiere.
His final play, *Jack*, was completed in 1977.

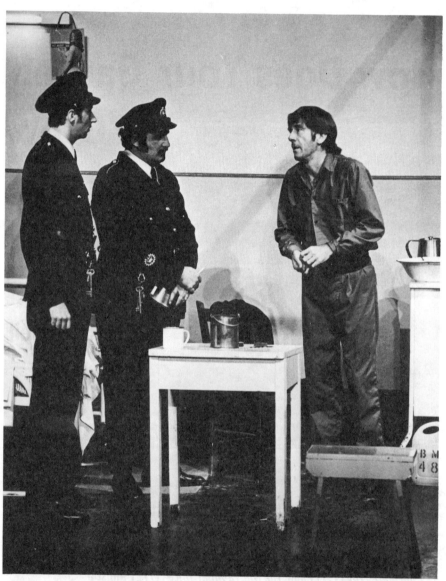

Left to right: George Shevtsov and Saviour Sammut as Wardens and Leslie Dayman as Sam in the 1975 South Australian Theatre Company production of How Does Your Garden Grow.

FIRST PERFORMANCE

How Does Your Garden Grow was first performed by the New Nimrod Theatre, Sydney, on 15 November 1974, with the following cast:

SAM	Max Cullen
FIRST OFFICER	Graeme Smith
SECOND OFFICER	Tony Llewellyn-Jones
SENIOR OFFICER	Don Crosby
MICK	Martin Harris
BRENDA	Darrell Hilton
SWEEPER	Don Crosby
LEVICK	Alan Tobin
WOMAN	Robyn Nevin

Directed by John Bell
Setting designed by Kim Carpenter

To Robert MacKinnon

ANOTHER BRAIN CELL DIED TODAY

Early to bed
early to rise—
how nice to be born
a sparrow.
But for a mind without feathers
you'll find
that a cell is too long
and too narrow.

CHARACTERS

SAM, a prisoner in his thirties
FIRST OFFICER, young, slightly intolerant and uncertain
SECOND OFFICER, older and more tolerant than the other
SENIOR OFFICER, a much older man
MICK, a prisoner in his thirties, younger than Sam
BRENDA, a prisoner about twenty-five years old
SWEEPER, a prisoner over fifty years old
LEVICK, a parole officer, a pleasant man of about forty-five
WOMAN, a dragon in her mid-twenties

SETTING

Scene One: Sam's cell after Saturday evening lock-up
Scene Two: The cell of Mick and Brenda, a little later
Scene Three: The prison exercise yard, Sunday morning
Scene Four: Outside the Parole Office, Monday morning
Scene Five: As for Scene Two, Monday evening
Epilogue: The exercise yard, the following Sunday morning

AUTHOR'S NOTE

Sam and Mick show a marked contrast in their dress. Sam is clean, but his clothes are crumpled and he needs a shave. Mick is clean-shaven and very neat in appearance.

SCENE ONE

SAM's cell. Bare regulation furnishings. A mirror above the table. SAM
*sits staring moodily at his tin food dixie on the table. He pokes at it with a
slow finger. He sighs and looks around the cell, sniffing in boredom, at a
loss for something to do. He cocks an eye at the radio box which is fixed
to the wall about ten inches below the small neon light fitting. He gets up
and goes over to pull the radio switch to and fro. The radio remains silent.
He frowns peevishly and turns to growl at the closed cell door.*

SAM: Cahn, it's time for me wireless.

> *Silence.*

Bludgers, yers are.

> *He scowls, hesitating, then flicks the switch to and fro again before
> returning to stand at the table. He catches sight of himself in the
> mirror and grins wryly.*

How yer garn? [*Nodding*] Shithouse. [*Lecturing*] Ah well, there yer go.
Yer will break the law, mate. Serves yer right.

> *He grimaces at the reflection. He looks at the dixie, then sits down,
> lifts the lid, grimaces and pushes it firmly away, shaking his head.*

Nah. I'm not gonna.

> *He broods into space for a moment, then again lifts the lid. He
> scowls at it again.*

Nuh. Yer can't get me.

> *He thinks for a moment and then brightens.*

Tell yer what. [*Rubbing his hands briskly*] We'll have a cheese sanger.
What about a cheese sanger, mate, eh? [*Nodding at his reflection*]
Yeah, glad yer thought of that, Sammy old mate, good on yer.
[*Chuckling happily*] Nothing like the old cheese sanger for a man on
the go.

> *He rises, smiling, and winks at his reflection.*

What do yer reckon, eh? [*Nodding at the mirror*] Righto, then! We'll
chop into her.

> *He rubs his hands briskly again and goes over to the cupboard.
> From the food compartment he takes out wrapped bread, a plastic*

knife, some margarine and a wedge of cheese in silver paper. He smiles as he puts it all on the table.

Ha-ha! There y'are, all the goodies.

He takes two slices of bread and spreads them with margarine. He begins to pick the silver paper away from the cheese. Seeing himself in the mirror again, he abruptly addresses his reflection.

Well then, you just go and wash yer grubby hands first. [*Nodding firmly*] Gahn, yer grub, have a bit of a wash before y'eat anything.

He scowls at himself, then moves as if reluctantly to pull the tin wash basin out from a corner. He takes up the water jug and pours water into the basin. He takes soap from the cupboard, removes his hat and coat and has a brisk wash. He dries himself with the towel hanging on the end of his bed, then replaces the towel. Taking out a comb, he goes to the mirror and combs his hair, nodding at his reflection.

Aw, yer look lovely. [*Smiling*] See? Don't yer feel better now y've had a dobie, eh? [*Nodding again*] Told yer, didn't I? 'Course I did. Now finish doing yer hair, and yer sanger'll be ready—when yer make it. [*Grinning*] No use eating it before yer've made it, eh?

He chuckles, sharing the joke with his reflection. He puts the comb in his pocket, removes the lid from the sanitary tub and empties the water into it. He replaces the soap in the cupboard, puts his hat and coat back on and stands happily, clapping his hands together once as if prepared for any action. Suddenly the radio comes to life. A band is half-way through 'I Wonder Who's Kissing Her Now'. He cocks his head and listens, smiling. The vocalist takes up the refrain on the radio.

RADIO: [*singing*] I wonder who's kissing her now...
SAM: [*harmonising pensively*] La-da-da-daaa.
RADIO: [*singing*] I wonder who's teaching her how...
SAM: Ha-ha-ha! That'd be the day.
RADIO: [*singing*] I wonder who's looking into her eyes,
　　　　Breathing sighs, telling lies...
SAM: [*joining in*] Listening to her half-pied lies.

　　He chuckles.

RADIO: [*singing*] I wonder who's buying the wine...
SAM: [*harmonising*] The awful swine.
RADIO: [*singing*] For lips that I used to call mine...
SAM: [*wryly*] What a goose—fair dinkum.
RADIO: [*singing*] I wonder if she ever tells him of me...?

SAM *joins loudly in the last line.*

RADIO & SAM: [*singing together*] I wonder who's kissing her now.

> *The music fades.* SAM *stands in an exaggerated pose for a second, then relaxes moodily. He stands there in thought. A radio announcer chatters brightly.*

RADIO: And now the time by our studio clock is... exactly... fifteen to five.

> SAM *reacts abruptly, flicking the radio off as music starts to play. Silence.* SAM *sneers at the radio.*

SAM: Up you and yer studio rotten clock !

> *He stands staring moodily at the radio. He gives a big sigh and stands thinking. Amused by something, he snorts and grins to himself. He recites into the air.*

Hickory dickory dock,
The clock, the clock, the clock.
The clock struck four, they shut the door,
Hickory dickory... fuck 'em.

> *He turns abruptly to the table, grimaces wryly as if at himself, and takes up the cheese. He strips the silver paper from it, cuts it and makes a sandwich. He takes the scraps and crumbs and throws them in the sanitary tub, and puts the other items back in the cupboard. He stands smiling down at his sandwich, then nods, smiling, at the mirror.*

Well now, mate, it's time f'yer tea. [*Winking at his reflection*] Yer gonna love this.

> *He suddenly peers at the mirror and frowns. He holds the mirror steady with his left hand and polishes it with his right sleeve.*

[*Nodding and grinning*] There, I can see yer now.

> *He sits down at the table and takes a bite of the sandwich. He savours it, nodding appreciatively.*

By jeez, yer make a bloody good sanger, mate, I reckon yer do. [*Shrugging*] Aw, well, I suppose yer wouldn't call it the world's best sandwich, like, but yer know what I mean, it's not too bloody bad in the circum-rotten-stances, which some people would refer to as the quality of our... ah... of our environment, actually, is what some people call this rose, is a rose, is a rose... not to be confused with a turnip, nor even an albatross... which flies in the air, and has feathers and eyes and a beak... none of which will be found on a rose, never at all, and so it doesn't do for us to confuse roses with bloody albatrosses—some people call them albatrossi... [*with a wide gesture*] ... and so forth. [*Nodding solemnly*] Which returns us, gentlemen, to the problem I mentioned—of whether our situation amounts to circum-rotten-stances, or whether it amounts to what some people call the quality of... ah... of our environment, as they say. [*Nodding at the radio*] You know who *they* are, of course, perhaps?

He takes another mouthful of his sandwich, chewing and gesturing.

Mmmn, I can see you know what yer talking about, mate. [*Smiling and shaking his head slowly*] Which won't do yer no good. No use knowing what *you're* talking about. It's what *they're* saying— [*nodding*] most important thing in the world, mate... yeah, what they're talking about—all that shit, it's essential you learn to understand it, mate.

He nods and takes another bite of the sandwich, gesturing with it as if to go on speaking. A bell sounds once, loudly, outside. He stiffens and cocks his head, listening. He rises gently and approaches the door with a frown. There is a faint sound of keys, etc. He nods knowingly.

Ah... there yer go... didn't I tell yer? Knew they'd lob again tonight, didn't I say so?

He turns around slowly, checking his cell, then moves about quickly, tidying here and there. He straightens his already-neat blankets. He takes the towel and swipes about on the floor, then folds the towel carefully again. He straightens the books on top of the cupboard. He tidies up the toilet compartment. He opens the food compartment door and blows furiously at the inside of the cupboard.

Gah! Bloody crumbs everywhere. Yer'll have to clean this out shortly, mate.

He shuts the cupboard and pulls a defiant face at the air, standing with hands on hips.

Well listen, I'll clean it out when I'm bloody ready! *I* live here, not them. They don't like it, let 'em stay out.

He suddenly stiffens and cocks his head, frowning uncertainly. Pause. He assumes a cunning expression.

Ahhh... I don't like it when yers are quiet... ha-ha... aw, no... Come on, where are yers? [*Grinning*] Don't tell me yers are gonna give me a miss? Forgotten me for once, have yers? Eh?

He listens open-mouthed, moving slowly towards the blank doorway. Pause. He frowns, uncertain, then moves to the table and takes another bite of his sandwich. He stands chewing, looking thoughtfully at himself in the mirror.

Know what? [*Nodding*] I reckon they're not coming, that's what. The bell rang, but they ain't here [*shrugging*] so they can't be coming or they'd be here. Simple as that, mate, elementary arithmetic. [*Nodding*] Point one, the bell's rung. Point two, they're not here. [*Pointing a finger at the mirror*] Which all adds up to the nice neat answer, mate [*shrugging*] that they've missed yer. [*Grinning*] Okay? Don't wanna complain, do yer? Eh?

> *He smiles and relaxes. He picks up the sandwich and has a bite. He sits down comfortably. The door opens. The* FIRST OFFICER *enters.*

FIRST OFFICER: Evening search. On your feet and face the wall, please, Eighty-seven.

> SAM *rises slowly to stand by the table, only half facing the wall. The* SECOND OFFICER *enters. They both stand regarding* SAM *briefly.* SAM *stands brooding.*

SECOND OFFICER: Have you emptied his pockets?

FIRST OFFICER: Empty your pockets, Eighty-seven.

SECOND OFFICER: Everything on the table, please.

> SAM *heaves a sigh. He reluctantly empties his coat pockets, putting down a comb, a pencil, several cigarette butts, matches, a scrap of paper, a piece of electrical flex about a foot long. Then he turns half-on to the wall again. The* SECOND OFFICER *nods, satisfied. He turns to* SAM's *bed and begins searching the blankets, unfolding and shaking them, tossing them back on the bed. He lifts the mattress and looks beneath, etc. The* FIRST OFFICER *pokes among the things on the table. He picks up the scrap of paper and reads from it with a frown.*

FIRST OFFICER: Two, nine, F, seven. [*He squints at* SAM *suspiciously.*] Well, what's this, then?

SAM: Dunno. I can't read.

> *Pause.*

FIRST OFFICER: I'm asking you a civil question.

SAM: Uh. Well, yer a civil servant, aren't you?

> *He smirks slightly at his wall.*

FIRST OFFICER: [*young and uncertain*] Now don't get smart.

SECOND OFFICER: Hold on, what's it say?

FIRST OFFICER: It says—here, you look. [*Handing over the paper*] Looks like some sort of code to me.

> *The* SECOND OFFICER *reads, then smiles.*

SECOND OFFICER: [*to* SAM] Two ounces on number nine in the seventh at Flemington? [*Grinning*] You must have plenty of weed. [*Laughing*] Did it win, Sam, or are these your wealth?

He indicates the butts on the table. SAM *stares bleakly ahead.*

FIRST OFFICER: You answer when you're spoken to, Eighty-seven.

He looks at SAM *angrily; the* SECOND OFFICER *looks at* SAM *with a smile.* SAM *ignores them both. Pause. The* SECOND OFFICER *rummages in the cupboard. The* FIRST OFFICER *stands looking at* SAM. SAM *watches the* SECOND OFFICER *out of the corner of his eye.*

Face the wall, I said.

SAM does not move. Pause. The SECOND OFFICER *proceeds through the articles in the cupboard then moves to the top where he briefly examines a few books, etc. The* FIRST OFFICER *regards* SAM *uncertainly.* SAM *is tense, brooding, unmoving. The* SECOND OFFICER *looks at the table.*

SECOND OFFICER: Check that lot.

He resumes his cupboard-searching. The FIRST OFFICER *begins picking up the items on the table one at a time. He picks up the flex.*

FIRST OFFICER: What's this, then?

SAM ignores the question and stares ahead.

I'm asking you, Eighty-seven.

Pause. The FIRST OFFICER *stands uncertainly. The* SECOND OFFICER *helps him out.*

SECOND OFFICER: What is it?

He comes over to examine the wire. He smiles, nods and looks at SAM, *who broods.*

Oh ho! You like your tea hot for supper, eh?

He smiles at his mate, tossing the piece of flex to him, nodding.

Uhnn... Well, you see the radio box there, with the light on top of it?

The FIRST OFFICER *nods in bewilderment.*

Ah. Well... [*taking* SAM's *tin mug from the table to demonstrate*] ... see, if we were to fill this mug with water, hmmm? And if we were to stand the mug on top of the radio box, under the light... see? [*Chuckling and glancing at* SAM] Then all we'd need to do then, would be to have a piece of wood...

He looks abruptly around the cell, sees a piece of wood on the table, picks it up, nods on seeing the hole bored in the centre of it, laughs and shows it to his mate.

See? A bit of wood like this? [*Nodding.*] Mmmm... then all we'd need would be a bit of metal—say, a small bedspring—and this bit of wire here... y'know?

The FIRST OFFICER *is getting the message.*

Ah, and we could make a little electric jug, sort of, hey?

He grins at SAM.

SAM: [*scoffing sullenly*] Tcha! Yer wouldn't want to try putting that fairy story in practice. Kill yer bloody self.

The FIRST OFFICER *seems inclined to agree. The* SECOND OFFICER *is confidently amused.*

SECOND OFFICER: Oh, come on! I know a boiling-up wire when I see one—like this one.

SAM: What one? [*Glancing at it quickly*] Never seen it before. Must be yours.

SECOND OFFICER: The wire doesn't belong to you?

SAM: Never even seen it—told yers.

SECOND OFFICER: Oh. Sorry. Well then, we'll get it out of the cell for you, no trouble. [*He throws it out the door.*] There we are, that's rid of it.

SAM: Thanks very much. I'm obliged.

SECOND OFFICER: All part of the service.

He winks cheerily at his mate. The FIRST OFFICER *shakes his head. They both start searching aimlessly about.* SAM *stands morosely. The* FIRST OFFICER *eyes the radio box. He reaches up and feels on top. He brings his hand down black with dust. He pulls a disgusted face and holds his hand as if wondering how to clean it.*

SAM: Heh-heh-heh!

He feigns a cough. The SECOND OFFICER *looks away. The* FIRST OFFICER *glares at* SAM. *The* SECOND OFFICER *goes on hands and knees to peer up under the table.* SAM *shuffles away a little to allow him enough room, remaining half-on to the wall.*

FIRST OFFICER: Face the wall properly.

SAM *steadfastly stands half-on.*

I'll call the Senior in.

SAM *heaves a sigh. The* FIRST OFFICER *regards him uncertainly, but with growing determination. The* SECOND OFFICER *straightens up and watches the silent issue between them. He pushes his cap back, scratches his head and looks glumly at his mate. The* FIRST OFFICER *looks back grimly.*

He's refusing an order.

SECOND OFFICER: [*sighing, shrugging, grimacing*] Ah, well, we're finished anyway.

FIRST OFFICER: Oh, no, we're not. We're not finished until such time as he does what he's told.

Pause. SAM *stares ahead of him. The* FIRST OFFICER *glares at* SAM. *The* SECOND OFFICER *watches them both unhappily. He looks an appeal to the* FIRST OFFICER. *The latter shakes his head grimly.*

I gave him an order.

SECOND OFFICER: [*sighing, to* SAM] Just face the wall will you, Eighty-seven, and we'll be leaving you.

The only movement is that of SAM's *chin. Pause.*

Oh come on, Jenkins, face the wall.

SAM *ignores their presence altogether.*

FIRST OFFICER: He's a real smartie, this one.

Pause. The SECOND OFFICER *reaches to gently nudge* SAM's *elbow.*

SECOND OFFICER: Come on, Sam—

SAM *explodes in hysterical rage, turning to face them violently.*

SAM: Don't put yer hands on me. Lemme alone. Keep your hands off me. Keep 'em to yerselves and don't bloody well touch me with 'em! That's the rules!

He glares at them defiantly. Pause. Both OFFICERS *are shocked and unbelieving.*

SECOND OFFICER: Oh, fair go, all I did was to just touch your…

He laughs uncertainly. SAM *glares maniacally at them. The* SECOND OFFICER *edges towards the door.*

SAM: Well, just you don't just touch me. I don't like yer touching me. That's the rules, you do what yer like, whatever yer think yer have to do; but none of that other stuff, none of your putting yer hands on me, that's all.

SAM *is hardly able to articulate, he has become so very upset. Pause. The* SECOND OFFICER *holds his hands out slowly.*

SECOND OFFICER: They're clean enough, aren't they?

SAM: Not for me they're not.

FIRST OFFICER: Hmph! An untouchable. [*To* SAM] Who do you think you are, so special, anyway?

SAM: [*broodingly*] I'm someone you better not touch.

FIRST OFFICER: And I'm someone might lock you up.

SAM: Well, don't talk about it. Do it.

FIRST OFFICER: All right, I will.

SAM: Well, gahn!

FIRST OFFICER: You're going the right way—

SAM: Tcha!

FIRST OFFICER: Oh yes you are.

SAM: Ah well, just do whatever yer have to do, whatever yer like.

FIRST OFFICER: My job is all *I'm* trying to do.

SAM: Yeah? And my lagging's all *I'm* trying to do! [*Furious again*] So why do *you* have to keep coming in here of a night and making it hard for me? Hey? Why do yer? Why me? Every bloody night!

> SAM *glares from one to the other. Pause. The* FIRST OFFICER *frowns, puzzled.*

FIRST OFFICER: What are you talking about? Who's been every night? What do you mean?

SAM: Tcha! Who else? Youse have!

FIRST OFFICER: Every night?

SAM: Yeah! [*Mumbling*] Well, bloody near, anyway.

> *The* FIRST OFFICER *looks at his mate and then at* SAM.

FIRST OFFICER: I was here once before, [*thinking*] and that was about four days ago.

> *He nods.*

SAM: Tcha!

FIRST OFFICER: Right, or not?

> *Pause.*

SAM: [*answering reluctantly*] Ah... well, it seems like every night.

FIRST OFFICER: This is the second time I've seen you in my life, that you've seen me.

SAM: That's an elegant sufficiency.

SECOND OFFICER: Well, what are you talking about?

> *Pause.*

SAM: About you keeping yer hands off me.

FIRST OFFICER: I haven't touched you.

SECOND OFFICER: And I hardly touched you.

SAM: Well, don't try it is all.

SECOND OFFICER: You were just asked to face the wall.

FIRST OFFICER: He was ordered to face the wall.

SAM: Tcha!

SECOND OFFICER: And you wouldn't oblige.

FIRST OFFICER: He refused an order.

SECOND OFFICER: Oh, well I wouldn't say it was exactly an order, you know. I mean, it wasn't exactly put to the prisoner as any direct command, would you say?

> *He looks from his mate to* SAM, *who tries to look quite uninterested.*

FIRST OFFICER: Oh yes it was, quite clearly an order.

SECOND OFFICER: Oh no, I wouldn't have thought so.

FIRST OFFICER: But I'm telling you so, Mr Jones!

SECOND OFFICER: And I'm telling you, Mr Braithwaite!

SAM: [to SECOND OFFICER] Wouldn't cop that if I was you.

SECOND OFFICER: [nodding to SAM] No. [To FIRST OFFICER] Now look, there's a bit of a difference between a request and an order, you know, if you'll think about it.

FIRST OFFICER: That's right. And I gave him an order, not a request and not a suggestion and not a pork chop. It was an order!

    Pause.

SECOND OFFICER: Don't raise your voice to me, mate.

FIRST OFFICER: I'm just telling you—

SECOND OFFICER: Well, don't try making a fool of me in front of a prisoner. If you don't mind.

FIRST OFFICER: No one's trying to do that.

SAM: Tcha! 'Course he was.

FIRST OFFICER: You keep out.

SAM: It's my joint, ain't it?

FIRST OFFICER: That's an order.

SAM: Well, how can I keep out, when I have to be locked in? Make yer minds up.

SECOND OFFICER: Shut up. [To FIRST OFFICER] Now have you finished making a spectacle in front of a prisoner?

FIRST OFFICER: What are you talking about? You're the one who's made the spectacle. I never put my hands on the man. It's against the regulations, if you need to know that, so I wouldn't overdo it were I you.

    The SENIOR OFFICER *enters and stands looking at them, unnoticed.*

SECOND OFFICER: What do you mean? I never put my hands on the man. I merely—

FIRST OFFICER: Oh yes, you certainly did!

SAM: My oath yer did. [Nodding] Didn't he?

SECOND OFFICER: I did not!

FIRST OFFICER: You did so!

SECOND OFFICER: Never did!

FIRST OFFICER: Did!

SECOND OFFICER: Didn't!

FIRST OFFICER: You struck him.

SECOND OFFICER: I did not!

    He turns to SAM, *who nods.*

SAM: Yes yer did.

SECOND OFFICER: [hurt by this betrayal] Well, you're a right one. I'm the one started off trying to help you.

SAM *shrugs whimsically.*

FIRST OFFICER: And I'm the one gave him an order to face the wall.

SAM: No yer never.

SECOND OFFICER: Oh yes he did.

FIRST OFFICER: Quite so.

> They both look at SAM *again. Pause.* SAM *catches sight of the* SENIOR. *He pretends not to have seen him.*

SAM: Please, officers. You shouldn't argue in front of me, it isn't right. If yers don't mind, I'll just face the wall until yers finish whatever yers are doing. [*Nodding to the* SECOND OFFICER] And don't worry about the way yer knocked me about before, I'll cop it sweet, no chance of me saying anything or making any complaints, y'know. Anything for peace, is my way. [*Mournfully*] But I do think it's a bit rough, the ways yers planted that wire on me. Yer know it's almost as bad as the way yers verballed me about not facing the wall. [*Nodding firmly*] Anyway, that's what I'm gonna do, whether yers like it or not.

> SAM *turns and faces the wall. The* OFFICERS *look at each other.*

FIRST OFFICER: He's... not the full deener.

SECOND OFFICER: Uhnn...'bout ninepence ha'penny...

> They look at each other, nodding. The SECOND OFFICER *takes out his book and pencil.*

[*Writing*] He refused an order...

FIRST OFFICER: And he had a boiling-up wire...

SECOND OFFICER: Uh-huh... [*Writing*] And insolence.

FIRST OFFICER: And a frivolous complaint. He said you touched him... you didn't.

SECOND OFFICER: Of course not.

> He writes. They smile at each other. The SENIOR *gives a loud cough. They turn in surprise.*

SENIOR: Don't mind me gentlemen. [*Smiling*] Carry on with your duties.

FIRST OFFICER: Oh, we, uh, we've just finished, sir.

SECOND OFFICER: Just this minute, sir.

SENIOR: Uhnn, you certainly have. [*To* SAM] Jenkins?

SAM: [*turning round*] Uh, yes sir?

SENIOR: Have you a complaint to make, Jenkins?

SAM: Oh, uh, well sir, I...

> He looks at the junior OFFICERS.

SECOND OFFICER: I'm a married man.

FIRST OFFICER: Me too.

> Pause.

SAM: Me three.

> *The three of them smile at each other.* SAM *remembers the* SENIOR.

Eh? Oh, no sir, no complaints from me, sir. Ha-ha! Just the usual search.

SENIOR: Mmmn? Well, I must say there seemed to be some sort of misunderstanding when I came in—that is to say the least.

> *Pause.*

SAM: Misunderstanding, sir?

SENIOR: Mmmn.

SAM: Oh! [*Laughing*] Oh, well so there was, sir, so there was; just for a bit there. [*Taking the piece of wood*] See this, sir? Ha-ha, it's the lid of me mug, yer see, to keep me tea warm?

> *He nods.*

SENIOR: Ah?

SAM: Ha-ha! Yeah... and, well, this officer found a bit of old wire that he thought was mine—but it wasn't, of course—and thought I might be making an electric apparatus for boiling up hot water or something. Ha-ha!

SENIOR: Ha-ha!

SAM: Yeah. Ha-ha! Y'know, he thought I might be using a bed spring, and wire, and wood, like in them Hollywood gaol stories... ha-ha!

SENIOR: [*nodding dubiously*] How silly... of course.

SAM: Ha-ha! Yessir. [*Gesturing with a smile*] Ha-ha! They thought I might be plugging into the light, and using the radio box for an earth, like. Ha-ha! Couldn't work, of course.

SENIOR: Couldn't it?

SAM: Oh, I wouldn't think so, sir.

FIRST OFFICER: Oh, certainly not.

SECOND OFFICER: No. When you think about it...

SENIOR: [*looking at them doubtfully*] Mmmmmmmn.

SAM: Ah no, of course not. It wouldn't work.

> *The* FIRST *and* SECOND OFFICERS *make noises of agreement. The* SECOND OFFICER *looks at his watch.*

SECOND OFFICER: Well, it's almost five...

FIRST OFFICER: So it is, time to go...

SAM: Ah. [*Smiling*] Yer finished?

FIRST OFFICER: Oh yes, thanks.

SECOND OFFICER: You're clean, Eighty-seven.

FIRST OFFICER: Got tub and water?

SAM: [*nodding happily*] Yes thanks, sir.

SECOND OFFICER: Oh well that's it, then.

FIRST OFFICER: We can all go home.

SAM: Uhnnhn. G'night.

He nods at them. They all turn to the SENIOR.

SENIOR: Well... everything all right, then?

SAM: Couldn't be better, thanks sir.

SENIOR: We'll leave you, then.

SAM: All right, sir. G'night, then.

> *The* SENIOR *gestures the junior* OFFICERS *out. They nod at* SAM *and take their leave.* SAM *nods after them fondly. He and the* SENIOR *look at each other.*

SENIOR: Jenkins...

SAM: Sir?

SENIOR: Jenkins... Goodnight, Sam...

> *He goes out.*

SAM: [*nodding after him*] Yeah, g'night, sir.

> *The door slams, the bolt bangs, the keys jingle, the lock clicks. Silence.* SAM *stands alone again. He smiles at the door, blows a long raspberry, makes a rude gesture, laughs aloud, goes to look in the mirror, and winks, grinning at himself. He looks at the table, sits down and takes up the last bit of his sandwich. He gestures with it.*

Now, where were we? [*Pause.*] Nah... can't think where we was. [*Chuckling*] Ah, the old memory's going on yer, mate. Hnnhn... can't even remember what we was saying ten minutes ago. Hmph, yer gone, mate. [*Pause. He finishes off the sandwich.*] Ahhh! Was that a good sanger, or what? [*Nodding*] I reckon it was, mate, the way yer wolfed it into yer. [*Thinking again*] Hmph! [*Grinning*] Can't even remember. [*Frowning defensively*] Aw, well it was them upsetting me, wasn't it? Yeah, 'course it was... Nothing wrong with the old brain box at all, not really... It's just them with their upsetment, is all... [*Pause. He brightens.*] Ah, yeah, that's what it was! [*Nodding*] We was talking about the arithmetic of this situation... that they wasn't coming tonight... [*Chuckling*] Never was no chop at arithmetic, were yer? No... ah, well.

> *He nods and smiles, then sighs. He looks around in boredom. The prison clock strikes five. He sits counting the strokes, nodding as he listens. Pause. He smiles whimsically.*

Hmmmn... Tea time, mate... the old brew.

> *He grins suddenly at the door and rises. He goes to the table, picks up the piece of wood and puts it down again. He goes over to the bed, lifts the mattress, and after fumbling beneath it pulls out a small three-inch spring. He puts this on the table. He begins to act*

chirpily, whistling tunelessly. He skips over to the water jug, brings it to the table, fills the mug, and puts the jug back. He takes a small jar of tea from the cupboard and puts it on the table. He stands regarding his apparatus. Suddenly he gestures pathetically, and smacks his forehead.

Ah... strike me! [*Crying plaintively at the door*] You've taken me wire! [*Hamming it up*] Oh, sir, please don't take me wire. Please don't take the wicked stuff yer find in me pocket because yers are so bloody clever. Please, sir...

He sags dramatically, pathetically, with supplicating hands reaching out to the door. Pause. He straightens, smiles and grins at the door.

Heh-heh-heh!

He goes to the mirror on the wall, and takes it down. He removes a length of plastic flex from the back of it, and holds it up.

Pardon, sir? This, sir? [*Shrugging*] Oh, well, sir... it's uh, it's a bit of wire.

He chuckles and makes another rude gesture. He smiles at his odds and ends, then takes up his mug, pulls the chair over to the radio, stands the mug of water on the radio box. He takes the wood, spring and wire, and climbs up on the chair. He is now ready to boil his water. He pauses, leans over to look down into the mirror, and winks.

Ahh, you clever little swine!

He laughs loudly.

SCENE TWO

The cell of MICK *and* BRENDA, *a little later. There are two single bunks. The cell has a 'homey' look: a length of string is stretched along a few feet of wall, on which hang a singlet, shorts and a scruffy orange wig; there are tin jugs, a wash-basin, a tub, books, floor mats, and so on.* BRENDA *sits on the floor, wearing trousers and singlet pulled off the shoulder. He holds a mirror and a small pair of tweezers. He is plucking his beard. Since he has hardly any beard, this is not a great task.* MICK *is also wearing singlet and trousers. He is exercising, throwing punches at the air, then touching his toes, then sparring again, his face a picture of ferocity for some imagined enemy.* MICK *slows down and stops. He stands huffing and puffing, then gives a slow grin as he observes* BRENDA.

MICK: Whooo!

BRENDA: Ow!

He frowns at a plucked hair.

MICK: Ha! [*Posing*] Fit as a mallee bull!

BRENDA: Moo.

MICK: Ha-ha-ha! [*Posing again*] How's that, eh? [*Proudly*] That's two thousand punches I done since breakfast.

BRENDA: Mmmmn!

MICK: That's counting lunchtime, like.

BRENDA: Uhunn.

He continues plucking. MICK *sits on a bed.*

MICK: Still saving blades.

BRENDA: Nearly finished.

MICK: What a way to bloody shave.

BRENDA: You be quiet. [*Frowning*] Oh I wish they wouldn't grow back!

He peers in the mirror.

MICK: Hnnhn… wonder they do, yer know.

BRENDA: I know.

MICK: Yer'd think they wouldn't.

BRENDA: Uhnn… they do, though.

MICK: Yeah. [*Pause.*] Wonder how old Sam's going down there. [*Peering at the floor*] I think they was down there before… poor old Sam.

BRENDA: Who?

MICK: The evening search.

BRENDA: [*feeling his face carefully*] Oh.

MICK: Lonely poor bastard he is.

BRENDA: Aren't we all?

MICK: Ha-ha! [*Dully*] I reckon. [*With a big tired sigh*] Whoo, I'm rooted.

He stretches.

BRENDA: Don't talk like that.

MICK: Ahhh.

BRENDA: Doesn't suit you at all.

MICK: [*grinning placidly*] Righto.

BRENDA: Mmmn, that feels better.

He stands, looks at himself critically in the mirror, and nods, smiling. He puts the mirror on top of the cupboard, the tweezers in a compartment, then takes the dustpan and broom to sweep up hairs. MICK *watches, smiling.*

MICK: Make sure y'get 'em both… haw!

BRENDA: Very funny.

MICK: Dunno why you go through all that. [*Grinning*] Do it just as easy
    with a chamois. Ha-ha!
BRENDA: You're not funny.

> *Pause. He puts the broom away, a bit huffy.*

MICK: Only having a go at yer.
BRENDA: Mmmmn...

> *He gives* MICK *a brief smile, then has a quick wash at the basin,
> while* MICK *watches.* BRENDA *takes a towel to dry his face.*

MICK: Putting yer glad rags on, are yer?
BRENDA: Don't you want me to?
MICK: 'Course I do.
BRENDA: Well, I will then.

> *He smiles, finishes drying himself, puts the towel away, and starts to
> comb his hair in the mirror, patting it this way and that.* MICK
> *watches as* BRENDA *makes a fuss of himself in the mirror.*

[*With an impudent grin at* MICK] God, I'm lovely.
MICK: Ha-ha! Yer got the cardboard bit?
BRENDA: You'll give me some.

> *He takes the mirror and sits on his bed with it, his feet on the bed
> and the mirror leaning against his legs. He admires himself.* MICK
> *feigns disgust. He takes out a packet of cigarette papers and
> waggles it with a show of reluctance.*

MICK: Aw, that's me last packet of papers. Yer wouldn't ask a man to bust
    his last packet, now would yer?

> BRENDA *jerks an impatient hand for them, grinning a demand.* MICK
> *shakes his head in mock misery.*

No one'd ever believe it...

> *He grins, tears the packet apart, and extracts the cardboard
> backing from behind the folded papers. He hands the cardboard to*
> BRENDA.

Here y'are then, Madame...
BRENDA: Thank you, slave. You can tell the cook I said to give you three
    extra peas for tea.

> *He returns to the mirror.*

MICK: Three? [*Growling*] I want four.

> *He pretends to menace* BRENDA.

BRENDA: Don't ask me to spoil you, boy.
MICK: [*grabbing*] Give us back me gear, then.
BRENDA: [*resisting*] Get away from me.

MICK: [*grabbing* BRENDA] Down with the tyrant!

BRENDA: [*struggling, a muffled shriek*] Guards!

> MICK *pretends to punch and throttle him, while* BRENDA *puts up a show of calculated weakness.* BRENDA *calls it off abruptly.*

Oh, no more! I give up.

MICK: Four, is it, cruel queen?

BRENDA: [*gasping*] Yes, yes! Tell the cook.

MICK: [*releasing him*] Righto, then.

> *He stamps over to sit on his bed.*

BRENDA: [*pulling a face*] You'll pay for that.

> MICK *laughs and sits grinning happily.* BRENDA *returns to the cardboard. He puts out a hand with a snap of his fingers.*

MICK: What?

BRENDA: Match.

MICK: Ah. [*He frowns suddenly and feels in his coat, which hangs on the back of the chair.*] Jeez, I tell yer what... [*pulling out a matchbox and looking inside*] ... we're a bit light on for matches.

BRENDA: [*waggling his head impatiently*] Give!

MICK: No, fair dinkum... only three in it... wouldn't it ruin you? Meant to get some off Wocko.

BRENDA: I only want one.

MICK: Ah. [*Reluctantly*] I'll be wanting a smoke, y'know.

BRENDA: I rolled you some. On top of the cupboard. [*Flicking his hand again.*] Come on, give us.

MICK: Aw... here y'are.

> *He is about to strike a match.*

BRENDA: No, let me do it.

> *He takes the match and matchbox.*

MICK: Ah, I could have done it.

> *He sits on the bed again.* BRENDA *strikes the match and lights the cardboard strip. He blows out the flame after letting it burn a few seconds. He carefully knocks away the loose bits from the blackened end. He puts the matchbox down on the bed, and leaning over the mirror, proceeds to apply the burnt cardboard to his eyebrows, lashes, the corners of his eyes. He is very absorbed in his own face.* MICK *sits watching with a smile. Suddenly* BRENDA *frowns, looks impatiently at the cardboard, rubs it with a finger, and frowns at his finger.*

BRENDA: Tch, tch!

> *He takes another match from the box.*

MICK: Now just you hang on a minute.

He goes to claim the matches, waving an admonitory finger at BRENDA.

You'll have a man without a light.

He bends to untie a shoelace, pulls it from his shoe and stands with the lace dangling.

BRENDA: Oh... the smoke... don't do that.

MICK: Better than no smoke, I'll tell yer.

He goes to the cupboard, takes a cigarette and puts it in his mouth. He puts a book on one end of the shoelace, letting the length of it hang down from the top of the cupboard. He lights a match, lights his cigarette and then the hanging lace. He lets the lace burn for a couple of seconds, then blows it out. The lace hangs smouldering. He nods, satisfied, and throws the matchbox to BRENDA.

There y'are, the last one.

BRENDA: [*catching the box*] I wish you wouldn't do that.

MICK: Humph... old habits die hard.

BRENDA: [*giggling*] I know.

He flutters his eyelashes, grinning at MICK, *then returns to the mirror. He relights the cardboard with the remaining match, and goes through the same procedure as before.* MICK *smiles, and drags on his cigarette. It has gone out. He scowls and spits loose tobacco.*

MICK: Rotten weed! No sooner light it than it's out. [*Grumbling as he goes to the burning lace*] No wonder a man runs out of matches.

He lights the cigarette from the lace.

BRENDA: I heard they're changing it.

MICK: What? Tobacco?

BRENDA: Mmmnn.

MICK: Hmph! [*Wryly*] Yeah... I heard that too...

BRENDA: Not that it will matter.

MICK: Know *when* I heard it?

BRENDA: You'd complain whatever it was. When?

MICK: Ten bloody years ago, that's when.

BRENDA: Oh.

MICK: I heard it me first lagging, I heard it me second lagging...

BRENDA: Must be the old, old story.

MICK: And now you've just told me again. [*Registering what* BRENDA *has just said*] Eh? Hmph. Orright for you to talk about complaining, seeing as yer don't even smoke at all. [*He puffs peevishly and glares at his cigarette.*] Every time they change it, it's worse.

BRENDA: You'd be lost without it.

He smiles at himself in the mirror, satisfied. He gets up, puts the mirror back and disposes of the burnt cardboard. MICK *watches.*

MICK: What, without their rotten weed, you mean?

BRENDA: Without something to complain about.

MICK: Well, who wouldn't complain? [*Scowling at his cigarette*] Man has to use three matches for one smoke.

BRENDA: You're doing all right. Be glad. [*He smiles, winks, poses dramatically.*] Am I beautiful, or what?

MICK: Bloody gorgeous.

> *They grin at each other. Pause.*

[*Playfully*] Where'll we go tonight, then?

BRENDA: [*considering*] Oooh, I thought you might take me to dinner first, then perhaps to the Opera House. [*Sighing*] We can look at all the lovely ladies in their lovely jewels... mink and everything... diamonds galore...

MICK: Ah, yeah, dinner at the Chow's first...

BRENDA: Mmmn... and lovely wine.

MICK: Nah... don't drink wine... Resch's.

BRENDA: A little wine... just to please me.

MICK: Ah. I'll have half a glass, then.

BRENDA: Wine! Red wine!

MICK: Orright.

BRENDA: The nightingale cried to the rose.

MICK: Eh?

BRENDA: Nothing.

MICK: Oh. Well, anyway, I'll have me beer.

BRENDA: Of course you will.

MICK: Then we'll go to the show.

BRENDA: Mmmn... [*Dreaming*] We'll be in evening dress, [*winking*] tuxedo and heavy drag.

MICK: Of course. [*Posing as a butler*] Like, the mug'll announce us, m'dear: Mistah and Missis Otis P. Bunglethorpe.

> *They hook arms and make an entrance.*

BRENDA: Not Missus. I'm *Lady* Bunglethorpe.

MICK: True, and you look beautiful tonight.

> *They pose again.*

BRENDA: I know I do. All the women hate me.

MICK: Ah?

BRENDA: And their husbands all adore me.

MICK: Ha-ha!

BRENDA: And I'm terribly, terribly happy!

They both laugh and stop posing, giving each other a push as they half stagger to sit on their different beds.

MICK: Ha-ha! Dunno which of us is maddest.

BRENDA: Oh I am! I've been at it the longest.

MICK: Hmph. Yeah. [*Fondly*] I suppose y'have. [*Pause.*] Yer look grouse. [*Nodding*] Yer do.

    BRENDA *preens gratefully.*

Where's yer bangle?

BRENDA: Oh!

He jumps up and gets a length of light chain from the cupboard, winds it around his wrist, then offers the wrist limply to MICK.

Do it up for me?

MICK smiles, fiddles with the chain, nods, then steps back as BRENDA *poses with the bangle.*

MICK: Ah. [*Nodding*] That's it. Wouldn't want a whack in the ear with it. Ha-ha!

BRENDA: Treat me nice, then. [*Examining the bangle critically*] Wish it was real.

    He sighs.

MICK: It looks real. It suits yer grouse.

BRENDA: True?

MICK: Wouldn't say it if it wasn't.

    Pause. BRENDA *smiles at the serious* MICK.

BRENDA: Oh well, what will we do?

MICK: Ah. Oh, I dunno. What do y'reckon?

    They both fall to considering.

BRENDA: Mmmn. [*Shrugging*] Well, whatever you like.

MICK: Aw, I dunno. Want a game of draughts?

BRENDA: Nuh.

MICK: How about euchre, then?

BRENDA: No! [*Scowling*] I feel like some fun.

MICK: Ah. [*Pause.*] Wish we had some beer.

BRENDA: Oh, I could kill you sometimes!

MICK: Eh? Ah! Well, what's there to do to have fun, I might ask yer?

BRENDA: I don't know.

MICK: [*at a loss*] Ah, well, I dunno, love. [*Gesturing vaguely*] Keep doing yerself up or something. Put some more soot on yer mush... and that. Where's yer dress? [*Pointing to the clothesline*] And what's *that* thing, I meant to ask yer? Where'd yer drag *it* from?

BRENDA: I got it...

MICK: I can see that. Where from? What is it? [*Pause.*] Eh?

BRENDA: It's a wig. What's it look like?

MICK: A wig... that? It's bloody orange!

BRENDA: Myrtle left it to me.

MICK: Left it to yer? She gone out?

BRENDA: Today.

MICK: Ah. Never said goodbye to me.

BRENDA: I washed it.

MICK: That's good. Been on *her* head.

BRENDA: I thought you might like it.

> *Pause.*

MICK: Yer know it's a *pinch*, I suppose? Get sprung with it and yer off tap, yer know that?

BRENDA: I know.

MICK: Yer know! Three days pound it's likely to get yer. And you've got it hanging on the line.

> *Pause.*

BRENDA: I thought you might—

MICK: Yer thought I might like it.

BRENDA: Yes, for fun.

> MICK *frowns, then he smiles.*

MICK: [*fondly*] Did yer?

> BRENDA *hangs his head.* MICK *grins, wagging his head. He gets up and goes towards the clothesline.* BRENDA *leaps to his feet and beats* MICK *to the wig, pulling it from the line.*

BRENDA: Let me! You'll crush it.

> MICK *stands with a wry face.* BRENDA *skips back to the bed and sits with a coaxing smile, the wig in his hand. He shakes it.*

Will I?

> MICK *chuckles and sits down.*

MICK: Please yerself. Is it dry properly?

> *He chuckles with fond humour.*

BRENDA: Like a bone.

> *He feels it, smoothing it out.* MICK *laughs.*

MICK: A bone, eh? Lucky I'm not a dog, I'd likely bite yer head off! Haw!

> *They both laugh, becoming a little hysterical, as cell-dwellers do.*

BRENDA: You're savage enough as it is.

MICK: Better put me on yer chain.

> *They laugh noisily.*

BRENDA: Shush! They'll think something's wrong, with the noise we're making. [*Hopping up to stand at the mirror*] Just be quiet, while I turn into a fairy.

> *He starts fitting the wig on his head.*

MICK: Haw! Fairy! Yeah, that's grouse.

> MICK *laughs heartily, watching* BRENDA, *who turns with the wig on his head.*

BRENDA: Am I ravishing, or what?

> *He grins and turns back to the mirror.* MICK *wags his head, mock-serious.*

MICK: And they make such a *fuss* about Sophia Loren.
BRENDA: That *bag!* Aren't I lovely?

> *In fact, he looks like an orange squash. Pause, while* BRENDA *poses and* MICK *admires.*

MICK: That does it, they can throw the key away.

> BRENDA *goes back to the mirror.* MICK *gets up with a growl.*

I could go for you, chick.
BRENDA: Scram or I'll call a copper.
MICK: Yeah? So what's the charge?
BRENDA: [*giggling*] Being a hardened criminal!
MICK: [*laughing, greatly amused*] Don't flatter yourself.

> *They laugh for seconds, then sit at a loss for something to say.*

BRENDA: Look out, now.

> *He goes to fossick in the cupboard and pulls out a large square of bright material.*

[*Smiling*] I know what.
MICK: Eh?
BRENDA: I want to change. Look away somewhere, do something for a minute or something. Go on. [*Starting to undo his trousers*] Come on, look somewhere else!

> *He waits.* MICK *hams it up again, grinning.*

MICK: [*screwing up his eyes*] I can't see nothing.
BRENDA: Come on, I said.
MICK: [*feigning blindness*] Wah! Who pinched me white walking stick?
BRENDA: Oh! Stop holding me up!
MICK: [*suddenly clutching his ankle*] Ow! Aw! Me seeing-eye dog just bit me!

> *He wails.* BRENDA *waits impatiently. Pause.* MICK *stops playing and grins.*

BRENDA: Finished?

MICK: Ah, go on, I'm not looking at yer.

BRENDA: Well, have your wash. Do that, then.

MICK: Can't. Still haven't finished me push-ups.

BRENDA: Finish them now, then, and then wash.

MICK: Thirty more. That'll make three hundred.

BRENDA: All right, then. Go on.

MICK: Pretty good, isn't it, hey?

BRENDA: Terrific.

MICK: Well, I reckon it's not bad. Only a couple of months, y'know since I started on 'em... and now I'm in the hundreds.

BRENDA: That's good. You'll go home fit as a fiddle.

MICK: A hundred and seventy at lunch time.

BRENDA: Mmmn.

MICK: And a hundred at breakfast, was it?

BRENDA: I think it was.

MICK: Yeah. I have to do thirty.

BRENDA: Uh-huh.

MICK: Righto, then! Here we go!

> *He throws himself down on the floor and does his push-ups, not too fast and with much huffing.* BRENDA *slips out of his trousers and wraps the material around him, sarong-like. He stands smiling at* MICK*'s efforts.* MICK *counts the last few out loud.*

Seven. Eight. Twenty-nine. Up!

> *He bounds to his feet, does a bit of a dance and throws a few punches. He turns to* BRENDA *with a grin.* BRENDA *poses slowly with a languid arm up against an imaginary doorway in an imaginary street, and smiles vampishly.*

Now I'll have me wash.

> *He looks askance at* BRENDA*'s pose.*

BRENDA: You spending money, big boy?

> *He gives a bit of a bump and grind.*

MICK: How much, baby?

BRENDA: To you, handsome, ten dollars.

MICK: [*leering*] Do it my way and I'll make it twenty.

BRENDA: Filthy.

MICK: Well, what do yer say?

BRENDA: I say it's a deal. Your way.

MICK: A deal is it?

> BRENDA *nods.*

Right! My way is a dollar down and a dollar a week!

They laugh as if the joke was new. They sit on their beds and fall silent, smiling.

Yer look pretty sexy.

BRENDA *smirks and poses.*

I'd better have me lemon.

MICK *stands to have his wash.* BRENDA *bounces up.*

BRENDA: Let me first.

He prepares the water, soap and clean towel for MICK. MICK *removes his singlet and socks. He washes his face, splashing water everywhere, then washes his feet by plonking one and then the other in the basin.* BRENDA *takes the singlet and shorts from the clothesline.*

I'll put these on the bed.

He does so. MICK *begins to dry himself.*

MICK: Ta.

BRENDA: All right.

He watches as MICK *takes the singlet and puts it on, tucks it into his trousers, then sits on his bed and holds up the shorts.*

MICK: I don't want these now.

BRENDA: In the morning you will.

MICK: Yeah, well, put 'em somewhere now.

He holds them out. BRENDA *takes them and puts them somewhere in plain sight.*

BRENDA: There they are there, then.

MICK: Yeah.

BRENDA: Don't forget.

MICK: Sweet.

He looks at a bare foot, grimaces and takes the towel to dry it properly. BRENDA *takes a comb from the cupboard.*

BRENDA: Hold still.

He begins to comb MICK's *hair.* MICK *pulls a face, shrugging.*

Keep still.

MICK *suffers it out.* BRENDA *steps back, pats his head a little, then looks approving.*

You'll do.

MICK: [*wagging the towel at him*] Here y'are.

BRENDA *takes it, balls up all the grubby gear and puts it away.*

BRENDA: I'll wash these tomorrow.

MICK: Dunno why yer don't just send 'em to the laundry like everyone else does.

BRENDA: Because we're not everyone else is why. [*Smiling*] I like to do it, Mick.

MICK: [*smiling*] Yeah, I know yer do.

He watches, smiling, as BRENDA *takes a cloth to clean the mess on the floor, losing interest when* BRENDA *rinses the cloth in the basin, wrings it out once or twice, then hangs it on the line. He turns to* MICK *with a sigh of relief.* MICK *is staring absently at the floor.*

BRENDA: Well, where have you gone? Mick?

MICK: [*looking up*] Uh?

BRENDA: What were you thinking about?

MICK: [*smiling*] Oh, about a girl called Brenda.

BRENDA: [*wryly*] About me?

MICK: Sure.

He falls pensive again.

BRENDA: Hmmmn... why are you sitting like that?

MICK: [*mildly complaining*] Oh lemme alone.

Pause. MICK *sits moodily.*

BRENDA: Are you sad?

MICK: [*with an impatient sigh*] Nah, I'm just thinking.

BRENDA: I can see that. What about?

MICK: Nothing. I told yer.

BRENDA *grimaces, flops on the floor near* MICK, *grasps one of his ankles and tugs at it, gently shaking his leg.*

BRENDA: Tell me!

MICK *frowns impatiently.*

Come on. Tell me what it is. [*Pause.*] I know what it is... anyway.

MICK: Shit yer do.

BRENDA: No need to swear.

MICK: Oh well, you know everything. [*Bitterly*] Think yer do, anyway.

BRENDA: About you I do.

MICK: Tcha!

BRENDA: Yes I do so.

He leans his cheek against MICK*'s leg and is silent. Pause.*

MICK: I was thinking about me parole.

BRENDA: Yes, I know.

MICK: I've got to see him tomorrow. No, Monday.

BRENDA: Mmmn. Well, that's all right. He's been nice to you so far.

MICK: Aw, yeah, but this is the—Well, like, if the Board sat on me case last Friday then this'll be the important one for me.

BRENDA: Well, there's no use worrying now, then, is there? If they've heard your application then nothing you can do will change whatever they decided. [*Coaxing*] Will it now?

MICK *worries grumpily.*

Anyway, you've got the best parole officer too. Everyone likes him the best.

MICK: Hmph. But does *he* like *me?*

BRENDA: Of course he would.

MICK *is dubious.*

You are likeable.

MICK: [*wryly*] Good on yer.

Pause. MICK *broods.* BRENDA *leans against him.*

Ah! How the hell would *I* get parole?

BRENDA: [*exasperated*] Oh! The same as everyone else does, of course. Because you've served four and a half years out of seven is how!

MICK: Ah...

BRENDA: So come on. [*Shaking his leg*] Wake up.

MICK: Aw. [*Nodding*] I know they'll say no.

BRENDA: They will not.

MICK: Yeah they will.

BRENDA: What makes you think they will?

MICK: [*with a martyred smile*] What makes you think they won't?

BRENDA: But you've had good behaviour.

MICK: Haw!

BRENDA: Good work reports.

MICK *nods agreement.*

And all that... to help you.

MICK: [*being practical*] Me record.

BRENDA: What about it? It's just your third time.

MICK: Hmph! [*Grinning*] Just!

BRENDA: Oh well, anyway it isn't the past they care about. It's... it's what you're going to do in future. That's what it's for: a chance.

MICK: Yeah, yeah. I know.

BRENDA: Well?

MICK: But I've had two chances before, that's what they'll say. You watch 'em.

BRENDA: But they won't. Why should they? The other times you went out weren't parole.

MICK *agrees with a shake of his head.*

No, well there you are. As far as they'll be concerned this is your first chance at parole, *and you will get it so stop worrying!*

Pause.

MICK: Ah... yeah... I know all that.

BRENDA: Well, why are you saying things?

MICK: Aw... I just know, that's all.

BRENDA: What? What do you know?

MICK: I know I won't get it.

BRENDA: But why won't you?

MICK: Just my luck, that's all.

BRENDA: Phooey!

MICK: You'll see. Never cracked it in me life.

BRENDA: Well, shut up. You will this time.

MICK: Hnhnn... I hope you're right.

> *He puts a hand absently on* BRENDA's *head.* BRENDA *raises his hand to cover* MICK's. *They sit in silence.*

BRENDA: Mr Levick is a very nice man. [*Pause.*] Everyone says so... that he's a nice man. I haven't heard anyone yet said otherwise.

MICK: Mmmn... I suppose he is.

BRENDA: He is. You can tell just by looking at him... the way he looks at you, as if he doesn't think you're just a number... y'know?

MICK: Hnhnn... there's that... [*Abruptly*] Hey, that reminds me: the number. [*Apologetically*] Me number's come loose again.

BRENDA: [*sitting up crankily*] Oh! [*Looking about for* MICK's *coat*] Where? [*He stands up and grabs the coat from where it hangs on the end of* MICK's *bed. He fusses over it.*] Tch, tch!

MICK: Me rear plate it is.

BRENDA: [*examining the loose number patch*] How do you always manage to do it?

MICK: Sam done it mucking around.

> BRENDA *fossicks in the cupboard and takes out needle and thread.*

BRENDA: I'll Sam him.

> MICK *grins and watches as* BRENDA *sits on a bed to sew.*

MICK: Yer shouldn't say things about old Sam. He's yer best admirer, matter of fact. [*Chuckling*] Just waiting for me to go home, Sam is.

BRENDA: Hmph! [*In mock disgust*] He needn't bother. I'd sooner go with the garbage man.

MICK: Heh! Sam is the garbage man.

> BRENDA *huffs his displeasure and turns to concentrate on his sewing.*

What would I do without yer?

BRENDA *glares but is pleased.*

I'll have to take yer home with me. [*Grinning at the thought*] Hoo! Wouldn't *she* be pleased!

BRENDA *shoots a peevish look at him.*

Not that it'd be any of her business anyway, seeing as she can't even hardly write a man a bloody letter. [*Irritably*] Yer know it's getting on for seven months since she bothered to pick up the pen? [*He pauses, chewing it over quietly, bitterly.*] Hmph! I reckon I'll give *her* something for her corner... bitch it is. [*Pause.*] So yer reckon I'll get it then, do yer?

BRENDA: [*finishing the sewing and standing*] You tell that Sam that I'm not here to sew on numbers that he tears off. And that's the last time I'll be doing it.

> *He replaces the coat, needle and thread, then goes to the food compartment of the cupboard for a tin of Milo, sugar, condensed milk and the two mugs, taking them to the table.*

MICK: Probably is too.
BRENDA: Mmmn?
MICK: The last time yer'll have to sew me number.
BRENDA: [*peeved*] You haven't got it yet.

> *He makes the drinks.*

MICK: Aw, come on, pie-face.

> *He nudges* BRENDA *affectionately.* BRENDA *smiles. As* MICK *returns to sit down, the prison clock strikes seven slowly.* MICK *counts the strokes, nodding. He misses one stroke.*

Only six o'clock... already.
BRENDA: Seven.

> *He brings* MICK *a drink.*

MICK: [*tasting it, nodding*] Ah, that's grouse. [*Grinning clownishly*] I missed a dong then, did I?
BRENDA: No, it was a ding.

> *He gets his own drink and settles on the floor by* MICK*'s leg again, grinning.*

MICK: [*chuckling*] Not me, I wouldn't miss a ding.
BRENDA: [*in mock reproach*] Oh?
MICK: Might have been a ding-dong.
BRENDA: No, that would have been eight o'clock.

> *They giggle like idiots and drink their Milo.*

MICK: Ha-ha! [*Nodding*] We're mad, yer know.

BRENDA: [*giggling*] I know we are.

MICK: Right off.

BRENDA: Hnhn. [*Shaking his head*] No, not really.

> *Pause.*

MICK: Nah. [*Wryly*] Always carrying on as if we were, though. Wonder why we do?

BRENDA: So we don't go mad, of course.

> *He laughs. Pause.*

MICK: Yer right, yer know.

BRENDA: I know.

> *They sip their Milo silently.*

MICK: Ah, I dunno. [*Sighing heavily*] What am I gonna do without yer?

BRENDA: [*with a false smile*] That's what they all wonder.

MICK: [*with false humour*] Ah!

> MICK *laughs uncertainly.* BRENDA *returns him a peeved grimace. They sigh and sip their Milo.*

BRENDA: What about your wife, anyway?

MICK: Eh?

BRENDA: Well, you'd better start thinking about her, hadn't you? She hasn't written...

MICK: [*defensively*] Aw, well there's no worries about her, though. Like, she's been seeing the parole mob and all that for me. [*Shrugging*] 'S just she's been not able to visit and write much, that's all. [*Shrugging*] Like, she's been sick when she hasn't been busy, and busy when she hasn't been sick.

> *He nods, satisfied.*

BRENDA: As long as you're happy.

MICK: What, with her?

BRENDA: With everything.

MICK: Yeah... yeah, well, everything's all right.

BRENDA: I thought you got a letter today.

MICK: Yeah.

BRENDA: I thought it might have been her.

MICK: Nah.

> *They drink quietly.*

BRENDA: Who was it then... secret?

MICK: 'Course it's not a bloody secret! [*Pulling a letter viciously from his hip pocket*] See? It's from her mother... the old dragon! Sent me some photos, too, of the set-up they've got waiting for me. [*Sarcastically*] Orright?

BRENDA *ignores him altogether. Pause.*

Want to see the photos?

BRENDA: Of course. What are they?

MICK: Photos of home. She's got some grouse stuff while I've been in here, I'll say that for the bitch. On the never-never, of course.

He drags out some photographs and holds them singly for BRENDA's *attention.*

That's the new house she's gone and got... from the front. Not a bad-looking joint, eh?

BRENDA: It looks lovely.

MICK: Yeah. [*Grinning*] I'll bet the rent's lovely too. [*Selecting another sample*] There y'are, there's the new bomb she's got. Holden sixty-nine it is.

BRENDA: [*nodding at the snap*] Mmmn... you will be flash.

MICK: I reckon. Dunno how she does it. [*Producing another one*] This is the, uh... [*Grinning*] Reckon I'll be able to fit some beer in her, or what?

BRENDA: Mmmmn! [*Smiling*] It's a beauty.

MICK: Biggest bloody fridge you ever saw.

BRENDA: Must have cost a fortune.

MICK: Ah! What's it matter? She's happy.

BRENDA: Yes.

MICK: [*returning the snaps and the letter to his pocket*] Well, that's what me letter was.

BRENDA: Mmmn... Oh well, you'll see them soon.

MICK: [*with a pessimistic sigh*] Yeah, maybe. Maybe I will.

BRENDA: Oh, don't start that again.

MICK: Uhnhn. [*Meanly*] Oh well, as soon as they like'll do.

BRENDA: No need to get nasty.

MICK: Err...

He scowls. They both smile. Pause. MICK *brightens.*

Oh well, come on! What about a game of draughts? Cahn, one game.

BRENDA: You get the board, then.

MICK: [*going to the cupboard*] Orright.

He gets out the draughts set, smiling at BRENDA *as he sets it up on the bed.*

BRENDA: You want some more Milo?

MICK: Nah. [*Grinning*] Never know, yer might just manage to beat me before I go... if I go.

BRENDA: [*watching him with a smile*] I doubt it. I never do.

MICK: [*gesturing to the draughts, which are now ready*] Come on. [*Grinning*] Yeah, that's funny, hey? I mean, over all the games we've played, yer'd think you would have won some of 'em, like on the law of averages and that, y'know?

BRENDA: [*handling the pieces, firmly*] I'll win this one.

MICK: Well, yer just might too. [*Grinning at him across the board*] Still, they reckon a good colt'll always beat a good filly, eh?

BRENDA: Not any more.

MICK: Eh? Why not any more?

BRENDA: [*smugly*] You'll soon be finding out. Come on, play.

MICK: Find out what?

BRENDA: [*laughing*] Don't you know? There's a freedom for fillies movement going on out there.

MICK: [*scornfully*] Tcha! Yer mean that ladies' lib bullshit? That stuff in the magazines?

BRENDA: It's not bull. [*Giggling*] It's cow.

MICK: [*laughing*] Aw, yeah, well, they won't be worrying me. [*Guffawing at the thought*] All them great big wharfies with their female gelding books.

BRENDA: [*smiling*] Eunuchs.

MICK: [*laughing*] Yeah, well call 'em what yer like, they're not exactly having a ball, are they? Ha-ha! [*Clapping his hands above the board*] Cahn, let's play a game.

BRENDA: Who says they're not having a ball?

MICK: Eh? [*Grinning*] Well, they do. That's why they write their stupid books and that... stupid molls.

BRENDA: Hmph! [*Wryly*] Have you got a surprise coming.

MICK: Yeah, pigs I have. [*Nodding*] Don't you worry about me being able to find a seat in the tram. [*Scowling*] I'll be taking me natural place same as it always was. Never mind them. Bloody enemies of nature, the lot of 'em... bitches.

BRENDA: [*grinning*] What's that make me?

MICK: Haw! [*Gesturing at the board*] Now come on, it's my first move! [*Moving a token firmly*] Right! Black to move and win!

He watches BRENDA's *move and chuckles.*

Ah, jeez. I wouldn't be dead for quids.

They play the game.

SCENE THREE

The exercise yard. Sunday morning.

VOICE: [*off, bellowing*] In the yard! Come on! In the yard!

> *A rumble of feet and voices, sounds of keys jingling, bolts rattling, a gate squeaking.* SAM *and* MICK *wander on. Each carries a tin mug.* MICK *has a newspaper. They amble straight over to the fence.* MICK *puts the newspaper on the ground and sits on it, leaning back comfortably against the fence.* SAM *stands, yawns, stretches, looks around him and up at the sky, smiles down at* MICK, *then sits down side-on to him.* MICK *leans back and closes his eyes.* SAM *stares around vacantly, as if watching others in the yard, occasionally nodding to someone offstage. We hear the gate being shut and locked.*

SAM: We're all in.

VOICE: [*off*] Three Yard all correct, sir!

SAM: [*wryly*] Hmph! Correct, for Christ's sake.

> *He looks at* MICK *with mild interest.* MICK *lies with eyes closed.* SAM *stares around contentedly, smiles at the sky and then at* MICK.

Ah yeah, bonzer spot this. [*As* MICK *does not respond*] Looks like being a decent sort of day, too.

MICK: [*opening his eyes*] Hnhnn?

SAM: I just said this ain't a bad possie.

MICK: Ah...'swhy we sit here, ain't it?

> *He sighs and closes his eyes again.*

SAM: Ah... I suppose it is, mate.

MICK: Uhnhn.

SAM: Don't alter the fact, though, does it?

MICK: Uhnhn.

> *Pause.*

SAM: [*fidgeting, looking a bit peeved*] Oh, yer great company, mate. Late night, did yer?

MICK: [*growling, his eyes shut*] Errr!

SAM: Ah. Knocks yer about, don't it?

MICK: Uhnn.

> *He sighs deeply, eyes still closed.*

SAM: Oh.

He sits looking at MICK. *He clears his throat. He breathes deeply, looks at the sky, exhales, stretches. He looks at* MICK *again. He scratches himself, shifts a bit uncomfortably on the concrete.*

Ahhh! [*He stares offstage suddenly, as if observing some activity down the yard.*] They're gonna play tennis again.

MICK: Uhnn.

Pause. SAM *looks idly at the ground near his leg. He picks up a piece of wood, or a dead match, and begins gently scratching the ground with it.* MICK *opens his eyes and growls.*

Shush, will yer?

SAM: [*dropping the wood*] Sorry.

MICK *closes his eyes. After a short pause, he opens them again and frowns.*

MICK: I was trying not to think.

SAM: Oh.

MICK: Y'rooted it with yer scratching.

SAM: I wasn't thinking.

MICK: Doesn't matter.

He sighs and closes his eyes again. Pause. SAM *fidgets. He takes up the piece of wood and picks at his teeth. He takes it out and explores his tooth with his tongue. He pokes with the wood again.*

SAM: Yer thinking?

MICK: Nuh.

SAM: Ah. [*Sucking juicily at his tooth*] What about?

MICK: [*complaining*] Stop sucking y'choppers.

SAM: [*stopping his dental care*] Didn't know it was that loud.

MICK: Sounded like a broken shithouse.

SAM: Mmmn... [*Pause. Chuckling*] I'll have to get it fixed.

MICK: Hmph.

SAM: Yeah. [*Looking at the sky, bored*] Not a bad day.

MICK: So yer said.

SAM: Better'n the winter, anyway.

MICK: I reckon.

SAM: Can't cop the winter... never could.

MICK: Uh-huh. Shits yer, all right.

SAM: Yeah, me it does.

MICK *nods, his eyes closed. Pause.* SAM *daydreams for a bit, then stretches.*

Know what I feel like?

MICK: Uhn.

SAM: One of them big fat German sheilas.

MICK: Ah.

SAM: [*smiling*] Yeah, one of them... [*Dreaming and sighing*] Ah yeah... wouldn't even matter if she wasn't German, I suppose. What do yer reckon?

MICK: Hnhn, or fat either.

SAM: [*laughing*] Nah! [*Chuckling softly*] Long as it had one head.

MICK: [*bored*] Ha-ha.

SAM: But German for preference, like... and fat. [*Grinning*] If yer gonna dream, well yer might as well order the grouse, hey?

MICK: Ah. [*Sighing*] Whatever yer fancy.

SAM: Yeah. [*Pause.*] Yeah, well, that's what I fancy: a big fat German sheila from Germany.

MICK: Heh!

SAM: What?

MICK: [*waking up with a grin*] You're not real.

SAM: Huh. [*Grinning*] Don't even feel real.

MICK: You'll be right. Long as yer keep on dreaming about fat frauleins, can't be too much wrong with yer.

SAM: Ha-ha. No.

> *Pause. They glance around idly.*

MICK: What was in yer tooth?

SAM: Uh?

MICK: That yer siphoned out.

SAM: Oh. Bit of something.

MICK: Ah. [*Pause.*] Hole in it, is there?

SAM: I reckon.

MICK: Um. Bastard, that.

SAM: Bit of apple, it was.

MICK: Uh?

SAM: Yeah.

MICK: When from?

SAM: Eh?

MICK: When did you have an apple?

SAM: I never.

MICK: Oh.

SAM: Bloke gimme a bite of his.

MICK: Oh yeah. When was it, then?

SAM: Other day.

MICK: No wonder yer got a hole.

SAM: Ah. Tomatoes are the worst.

MICK: I believe yer.

> *Pause.* MICK *begins to chuckle.*

SAM: What?

MICK: You. [*Laughing*] Bloody hypocrite, y'are. After my Brenda one minute, and talking about big fat sheilas the next. Hmph!

SAM: Oh, that's a different thing.

MICK: Oh no it ain't. Yer've lagged yerself. [*Nodding firmly*] Consider y'self uninherited!

> *He wags a finger at* SAM, *smiling.*

SAM: Aw, don't pull me leg about that, mate. [*Grinning*] Yer know I'm waiting in hopes there.

> *He gestures an appeal.*

MICK: [*mock-solemn*] Aw, no, it's no good. Afraid I'll have to reconsider the matter now, mate. I mean with regard to what yer've just told me about yer dreams of female women...

SAM: Oh turn it up, will yer?

MICK: [*raising a hand firmly*] Ah no! And with further regard, like, to certain property of mine... [*grinning*] ... to wit, my unlawful wedded, uh, domestic company, which you have asked I should leave in your care when I go forth from here into the world of *up*-side-up again... [*Frowning and shaking his head*] Ah yes, mate. I've got me doubts about leaving her in your hands... fair dinkum.

SAM: Oh, balls. What do you care, eh? Won't be taking her with yer, will yer, eh? Just as good for me as anyone else, ain't she?

MICK: [*solemnly*] Oh... well, I dunno.

SAM: Well, she has to finish with *some*one.

MICK: Hnhnn!

SAM: So why not me? [*Pause.*] Eh? Why not, then?

MICK: Yer don't clean your teeth.

SAM: Oh. Oh, well I will. I mean I would, if I was, like, if I had a reason like that.

> MICK *chuckles. Pause.*

MICK: Hnnhn. She is a good reason, ain't she?

SAM: Ha-ha. [*Nodding.*] Reckon she is.

MICK: Hah. I should reckon you'd reckon.

SAM: Ha-ha-ha. [*Pause.*] Well what about it, then?

MICK: What?

SAM: Well, will yer or won't yer?

MICK: Aw. [*Considering*] Yer jumping the gun a bit. I dunno yet.

SAM: How am I? Yer seeing the parole bloke tomorrow aren't yer?

MICK: Don't mean I'll get it.

SAM: Ah, balls! 'Course yer will. Yer been waiting long enough. Yer due. Yer got good reports and everything.

MICK: Hmph. So I have.

SAM: Well?

MICK: Huh.

> *Pause.* SAM *eyes* MICK *carefully.*

SAM: [*hurt*] Truth's known, yer've promised her to someone else.

MICK: [*smiling*] Nah. No I haven't. [*Nodding at* SAM] Not to nobody.

SAM: [*with a reassured sniff*] Ah, well what about me, then? Come on, I'm yer mate, aren't I? Done all the waiting with yer... thick and thin, like.

MICK: Ha-ha.

SAM: [*slightly hurt again*] What's funny about that, then?

MICK: Oh nothing. Forget it.

SAM: Well it's right, ain't it?

MICK: Yeah. Yeah, 'course it is.

> *He gives* SAM *a smile.* SAM *smiles back and shows some relief.*

SAM: Ah! Yer just having a go at me.

MICK: Ah.

SAM: Y'oughtn't to joke about being mates, but.

MICK: Ah.

SAM: 'Specially like you and me have been... like, sticking together, and...

MICK: Yer right.

SAM: You know, even sacrificing for each other.

MICK: Oh, ha-ha! Jesus!

> *He stops himself abruptly, a bit too late. Pause.* SAM *sniffs miserably.*

SAM: Yer've done it again.

MICK: Aw, I was thinking of a joke.

SAM: [*considering*] Nah.

MICK: [*considering*] Aw, well I don't mean it like it might have sounded. I was just thinking of something.

SAM: [*sadly*] Nuh. Nah, you just don't believe in mates any more... do yer? Not since yer been with her. I've been watching.

MICK: [*frowning*] Oh, forget it will yer, Sam?

> *Pause.*

SAM: All right. Well, what about what I arst yer?

MICK: I bloody told yer!

SAM: No yer never! All yer've done is put me on yer waiting list. Yer've put me off and made sure *not* to tell me! And I want to *know*!

MICK: Well I *dunno*!

SAM: Well yer've got to know! Soon! [*Appealing*] Aw, what's the key t'yer anyway, Mick? Yer'll be going home now any day... out t'yer *right* missus... *any* bloody day.

MICK: Ahhh. [*Sighing heavily*] That's what I was busy not thinking about when you started with yer scratching and Juicy-Fruiting.

He leans back and closes his eyes.

SAM: Decide then, and yer won't have to think.

    Pause.

MICK: Aw… well, look—

    A tennis ball flies from offstage and hits MICK. *He starts, scowls and glares offstage.* SAM *grabs the ball, throws it angrily back where it came from, shaking a fist.*

SAM: Watch where yer hit that ball, yer nits!

MICK: It hits me again, I'll shove it where yer boyfriend'll find it. Mugs, y'are!

    They relax again slowly and look at each other.

SAM: Hmph. Mugs. Give 'em a ball and they're happy.

MICK: Mmph.

SAM: Wouldn't leave the rotten joint if they couldn't take their ball with 'em.

MICK: Nah. 'Course they wouldn't.

SAM: They wouldn't, yer know.

MICK: No. I know.

SAM: Makes me sick.

MICK: Hmph. [*Laughing dully*] Life's a ball.

SAM: Ha-ha. Yeah. [*Sniffing*] Nah, the thing is, though, I mean, what about the screws, what do they think, hey? I reckon they must laugh, yer know, seeing crims playing with bloody balls.

MICK: [*nodding*] Hmph.

SAM: Y'know they must think to 'emselves, like, all they have to do to keep crims in, is give us a ball to play with.

MICK: Bloody right.

SAM: It is bloody right. That's the trouble.

MICK: Ah.

SAM: Can't tell 'em, though.

MICK: Nah. [*Pause.*] Ah, well… that's how it goes.

SAM: [*sighing*] Yeah… just gives yer some idea, though, of the mentality of these gooses.

MICK: [*nodding*] Ah. Stupes.

SAM: I reckon. Top idiots. Imbos.

MICK: Shitmen.

SAM: Oh yeah, well that's it, yeah.

MICK: Mmmmn. Oh well, let 'em go.

SAM: Yeah, let 'em. That's what I say.

MICK: Me too.

Pause. SAM *fidgets. He feels his hollow tooth with a finger. He is at a loss for action. He spits copiously onto the ground. He picks up the piece of wood again and begins to stir the spittle with dull interest.* MICK *looks on in disgust.*

What are yer doing that for?

SAM: Ha-ha. It's full of little organism things. Liven 'em up a bit.

MICK: Full of germs, yer mean! Give it a miss.

SAM: Nah. Liven 'em up a bit. [*Chuckling*] Every time they think they're going somewhere, the old Sam gets 'em with his shit-stirrer. Ha-ha! They don't even know what's happening. Little nits.

His tongue protrudes. He is now absorbed in this new activity.

MICK: Ahh, you're right off.

SAM: [*still poking*] Yeah... I reckon.

MICK: Yer can't even see the bloody things.

SAM: Hnhnn! [*Grinning*] They can't see me, either.

Pause. SAM *stirs on.*

MICK: Oh, turn it up, will yer? [*He stares offstage, then back at* SAM.] Yer've got half the yard looking at us.

SAM: Let 'em.

He gestures rudely in the direction of offstage.

MICK: Well, stop putting *me* on show!

He glares at SAM *angrily.* SAM *laughs dully, throws the match away, suddenly losing interest in his spittle.*

SAM: There y'are. [*Laughing*] God's off for lunch.

MICK: Ahh! You're not the full deener.

SAM: [*laughing*] I wouldn't reckon. Yer got to be ninepence ha'penny to be here.

He laughs again.

MICK: [*sniffing*] Yer in yer right place, then.

SAM *chuckles, stretches, and grins vacantly around. He begins to fidget again.*

SAM: [*sighing*] Ahhh... Jesus.

MICK: What's the matter now?

SAM: Ah, nothing. I hate these weekends in the yard. They shit me to death.

MICK: Yer don't say.

SAM: Oh, all right for you. This might be yer last. [*Laughing dully*] All right for you.

MICK: 'Might' is the operational word.

SAM: Oh. Bit of luck...

MICK: Need more'n a bit.

SAM: ... and you'll be home with the missus.

MICK: Hmph. With the barmaid at the Prince.

SAM: Ah, well I mean when the pub shuts.

MICK: Better.

SAM: Ha-ha. [*Sighing*] Like to be halves with yer...

MICK: Mmmn.

SAM: 'Stead of being left in this... y'know.

MICK: Yeah.

SAM: All on me pat.

MICK: Uhnn.

SAM: Hnnhn. Yer'll be a fortnight at the most, now.

> *Pause.*

MICK: Ahhh... all right... I'll see what I can do...

SAM: [*grinning*] Yer will!

MICK: If you'll just stop rushing me.

SAM: Sweet!

MICK: And let me see if I get me parole first...

SAM: Oh yeah, yeah! I wasn't meaning to—

MICK: Then I'll fix it for yer with Brenda.

SAM: Grouse!

MICK: Orright?

SAM: [*nodding and beaming*] Grouse, mate. Grouse!

MICK: Orright... well, leave it to me.

SAM: Ha-ha! Sweet.

MICK: [*smiling*] Ah, yeah... sometimes it is.

SAM: Hnnhn.

> *He sits smiling at* SAM. *A voice starts bellowing offstage.*

VOICE: [*off*] Fall! Fall in for inspection!

> *They look glumly at each other.*

SAM: Ah, jeez. I forgot all about inspection.

MICK: Bloody pests.

> *They rise reluctantly.* SAM *brushes his clothes with his hands. His clothes are clean but very untidy and he needs a shave.* MICK, *on the other hand, wears a well-pressed coat and pants. His clothes fit him, in contrast to* SAM'*s. He is clean-shaven and looks very well indeed.*

VOICE: [*off*] Come on, now. Fall in, Three Yard. Move it!

> *They prepare reluctantly to fall in.*

SAM: How do I look?

MICK: Shithouse. Yer a grub.

He looks at SAM *and shakes his head.* SAM *looks from himself to* MICK.

SAM: Ah well, I got no cell-mate like yours.

MICK: Hmph. Yer not much chance of getting a cell-mate either, 'less yer smarten up a bit.

SAM: Oh well, I will now. Now I know yer'll be putting in the good word for me, like— [*He breaks off, glancing offstage.*] Here they come! Lively!

They both take their places in the inspection line-up, elbowing their way in as if other men impede them. SAM *stands to the right of* MICK. MICK *jabs an elbow left, grumbling.*

MICK: Give us some room, will yer?

SAM: [*jabbing an elbow to his right*] Don't need all the bloody yard, do yers?

They both obtain their territory. They stand straight, unbutton their coats and stare ahead of them. They wait. There is the sound of keys rattling and of an iron bolt banging.

Gate's open.

MICK: Yeah. Lot of bullshit this is.

SAM: Ah, you're all right. Look at me.

Pause.

VOICE: [*off*] Attention, Three Yard!

They lift their chests and drop them again.

SAM: [*whispering*] What do they bloody think it is? Bloody Holsworthy Army boob?

MICK: Shut up, here they are.

Enter the SENIOR *and the* SECOND OFFICER. *They pause on the edge of the stage, as if inspecting the first prisoners in line. Proceeding slowly along the line, the* SENIOR *does his inspection while the* SECOND OFFICER *tags along behind, taking down his remarks in a notebook.*

SENIOR: A haircut tomorrow, Fifty-seven... tuck that shirt in, One-nine-five... The shoes could be better, Seventeen...

They reach MICK *and stop. The* SENIOR *nods and smiles approvingly.*

Your appearance is a credit to you, Twenty-six.

MICK: [*smirking*] Thank you, sir.

SECOND OFFICER *makes a note of* MICK's *merit.*

SENIOR: [*with a knowing smile*] Well, now... ha-ha... you look like a man with an appointment. Eh?

MICK: [*smiling*] Yessir, with the parole officer, sir. Not till tomorrow, though.

SENIOR: Ah, yes, yes. That's right. Well, he won't find fault with the look of you, Twenty-six.

He nods more approval at MICK.

MICK: Ha-ha. I hope not, sir.

SENIOR: You'll be all right, lad. [*Winking*] I'd say a fortnight at the most.

He smiles at MICK *reassuringly.*

SAM: [*aside to* MICK] Hey! What'd I tell yer?

They all become aware of SAM, *who realises the fact and again stares straight ahead, regretting having spoken. The smile leaves the* SENIOR's *face. He and the* SECOND OFFICER *move along and stare at* SAM. *The* SENIOR's *expression becomes more horrified at* SAM's *disreputable gear and unshaven face. He looks to the* SECOND OFFICER, *who shakes his head in silent answer. They both turn to stare at* SAM *together.* SAM *turns his head to look at them, his expression whimsical, then looks away.*

SENIOR: Jenkins…

SAM: Sir?

SENIOR: Tell me, Jenkins…

SAM: Sir?

SENIOR: Tell me about the bushfire.

SAM: Ha-ha, sir.

SENIOR: Uh, ha-ha! You have been in one?

SAM: Oh, uh, well not exactly, sir.

SENIOR: Oh?

SAM: No, sir.

The SECOND OFFICER *is taking notes.*

SENIOR: Not even recently, Jenkins?

SAM: Not lately. No, sir.

Pause.

SENIOR: An explanation, please Jenkins? [*Pause.*] Smartly, Jenkins. [*Pause.*] Anything will do, Jenkins.

Pause. SAM *considers, glancing at* MICK.

SAM: Ah.

SENIOR: Mmmn?

SAM: Oh well, sir… it has been said… I mean they do say, sir, that I'm… ahh, well, they do say I'm not the full deener, sir.

SENIOR: Oh… they do?

SAM: Oh, Yes sir. [*Shrugging*] Oh, I don't mind having to admit it, sir. It's true enough, I suppose, about me deprived background… sufferings I went through as a little kid, sir, with me drunken old man used to punch and kick me in the cot… me mum drinking wine out of the bath, and all that... [*Sniffing back a sigh*] I'd rather if I could forget it, of course, sir, but seeing as you bring it up I suppose a man can't deny it. I have had a rough trot, sir, all me miserable life, sir, and it's left me about tuppence ha'penny short of the deener. [*Looking bravely at the* OFFICERS] And it shows. It's noticeable... I know that.

> *He sighs and looks down at his feet, then straightens again. The* SECOND OFFICER *is quite sad. The* SENIOR OFFICER *shakes his head.* SAM *hangs his head, then looks up.*

SENIOR: Jenkins?

SAM: Yes, sir?

SENIOR: Are you pleading insanity?

SAM: Uh... diminished responsibility, sir.

> *He nods seriously, apologetically. Pause. The* OFFICERS *look at each other. The* SECOND OFFICER *shrugs, believing. The* SENIOR *rounds on* SAM.

SENIOR: Jenkins!

SAM: Sir! Here sir! Present sir!

SENIOR: Have a wash!

SAM: Yessir!

SENIOR: Have it twice!

SAM: Yessir! A double dobie, sir!

SENIOR: Get those shoes shined!

SAM: Shoes, sir! Yes, sir!

SENIOR: Wake up to yourself!

SAM: Wake up, sir!

SENIOR: And sleep in your *pyjamas!*

SAM: Right away, sir!

SENIOR: Or I'll put you on the mat, Jenkins!

SAM: Yessir! On the mat, sir!

SENIOR: [*cooling down*] So report to me in the morning and let me see you looking like—like—like Twenty-six here.

> *They all look admiringly at* MICK, *who looks modest about it all.* SAM *considers briefly, then appeals to the* SENIOR.

SAM: I tell you what, sir. It might take me a few days, sir, but I'll tell you, sir. [*Gesturing at* MICK] Make it a fortnight at the most, and I'll have meself looking exactly like Mick here, I will, sir.

> *Pause. The* SENIOR *considers, then he nods encouragingly.*

SENIOR: Ah, well that's the spirit. Try, lad.

SAM: Oh I am, sir—I mean I will, sir.

> *Pause.*

SENIOR: [*giving* SAM *a fatherly pat on the arm*] Good lad.

SAM: Thank you, sir. No one ever said that to me before, sir.

SENIOR: Well, see you manage it, now.

SAM: Yessir. Well, I mean, would it be okay then, sir, about the fortnight, sir?

> *The* SENIOR *considers. The* SECOND OFFICER *waits with pencil poised. The* SENIOR *nods at the* SECOND OFFICER, *who nods, smiles and writes. The* SENIOR *nods at* SAM.

SENIOR: Try, Jenkins, just try.

SAM: Depend on me, sir.

SENIOR: I'm taking your promise, then.

SAM: [*raising two fingers, crossed*] Crim's honour, sir.

SENIOR: [*raising his eyebrows*] Oh, well then...

> SAM *and the* SENIOR *nod at each other. The* SENIOR *moves on slowly to the next man, then more quickly, the* SECOND OFFICER *after him, until they almost dash offstage.* SAM *and* MICK *continue staring ahead.*

VOICE: [*off*] All right, Three Yard. Break off!

> *They relax and sag and sigh.*

SAM: Whooo!

MICK: Gawd strike me. Bloody marathon.

> *They stand easy, then wander back slowly to their place by the fence.*

SAM: [*glaring after the* SENIOR] Bloody old fusspot.

MICK: Pigs he is. Wasn't him, it was *you* and yer warby self kept us all propped there.

SAM: Ah, orright, orright! I just heard it all off him, didn't I? [*Sighing*] Give us a go.

> *He sits down carelessly.* MICK *sits down after carefully placing his newspaper beneath him, answering* SAM *as he does so.*

MICK: He just give yer a go.

SAM: [*directing a scowl offstage*] Hmph! Screw.

> *He blows a brief raspberry.*

MICK: [*flatly*] Good on yer.

SAM: Eh?

MICK: [*censuring him*] He just give yer a go, didn't he?

SAM: Ah, well so what?

MICK: Well, so yer don't shitcan someone gives yer a go, that's what.

> SAM *broods.*

He's not a bad old bastard.

SAM: Aw.

MICK: No he ain't. Yer treat him all right, he treats you all right. Always has.

> *Pause.*

SAM: [*scowling impatiently*] Ah well, he ain't the lot of 'em, is he? There's more to it than him. Plenty of 'em all just dying to pinch a man... millions of 'em.

MICK: [*scoffing*] Tcha! Haw... millions of 'em. Give it a go, Sam. And anyway, if there was, no need to take it out on him. Just don't shitcan a bloke gives yer a go, is the point I'm making.

> *Pause.*

SAM: Aw, yeah. Well, I suppose so. A man gets in the habit, I suppose. Y'know.

MICK: Mmmn. Well, it won't solve a thing.

> *Pause.*

SAM: No. I suppose not.

> *The tennis ball flies on from offstage again and hits* MICK, *who manages fumblingly to catch it. He scowls, hesitates, then bowls it back with a resigned sort of action.*

MICK: [*calling to offstage*] Right, that's yer last go! [*Gesturing skywards*] Next time it gets pelted right over bloody A Wing!

SAM: [*grinning*] Yer been saying that every Saturday for the last eighteen months *I* know about.

MICK: Hmph. I'm running out of patience, though. [*Complaining in some amazement*] Why's the rotten thing have to hit *me* all the time for, I wonder? Never hits you.

SAM: Mmmnn.

MICK: Always me. Never misses.

SAM: No.

MICK: Never hits you.

SAM: Oh yeah. It has. Couple of times.

MICK: Oh yeah, but nothing like it hits me. It's hit me every time you've been sitting here with me. Never hit you while I've been here, has it, eh?

> *Pause.*

SAM: Not sure whether it has.

MICK: I'm telling yer. Man's not likely to make a thing like that up, is he? I *tell* yer, it's just that you never watch which one of us it hits, but I've been on it all the time and it bloody well always hits me!

> *He nods emphatically.*

SAM: [*surrendering graciously*] Aw, well, you'd know then, if yer've been on it.

MICK: Four years, mate, I've been remarking the fact of that thing always bouncing off me. Every Sunday I just wait for it; and every Sunday I get collected by the thing. Makes a man wonder, y'know. Why me?

>*He sighs.* SAM *nods thoughtfully.*

SAM: Mmmmnn. Yeah... probably what it is, y'know... it's probably that yer thinking about it. Like, yer probably the only bloke in the yard's got a sort of mentalised contact with the atoms in the ball, see? And it gets attracted to you, 'cos yer mind attracts it to yer. Mind over matter sort of thing. Yer've read about that, ESP and all that, I suppose?

MICK: [*nodding*] Uhnn... ESP... could be, too.

SAM: [*enthusiastically*] Oh yeah, my oath it could! Bloody marvellous what the mind can do nowadays. [*Nodding*] I've read a lot of stuff all about it, that yer'd never believe unless yer saw it in black and white, not 'less yer'd read the right books, like; cosmetic vibrations and that...

MICK: Oh, I know what yer mean. I'm up with it, it's pretty common knowledge, really, when yer think of it. Y'know, I've got on to it in a few books.

SAM: *Digests*, you mean?

MICK: Ah. Yeah. Y'know, [*nodding*] and other stuff.

SAM: Marvellous bloody thing, I reckon.

MICK: Oh well, it's natural enough. Y'know, when you say it's marvellous yer don't want to mean anything that's unnatural, 'cos in fact—as they'll tell yer—what we think is a miracle, or something extra-natural, like, well really it's not, because it's just some natural thing we never knew about and when it works we think it's a big deal, but it isn't because it's a natural fact we just never knew about.

>*Pause.*

SAM: Oh, yeah... understood.

MICK: Yer know what they say: there's more things in heaven and earth than y'can poke a stick at.

SAM: Yeah, I read that.

MICK: In the *Digest?*

SAM: Mmmn.

MICK: Well, there yer go.

SAM: I reckon. [*Pause.* SAM *has a surge of compassion.*] Hey, what about them poor bastards can't even read or write, eh? [*Shaking his head*] Must be a nice rotten way to be, not knowing what's there when it's written down for yer.

>*Together they nod in sympathy for others.*

MICK: Ah. They miss a lot.

SAM: Uhnn and never even know.

MICK: That's the sad part about it.

SAM: Makes a man realise how lucky he is.

MICK: I'll say it does.

> *Pause.*

SAM: That was in one of the *Digests*...

MICK: What?

SAM: I used to complain 'cos I had no socks... [*nodding profoundly*] ... till I met a man with no plates.

MICK: [*nodding, remembering*] Ah, yeah.

SAM: Makes yer think, all right.

MICK: Yeah, it's a good one that.

SAM: There's a few good ones.

MICK: I know there is.

SAM: Oh yeah, I thought yer would.

MICK: Yeah. I do.

> *Pause.* MICK *leans back and shuts his eyes.* SAM *fidgets, wiggles a foot with interest, staring about aimlessly and sighing.* MICK *yawns and opens his eyes.*

Ahh. [*Grinning*] Wish I had a yo-yo.

SAM: Ah?

MICK: Something to slow the old brain down a bit. Stop me thinking for a while. Can't stop.

SAM: Mmmn. Better watch that ball, then.

MICK: Yeah. I am. It'll come.

> *He yawns again.*

SAM: Nah. I don't think so, not while yer on to it, it won't.

MICK: Yer reckon?

SAM: Mmmn. Know what I mean, like? [*Considering what he means*] It's a bit hard to put into words, but it'll only catch yer when yer thinking of it but not expecting it, like, but not when yer thinking about it that it might lob. [*Nodding*] If yer try to make it happen, like, it won't.

> *He shrugs and gestures in explanation.*

MICK: Uhnn. Oh well, that's the way life is.

SAM: Pretty much, yeah.

MICK: Yer never know the day or the hour.

SAM: Yer do not, no.

MICK: Very true old saying, that.

SAM: Can't beat the old ones.

MICK: I don't reckon.

SAM: Nuh. Yer can't.

Pause. They sit at a loss for action, staring vacantly at nothing, each absorbed in his thoughts. The prison clock strikes nine. The sound fades away. SAM *and* MICK *do not react.*

MICK: [*abruptly*] What was that?

SAM: Uhnn?

MICK: Nine, was it? That all it is?

SAM: Never heard it. Clock, you mean?

MICK: Must have been nine...

SAM: Yeah, it would have been.

MICK: Hasn't been tea-up yet.

SAM: No. Yeah, nine it'd be. Inspection's just over, remember?

MICK: That's right.

SAM: Yeah.

MICK: [*sighing*] Ah. Jeez it drags.

SAM: [*sighing*] I reckon. [*Pause.*] Anyway, that's probably it. Yer've probably got abnormal mental powers, and it somehow works on the ball.

MICK: [*modestly*] Oh, I dunno.

SAM: Ah, no yer must have.

MICK: Oh well. It might be that.

SAM: I'd say it has to be.

MICK: Yeah. Well, it probably is.

SAM: Yer'll just have to not think about it.

MICK: That's what I have been doing.

SAM: Yeah. Oh, well. [*He suddenly becomes alert, staring offstage.*] What's he doing at the gate? Unlocking it, by the look of him... Yeah, [*nodding*] it must be tea-up now.

MICK: Yeah, 'tis. [*Staring offstage, then at* SAM] Yer bring any sugar?

SAM: 'Course. [*He digs in his jacket pocket and pulls out a small plastic bag of sugar.*] I should have brought a spoon. [*Staring around*] Nothing to stir it with.

MICK: Yeah, I got me Biro.

He pulls out a pen.

SAM: Ah. We're right, then.

MICK: Sweet.

He takes the two mugs and puts them on the ground conspicuously before them.

SAM: Here she comes.

They look expectantly to the gate. The SWEEPER, *a shabby man past middle age, comes towards them carrying a large bucket of tea. He looks tired.*

MICK: Here, old soldier, lemme do it.

He takes the bucket. The SWEEPER *nods gratefully and sighs, then bends abruptly to scoop a cigarette butt from the ground. He takes a tin from his pocket, and after sniffing the butt and nodding approval of it, puts it in the tin and pockets it. Meanwhile,* MICK *fills the mugs from the bucket. Then he turns and smiles at the* SWEEPER *as he hands the bucket back. The* SWEEPER *sighs, nods at them and shuffles off.*

[*Calling after him*] Thanks, old soldier. Good on yer.

They sit down again, their mugs of tea in front of them. SAM *shakes sugar into the mugs.* MICK *stirs them carefully with his Biro. He wipes it on* SAM'*s coat and pockets it. They nod at each other satisfied. They sip the tea tentatively.*

SAM: Not too bad.

MICK: [*nodding*] Better'n a kick in the arse.

They nod philosophically together.

SAM: [*nodding after the* SWEEPER] What do yer put him on the old soldier for? Never been in the army in his life.

MICK: Ah...

He drinks.

SAM: Hmph. That's the only uniform he ever had.

MICK: I know. That's why I say it for him.

SAM: Ah! Reckon it makes him feel better, do yer?

He chuckles, mildly contemptuous.

MICK: Oh I dunno. I just say it, that's all.

SAM: Hmph. Saying one thing won't make another. [*Patting his pockets abruptly*] What about a smoke?

MICK *fishes out tobacco, matches and so on. He takes some himself and passes it to* SAM. SAM *takes the makings and gives it back.* MICK *returns the tobacco to his pocket. They roll their cigarettes.*

MICK: A man might be back on the Camels shortly.

SAM: Well, strike me lucky! [*Cackling*] Get it? Strike me lucky... Lucky Strikes!

MICK: Ha-ha. Yeah. Good one. Camels are my go. Best smoke of the lot, for mine. Always was.

SAM: Medical authorities warn... that smoking Camels... are usually on fire. Ha-ha-ha!

MICK: Ha-ha. I suppose they would be.

He smiles and strikes a match. They light up.

SAM: [*blowing out smoke*] Aw, hey what about the other morning when that earth tremor thing went off? Ha-ha! [*Grinning*] Yer hear about Wocko and Swampguts in the peter?

MICK: No. What happened?

SAM: Ah, well y'know how the whole bloody joint just shook and moved for a minute?

MICK: I reckon I do. Near wet meself... it was—

SAM: Yeah, yeah. [*Grinning*] Well... y'know Wocko and Swampguts are in the top and bottom bunks, like?

MICK: Ah.

SAM: Yeah, well Wocko's in the top one, see, and Swamper's under him... and anyway, Wocko's feeling a bit frisky up top, and having a bit of a sly go, see? [*Nodding, grinning*] But he's not knowing that Swampguts is awake, so the old bunk's rocking a bit, like, but old Swamper's putting up with it and not saying anything like, you know?

MICK: [*grinning, nodding*] Ah, hah-hah.

SAM: [*getting convulsed*] Yeah... well, anyway, what do you reckon? All of a sudden that earth tremor hit [*cackling*] and the whole joint rocked and rolled; and Swamper leaned out from the bottom bunk at Wocko and said... he said, 'Ah, you're *over* the bloody fence!'

They both collapse with laughter. They eventually laugh themselves to a halt. Pause.

[*Almost crying*] That's fair dinkum.

MICK: [*the same*] Ah, that bloody Wocko...

They sniff and control themselves. Pause. They gasp and cackle softly.

SAM: [*softly*] Ha-ha... what a bloody thing to happen at five o'clock in the morning.

MICK: Ah. Poor old bloody Wocko.

SAM: Yeah. That Swamper's a funny bastard too.

MICK: Yeah, I know.

SAM: Uh, ha... hmmn.

MICK: Mmmnn... hnnhn.

They finally calm themselves with tea. They puff happily on their cigarettes.

SAM: Ah, it's a funny joint, this.

MICK: I reckon it is... [*Sipping his tea*] Gimme a fright, though, that earthshake.

SAM: Yeah. Nice if it come down on yer.

MICK: Jesus.

SAM: Yeah. Yer'd have been talking to Him.

MICK: That's one thing about this joint... made to last, mate, none of yer ramshackle building when they built this lot.

SAM: Ah. just the place to be when earthquakes are on tap. [*Nodding*] Bloody oath.

They drink.

Ahh. Nothing like the old cuppa.

MICK: Huh.

SAM: [*appreciatively*] The old cuppa tea.

MICK: Yep… [*Smiling and toasting* SAM] Bit of luck with this parole, I'll never have to drink the rubbish again.

SAM *toasts him back. The tennis ball arrives again, hitting* MICK. *He grabs it and throws it back with a shout.*

Can't yers even knock off for smoko, yer ratbags! [*He scowls and turns with a sigh to* SAM.] I must have been doing it unconscious.

SAM: That's just what I was thinking.

Pause.

MICK: Ah, let's not worry about it.

SAM: Nah. It'll only get worse.

Pause. They sip and smoke. SAM *shakes his head thoughtfully.*

Funny, that…

MICK: What?

SAM: What yer said before… the way one'll give yer a go, like, if you do the same…

MICK: True wherever yer go.

SAM: Ah. Would be, I suppose. Thing is, though, why is it there's some yer can't handle?

MICK: [*after considering briefly*] Oh, well it's just human nature, like. Yer get those'll treat you like you treat them, and yer get those don't give a stuff what you do but they'll do what they do anyway…

SAM: Ah, yeah. [*Nodding*] That's screws all right.

MICK: Um. And crims.

SAM: Aw…

MICK: It's people, matter of fact.

Pause. SAM *considers it.*

SAM: [*abruptly*] Ah yeah, but what about the night shift this bloody week? What about 'em lobbing in *my* peter every night of it, every night on the search—in *my* peter!

MICK: Well, so what? Got nothing, have yer?

SAM: No, but that ain't the point. What about the same one pulling me blankets apart every night, and poking about and pulling me joint to pieces? The same lair every night! Not one night this week he ain't got me. [*Appealing*] There's a couple of hundred other peters he could pick on, ain't there, without mine?

MICK: [*grinning*] Well… he might like yer face.

SAM: [*huffing*] Ah no, fair dinkum. [*Drinking*] Jeez, I get wild.

MICK: Hmmhn. [*Smiling, understanding*] What's he, one of the young blokes?

SAM: 'Course.

MICK: Ah, well he's just learning, I suppose.

SAM: Let him learn on some other mug, then. [*He thinks about it and sulks.*] All right for you... different thing.

MICK: Oh. Dunno about that.

SAM: Well I do. 'Course it is. You got yer little Home Sweet Home going. Someone to keep the ship tidy and you happy—Home Sweet Home. [*He nods at* MICK, *drinks and nods again.*] It'll do me... if it's on.

> He looks doubtfully at MICK. Pause. MICK *drinks, looks at* SAM, *smiles.*

MICK: Don't worry. You'll be all right. Told yer, didn't I?

SAM: Uhnhn. I know yer did. I hope so though. [*Considering dismally*] *She* mightn't want to cop me, though—yer thought of that? Might tell yer no when yer mention me...

MICK: [*reassuring*] Nah! Just don't worry... And *don't* start at me again about it now! [*With a raised hand*] It'll be sweet... but like I said, see if I get me parole first.

SAM: [*emphatically*] Yer will.

MICK: Yeah, well, we'll see if I will first.

> He nods firmly at SAM.

SAM: Yeah, all right, all right, I [*He spies someone coming.*] Hey! Here she *is!*

> He jumps to his feet grinning. He pulls his hat off and clutches it excitedly.

MICK: What? [*Looking and grimacing*] Aw, yeah... I might have known she'd be around.

> They both look offstage welcomingly, MICK *a little reluctantly.* BRENDA *arrives and stands smiling. He is wearing only pants and shirt and tennis shoes.*

BRENDA: Hello. Having tea?

MICK: [*grumpily*] Nah. Eating tin mugs.

SAM: G'day, Brenda! Gonna sit down?

MICK: [*reacting angrily, with an anxious glance towards the gate*] You nit! Shut up! She's *George*, yer fool! *George!* [*Gesturing towards the gate*] You want 'em to know the facts of life?

> SAM *looks crestfallen and apologetic,* MICK *gestures tiredly to* BRENDA.

Oh come on... Sit down for Christ's sake—George.

SAM: Yeah, George! [*Grinning*] Gahn—sit down.

BRENDA: [*looking at the ground, shaking his head*] No, I'll get too grubby.

> SAM *reacts immediately. He pulls off his coat and spreads it on the ground, gesturing.*

SAM: No yer won't. Look, here y'are!

BRENDA: Oh! But—oh no, please! Put it back on. I'd feel terrible. Honestly, I have to go...

SAM: No, go on. Sweet, no worries. [*Insisting*] Yer can't make it no—I mean it has to go down the laundry on Thursday, anyway. Gahn!

BRENDA: Oh. No, please. I can't stay. Truly, I—

MICK: [*flatly*] Will yer sit down and stop putting us on show?

> *He gestures at* SAM's *coat.* BRENDA *sighs and sits down. He nods nicely at* SAM.

BRENDA: Well... thank you very much.

SAM: [*staring, grinning*] How yer gahn?

BRENDA: Good, thanks.

SAM: That's good.

BRENDA: [*politely*] And you?

> SAM *grins. He nods a couple of times, grinning and staring.* BRENDA *nods back, hesitantly smiling.*

That's good.

> SAM *continues to grin and paces the yard, nodding occasionally.* BRENDA *nods to him once, he nods a salvo in reply.* BRENDA, *becoming uncertain, looks askance at* MICK.

MICK: Where y'been?

BRENDA: Is he all right?

> MICK *inspects* SAM, *who is still grinning at* BRENDA.

MICK: Sam? Sam!

> SAM *returns to the pair. He looks uncertainly at* MICK.

SAM: Ha-ha...

MICK: George just spoke to yer.

SAM: [*to* BRENDA] Oh. Sorry, George. Must have been thinking of something else. What y'say?

BRENDA: I said thanks very much.

SAM: That's all right.

BRENDA: It's very good of you. [*To* MICK] I've only been in Two Yard... had a game of tennis.

SAM: I love a game of tennis.

MICK: What've yer got for tea—anything?

BRENDA: I think some tomatoes. I've got us a nice couple of cups of milk—you can have it with your Milo.

MICK *nods.*

It's too early yet to see what's about. We'll have something.

MICK: Ah, good enough. Lunch'll be all right. Sunday special, plum duff and custard. A baked spud too. Hope there's parsnip.

SAM: [*nodding at* BRENDA] I love it, plum duff.

BRENDA: [*smiling*] Mmmmn?

SAM: Yeah.

MICK: Baked parsnip, I love.

BRENDA: Oh, you love food.

SAM: Me too.

BRENDA: Well, food is good for you.

> *Pause.*

SAM: Man does not live by bread alone... [*Pause.*] That's true.

MICK: Yer need fluids.

SAM: Aw, no, it means... aw...

BRENDA: I know what it means.

> *Pause.*

SAM: Do yer?

BRENDA: [*smiling*] Mmmn.

> *Pause.*

SAM: You Catholic?

BRENDA: Well... [*smiling*] ... in a way.

MICK: Bullshit. What are yers talking about?

> *Pause.*

BRENDA: Heaven.

MICK: Jesus!

BRENDA: Don't swear.

MICK: Ah, shit.

BRENDA: Oh, lovely language. [*Winking at* SAM] Just what the parole officer would admire.

MICK: Tcha!

SAM: [*to* BRENDA] I never swear.

> MICK'*s eyebrows fly up.*

BRENDA: Good for you. I'm glad. There's no need.

SAM: Ah. That's what I keep telling Mick here.

MICK: Ah. Silly looking bastard you are.

> SAM *manages to look hurt.*

BRENDA: Oh, he is not! [*To* SAM] You are not.

SAM: Ah, it's all right. [*To* MICK] Like, I know yer not the best, mate, waiting for news on yer parole and that... [*Coughing*] Not being able to think about anything except flying out of here to yer missus—yer wife... [*Coughing*] As yer was saying before.

MICK: What? [*Disgusted*] Ah, now look you—

> SAM *rises to his feet.*

What are you—? Where yer going?

SAM: I, uh... I'm in need of the toilet, as they say. [*Smiling and nodding*] Won't be a minute.

> *He walks off. They watch him disappear then look at each other,* MICK *scowling,* BRENDA *smiling.*

MICK: [*accusingly*] Dunno what you think yer doing.

BRENDA: Oh! I'm just having fun.

MICK: [*growling*] Yerr. [*Pointing a finger*] Listen, you. Yer want to go flirting with mugs, then just don't go doing it with my friends.

BRENDA: Tcha! How could I do that? I'm never allowed anywhere near them.

MICK: Yeah, well yer here now... so...

> *He is at a loss.*

BRENDA: [*giggling*] So?

> *Pause.*

MICK: [*gesturing decisively*] So piss off.

BRENDA: [*sulkily*] No.

MICK: [*menacingly*] Piss off, I said.

BRENDA: I was only playing...

MICK: Gahn, on yer merry. Scram! [*Pause. He jerks a thumb at the gate.*] Get going, I said. So get going.

BRENDA: [*sighing a sulky acceptance*] Oh all right, I will then.

> *He gets up.*

MICK: Well, do then. Go on, 'fore he gets back.

BRENDA: [*pacifying him*] I'll go and see about the tomatoes then. Are you really wild?

MICK: [*with a slow grin*] No. But ta-ta.

BRENDA: [*smiling*] All right. [*Moving off*] Give my love to Sammy.

> *He laughs and is gone.* MICK *flaps a hand after him, relaxing against the fence. He looks after* BRENDA *smiling, then turns to where he can see* SAM *returning.* SAM *bustles back a bit breathlessly and looks around in disappointment.*

SAM: Hey, where's Br—Where's George?

MICK: [*grinning*] She had to change the baby.

SAM: Coming back?

MICK: Nuh.

SAM: Oh. [*Sadly*] Oh, well.

> *He sits down.* MICK *closes his eyes complacently.*

What'll we do now, then?

MICK: [*with his eyes shut*] Hmph. What do yer reckon?

> *Pause.* SAM *looks around unhappily.*

We just wait, of course. [*Yawning*] Till it's time to go in.

SAM: Ah. [*Nodding*] Yeah. [*Singing*] Never mind.

MICK: Uhnnhn...

> MICK *dozes.* SAM *fidgets, takes up his coat, bundles it against his chest and sits absently. He looks glumly at* MICK, *puts the bundled coat against the fence next to* MICK, *then he too rests his head against the fence, lying on his back with the coat for a pillow. He changes his mind and sits up, then sighs and talks to* MICK *absently.*

SAM: What's to do, then? I dunno. [*Pause.*] Ah, jeez, I hope yer get yer parole, mate. I do. [*Pause.*] Makes yer wonder though, don't it, why they want to keep searching *my* joint... every bloody night. [*He sighs.*] Aw, Jesus. The nights, mate. I hate the bloody night time, yer know that? Hmph, I reckon I do. [*He stares around the yard.*] The days, well, all right... [*shaking his head*] ... but the nights. Hmph.

> *Pause. The tennis ball bounces on gently.* SAM *rolls it back slowly.*

Keep it up you bludgers. Keep it up.

MICK: [*stirring irritably*] Shush!

SAM: Sorry.

> *He lies back quietly against the fence.*

SCENE FOUR

Outside the parole office. Monday morning. A wall runs across the back of the stage, in front of which is a sad attempt at a rockery; a few shrubs and a miserable scrawny tree hang over the white-washed stones. The parole office is represented simply by a door at one side of the stage, with a sign reading 'Parole Office'. The ground is strewn with dead leaves. The SWEEPER *stands there with his broom, shuffling around slowly. He spies a cigarette butt, picks it up, examines it briefly, takes out his tin and puts the butt in it. He puts the tin away and begins sweeping slowly.* LEVICK, *a middle-aged man in civilian clothes, arrives briskly, smiling. The* SWEEPER *pauses to acknowledge him uncertainly.*

LEVICK: How are we today?

SWEEPER: Ah.

LEVICK: Not waiting for me, are you?

SWEEPER: No, not for you, sir.

LEVICK: Good, good then! And the name?

SWEEPER: Uh? Oh, ah, the name's Bruce, sir... but...

LEVICK: [*smiling*] Mr Bruce!

SWEEPER: I'm in under something else... this time. Like, another name...

> *He frowns.*

LEVICK: Oh? What's it, then?

SWEEPER: Ah, can't think offhand right now.

> *He thinks.*

LEVICK: But your name is Bruce.

SWEEPER: That's me name, yeah, it's... yeah.

LEVICK: Good! Well, how do you do, Mr Bruce!

> *He offers a friendly hand. The* SWEEPER *puts the end of his broom in it.* LEVICK *shakes heartily.*

SWEEPER: Ah... oh, well how yer gahn?

LEVICK: Oh, well, very well! And yourself?

SWEEPER: [*nodding*] Ah...

LEVICK: Well that's fine! [*Beaming and nodding*] My name's Levick, you know. Parole officer.

> *Pause.*

SWEEPER: Hnhnn...

LEVICK: [*nodding*] Hnnhn... [*Pause.*] Family man, are you, Mr Bruce?

SWEEPER: Ah... nah... I, uh, not now, no.

> *He shrugs.*

LEVICK: Anything, ah, I could do for you?

> *He smiles encouragement. The* SWEEPER *shakes his head.*

SWEEPER: Thanks all the same.

LEVICK: You're sure? Oh, well that's too bad. [*Looking abruptly at his watch*] I say, you haven't seen a lady?

SWEEPER: Huh?

LEVICK: [*gesturing at his office*] I'm expecting a lady, at ten. An appointment. She hasn't been by?

SWEEPER: Oh... ah, no, not while I've been here.

LEVICK: Oh good. Well, I'm in good time. [*Looking at his watch again*] And there's nothing you need, Mr Bruce?

SWEEPER: Nah, I'm pretty well fixed, sir. Only doing ten days.

LEVICK: Oh, well!

SWEEPER: Again.

LEVICK: You're okay, then.

SWEEPER: Yeah.

LEVICK: You don't need me.

SWEEPER: No.

LEVICK: Ah... oh, well...

SWEEPER: Hnnhn...

> *Pause. They nod to each other.*

LEVICK: Well! I suppose I'd better open up the old office. [*Fumbling in a pocket*] Key here somewhere.

SWEEPER: [*slowly starting to sweep again*] I'd best get a move on, meself.

> LEVICK *gets out his key and opens the door. He pauses and smiles as he is about to enter the office.*

LEVICK: [*waggling a couple of fingers*] Best of luck, then.

SWEEPER: [*pausing, nodding, sighing*] Ah...

> *He watches* LEVICK *go in and shut the door behind him. He grimaces, shakes his head and resumes sweeping. After a moment he stoops, fossicking among the leaves, and comes up with a butt. He examines it and throws it away with an air of professional distaste. He sweeps again. The prison clock sounds ten o'clock and, before it has finished, a prison* OFFICER *enters, followed by a* WOMAN. *They are moving straight towards the office, but pause at the sight of the* SWEEPER, *who also pauses. The* WOMAN *is plain enough, but her clothes are not so ordinary; she is dressed very aggressively, mannishly. The* SWEEPER *looks at her peevishly.*

WOMAN: [*to* SWEEPER] Hello.

SWEEPER: [*holding his broom on the defensive, muttering*] Gawd Jesus.

WOMAN: Hmmn?

OFFICER: Is the parole officer in, do you know, Five-thirty-five?

SWEEPER: [*staring*] Ah...

WOMAN: What's the matter?

SWEEPER: [*gesturing*] He's in there... lady.

WOMAN: Well, thank you.

> *She smiles at the* SWEEPER, *and at the* OFFICER, *who nods briskly and goes over to rap on the door. The door opens.* LEVICK *smiles, gesturing for the* WOMAN *to enter.*

LEVICK: Ah, good morning, here you are!

> *He draws her into the office, nodding to the* OFFICER.

Thank you, Officer, we'll be all right now.

The OFFICER *nods and walks off. The* WOMAN *disappears into the office.* LEVICK *winks and smiles at the* SWEEPER, *who nods slightly in reply.* LEVICK *closes the door. The* SWEEPER *shakes his head and shuffles to centre stage, where he removes his hat and raises his eyes to heaven.*

SWEEPER: Oh, Lord, whoever he is, whatever his state of grace what belongs to that... [*Gesturing sadly at the office door*] Lord, let a train run over the poor devil and take that cup from him...

He sighs, replaces his hat and starts to sweep again. He pauses, shaking his head.

Ah, it'd be one of them socio-ologist things from the university, no doubt about it. [*Sweeping slowly*] No wonder so many blokes are all turning poof these days...

He stands and looks at the office door.

Tcha! Fancy having to get its breakfast every day. [*Chuckling*] It sure wouldn't be getting yours for yer... no way in the world.

He potters about, muttering wryly to himself, looks a the door again and shakes his head.

A man don't know how lucky he is sometimes.

He sighs, then starts to sweep with a will. After a moment MICK *enters briskly. The* SWEEPER *pauses to look at him.*

MICK: G'day, old mate.

SWEEPER: G'day.

MICK: [*glancing at the door*] Parole bloke there, is he?

SWEEPER: Ah. Someone's in with him.

MICK: Oh. I'll prop, then.

They smile at each other.

Don't let me stop you.

SWEEPER: [*leaning on his broom*] Someone has to.

MICK: Ah? [*Grinning*] Get a go on, do you?

SWEEPER: Can't help meself. [*Indicating the leaves*] Been working me guts out all morning on this lot here.

MICK: Mmmn... Well, don't go overdoing it.

The SWEEPER *looks guilty.*

I know how it is, though. Yer sort of pitch in trying to make the time go, eh?

SWEEPER: [*sighing*] Yeah, that's about it.

MICK: I reckon, yeah. I know how it is. [*Nodding*] Yer got to watch it, though, case it starts to be a habit, like... wear yerself out.

SWEEPER: Oh well, it's the same in everything—habits, I mean —like, say, smoking's bad for yer...

MICK: Aw...

SWEEPER: Like, when it's a habit it is.

MICK: Oh, it's bad then, yeah, that's what I was trying to say. Any habit is no good—

SWEEPER: Like, it's not the smoking's bad for yer, not really, but the habit's what kills yer...

MICK: Oh yeah, yeah. Understood.

> *They nod. A slight pause.*

SWEEPER: [*eyeing his broom*] So any habit at all...

MICK: Yeah. [*Gesturing to the rockery*] You want to sit down for a while?

SWEEPER: Ah. [*Nodding wearily*] I suppose that'd be best. [*He sits tiredly on the rockery.*] Not that a man gets much chance of making it a habit—smoking, I mean.

> *He smiles.* MICK *smiles at him. Pause.* MICK *digs in a pocket to take out a tobacco pouch. He takes tobacco and a paper for himself and offers the pouch.*

MICK: One of these?

SWEEPER: Ta.

> *He takes the makings and returns the pouch. They roll cigarettes.*

MICK: That's all right. Doing long?

SWEEPER: Ten days.

MICK: Oh. Not enough to worry about.

> *He smiles. Pause. The cigarettes are lit.*

SWEEPER: It's enough to worry about, all right, when you get it as often as I do.

MICK: Ah?

SWEEPER: Never had a lagging over six months, I haven't. Six months, three months, fourteen days, ten days, seven days, even twenty-four bloody hours once, when I was a young feller.

MICK: Yer lucky.

SWEEPER: I reckon I've done about twenty-three years in the nick—a bit at a time.

MICK: Yer don't say!

SWEEPER: Ah.

MICK: Jeez. You have had a bad trot.

SWEEPER: In and out, in and out, round and round...

> *He sighs and looks down.*

MICK: You must've done a few capers?

SWEEPER: I drink a bit... always have.

MICK: Gor! That all?

SWEEPER: That's enough.

>   MICK *reflects on it.*

MICK: Jeez... twenty-something years!

SWEEPER: Dunno where it's gone.

MICK: Time flies.

SWEEPER: Yer can't... they fly too quick.

MICK: Eh?

SWEEPER: [*grinning*] That was a joke when I was a kid: Time flies, you cannot, they fly too quick.

MICK: Ha-ha. [*Pause.* MICK *considers the* SWEEPER.] I was you, I'd give it away.

SWEEPER: The bottle, yer mean?

MICK: I reckon.

SWEEPER: [*shaking his head*] Couldn't do that now.

MICK: Why not? Yer should try it.

SWEEPER: Uh. Wouldn't be patriotic.

MICK: Yer kidding.

SWEEPER: Nah. I've thought about it. I been tempted a few times, like, to turn it up. But see, the fact is they've go so many things going nowadays, organisations working to help the likes of me, if me and my mob gave it away we'd throw half the nation out of work.

MICK: [*impressed*] Ahh.

SWEEPER: Couldn't rightly do that.

MICK: Nah. I suppose yer couldn't, really.

SWEEPER: Nothing else to do, anyway.

MICK: Oh.

SWEEPER: Unless I go into business, which as a matter of fact I'm thinking of doing.

>   *He looks confidently at* MICK.

MICK: Oh, business, are yer?

SWEEPER: Ah. Small at first, like.

MICK: No need to rush at it. What, then?

SWEEPER: What sort of business, yer mean?

MICK: If it's all right me asking?

>   *Pause. The* SWEEPER *considers* MICK.

SWEEPER: It's sort of a manufacturing thing, like, plus being a sort of advertising affair.

MICK: Your own idea, like?

SWEEPER: Absolutely.

MICK: That's the main thing.

SWEEPER: It is so.

MICK: So they say, them that know.

SWEEPER: It's all me own idea, the lot.

MICK: Go on!

SWEEPER: Yeah. I tell yer what. Yer know these days how the blokes are wearing perfume after they shave and all that? [*Pause.*] Well, see, they're selling all these different shaped bottles of ladies' ware for men, all with different names like Moose and Rattler and that. So blokes'll buy the stuff and not think they're really poofs 'cos of the tough names... see?

MICK: Ah.

SWEEPER: Yeah. And then there's the advertising in the papers. Pictures of the bottles, with a bloke sometimes, but usually with a grouse sheila in the picture all ready to get her gear off if yer use whatever stuff they're trying to sell yer...

MICK: [*becoming impatient*] Well, what's your caper, then?

SWEEPER: Hang on. I'll tell yer...

He peers intently at MICK.

MICK: Come on, then.

SWEEPER: What would you say... if I showed you a bottle of *after-shave* that looked like a fair dinkum *hand grenade*?

MICK: Ahh!

SWEEPER: With a real-looking pin and all, instead of a top. Like, a ring that pulls out the pin that's really the top of the bottle that's a grenade.

MICK *considers.*

MICK: I reckon yer got something...

SWEEPER: And the name real big: Grenade!

MICK: Like, *Boom!*

SWEEPER: Exactly like a real bunger.

MICK: Yeah, and with the advertising picture yer put a bloke holding it in his hand, and with a sheila—a good sort, like—smiling at him... not much gear on her... and then yer slogan: [*posing as if with the bottle*] 'Grenade after-shave—Pull out the pin, and up yer go!' [*Beaming at the* SWEEPER] How's that for a best-seller?

SWEEPER: [*delighted*] That's it! That's me slogan!

MICK: My compliments.

SWEEPER: What was it again? Write it down. [*Producing a piece of paper*] Here, write it down for me.

MICK: [*taking out a pencil*] You do it for yerself. I'll say it.

SWEEPER: [*pushing the paper at him*] No, you write it.

MICK: [*waving him away*] No, you. I'm a rotten writer.

He will not take the pencil and paper. The SWEEPER *stands defeated.*

Righto. Here it is again. [*Posing*] 'Grenade after-shave—pull out the...'

He pauses because the SWEEPER *is still.*

Come on. Write it while I say it.

> *Pause. The* SWEEPER *holds out the paper and pencil.* MICK *slowly takes it from him. He writes, looking at the* SWEEPER.

Sorry, mate.

SWEEPER: Ah.

> MICK *hands him the paper, pockets the pencil and smiles.*

MICK: I'll be yer first customer.

SWEEPER: You're a good bloke.

MICK: Aw. [*He sits on the rockery and nods at the closed door.*] I hope *he* thinks I am.

SWEEPER: Who? The parole bloke?

MICK: Ah.

SWEEPER: Don't seem a bad feller.

MICK: Yer know him a bit, then.

SWEEPER: Just said hello to him today.

MICK: What's he like, I mean, do yer think?

SWEEPER: Don't seem a bad feller at all.

MICK: Well, that's good. That's what I reckon too.

> MICK *suddenly rises to his feet and begins pacing nervously. The* SWEEPER *watches placidly.* MICK *stops abruptly.*

What's today?

SWEEPER: Monday.

MICK: Yeah. I wasn't sure for a minute.

> *He begins pacing again.*

SWEEPER: Coming up for parole, are yer?

MICK: I suppose I'm some sort of chance.

SWEEPER: [*gesturing at the door*] Yer got to see him?

MICK: Ten o'clock, they said.

SWEEPER: Ah. Well, he don't seem a bad bloke.

MICK: Mmmn. He's been orright so far.

> *He sits down on the rockery again.*

SWEEPER: Can't say the same of her.

MICK: Who?

SWEEPER: Dragon with him.

MICK: What? You mean a sheila?

SWEEPER: Sort of. One of them lot from wherever they come from.

MICK: Uh?

SWEEPER: What do they call 'em... you know, social whatever it is... study yer, like...

MICK: Oh, yeah.

SWEEPER: And then they write a book about it.

MICK: Psychology and all that.

SWEEPER: Ah. Experts.

MICK: Mmmn.

> *They both nod wisely.*

Probably not a bad rort.

SWEEPER: I reckon not.

> *Pause. The* SWEEPER *chuckles to himself.*

Ha-ha. Y'ought to see her.

> *They grin at each other.*

MICK: What's it look like?

SWEEPER: Like a walking protest, mate. Yer can see it written all over her mush.

> *They laugh.*

MICK: Good sort or what?

SWEEPER: Head like a half-sucked jellybean.

> *They laugh.*

Butch-looking haircut. *Boots!* Haw!

> *They laugh again.*

MICK: Don't mind a bit of puss in boots.

SWEEPER: Ha! Wait'll yer see this one.

> *The* SWEEPER *laughs and shakes his head.*

MICK: Real monster, is it?

SWEEPER: Yer wouldn't take it to a shit fight.

MICK: Jeez, it must be a case.

SWEEPER: It's a case all right

MICK: How would you know?

SWEEPER: A case of belt it or bear it.

MICK: Oh, I thought yer meant—

SWEEPER: Nah.

MICK: Oh.

> *Pause.*

SWEEPER: Just got a *look* about her—you know?

MICK: Ah?

SWEEPER: Looks like a canary that's swallowed the cat.

MICK: Oh, ho!

> *They nod wisely together.*

SWEEPER: Like, if her head was a bumper I wouldn't pick it up.

MICK: Gawd! That bad is it?

SWEEPER: I reckon... [*Shaking his head*] Some poor bastard owns it.

MICK: Uhnn. [*Pause.*] Ah well, as long as it's not us.

> *They chuckle in relief together.*

SWEEPER: Yer'd go to gaol just to get away from it!

MICK: Haw! And yer wouldn't be the first bloke's done that!

> *They laugh together. They grin at the closed door. The door opens. LEVICK pops his head out. MICK and the SWEEPER stand abruptly.*

LEVICK: [*coming out, smiling*] Mr Harrison!

MICK: Ah, Mr Levick.

LEVICK: Well, we've been waiting for you!

MICK: Ah. Well, here I am.

LEVICK: Have you been here long? I didn't hear you knock.

MICK: Oh... nah... I, uh... [*Indicating the* SWEEPER] Me mate said yer had someone in there with yer.

LEVICK: Ah! [*Chuckling*] Oh yes, so there is. [*Beaming, he calls into the office.*] Mrs Harrison!

> *He gives MICK a huge grin. MICK looks in alarm to the doorway. The WOMAN appears, pausing demurely in the doorway.*

MICK: Jesus.

WOMAN: Michael.

MICK: It's you.

WOMAN: Yes.. how are you?

> *She comes out the door.*

LEVICK: [*taking MICK's arm*] Ha-ha! Oh well, you know, I thought for your last visit it would help to have the little woman along—last minute arrangements and all that. [*He chuckles, giving MICK a sporting nudge.*] Well, come on! She's not a ghost. Smile!

> MICK *continues to look aghast, ignoring LEVICK.*

WOMAN: [*encouragingly*] It's me.

> *Pause.*

MICK: [*scowling*] Yer wearing that get-up for a bet, or what?

WOMAN: Oh, don't start...

LEVICK: [*mournfully*] Oh, Mr Harrison.

MICK: [*snapping*] You shut up and keep out! [*To the* WOMAN] Just look at yer, yer silly-looking thing. What, have yer come here to put a man on show, have yer? Front of everybody in the bloody joint?

WOMAN: [*warning*] Michael...

MICK: Tcha! Don't bloody well Michael me, yer ratbag-looking imbecile. What are yer trying to do? Get a job on the bloody wharf or something? What's happened to yer?

LEVICK: Oh now, Mr Harrison.

WOMAN: [*sweetly*] Leave it to me, Mr Levick. [*Advancing on* MICK, *chin out*] Now you just don't start, Michael Harrison! [*Poking a finger*] Do you hear? I've taken a whole morning off my job just to come here and make arrangements to have you home tomorrow, you rude, useless, ugly, beer-gutted slob!

MICK: [*astonished*] Hey, just you listen... *Tomorrow?*

WOMAN: Shut up! I won't just listen at all. [*Smiling grimly*] That's all over, mate, when you did all the talking and I did all the listening; and you'd better get used to the idea because otherwise you're going to find yourself talking to yourself all the time because nobody wants to hear your big-boss drivel any more, especially me! You got that?

MICK: [*open-mouthed*] Err...

WOMAN: [*emphatically*] Yes, *err!*

MICK: Aw, but...

WOMAN: But what?

MICK: Ah... [*Helplessly*] Well, I dunno what's happened to yer...

WOMAN: No? [*Nodding*] Yes, well, you'll have plenty of time to find that out, mate. And this is for starters, that you don't try your tyrant tricks on me any more. Got it?

MICK: Hmmnn. well, I, uh... [*Pause.*] Looks like things've changed a bit, it seems to me... [*Pause. He sighs, thinks, looks hurt and pats his stomach.*] Dunno what you're talking about beer-gutted, though. Flat as a board I am, been exercising like a champion.

WOMAN: Oh. [*Examining his gut*] Well, I'll take that part back, then. [*Pleased*] Yes, you don't look too bad...

MICK: [*mollified*] Uhnn. Ah well, that's all right, then.

Pause. She smiles and poses for him.

WOMAN: All right... Well, come on then, grumpy, how do I look?

Pause. He hesitates, scowls, weakens and smiles.

MICK: Grouse. Yer look bloody lovely, mate.

They grin at each other. She rubs her nose impishly against his, pats his face and ruffles his hair.

WOMAN: 'Course I do! And so do you. I love you.

She takes his hand.

MICK: [*smiling*] Yeah, me too... now I remember.

LEVICK *smiles on them. He claps* MICK *on the shoulder, walking into the office.*

LEVICK: Well, come on in, both of you. We've got things to arrange for tomorrow.

He goes in. She follows, tugging MICK *by the hand. He pulls his hand loose as they reach the door and smilingly gestures her in.*

MICK: Go on, I'm coming in in a second.

She goes in. MICK *turns swiftly and goes back to smile very meanly at the* SWEEPER. *The* SWEEPER *shrugs philosophically.* MICK *reaches out and pulls the piece of paper from the* SWEEPER*'s pocket. He shakes it briefly under the* SWEEPER*'s nose, then deliberately tears it into small pieces, his smile turning to a scowl.* LEVICK *appears in the doorway.*

LEVICK: Well, come on, Mike!

He disappears again.

MICK: Yeah, here I come now.

He presses the torn paper into the SWEEPER*'s hand, leaves him and goes into the office, shutting the door behind him. The* SWEEPER *stands alone, clutching the paper. He stares down and opens his hand, allowing the scraps of paper to fall among the leaves. He sighs and begins sweeping slowly.*

SCENE FIVE

MICK*'s and* BRENDA*'s cell. The bell is ringing faintly off.* BRENDA *enters, then turns back to the door, beckoning.* SAM *staggers in with rolled-up mattress, pillow and blankets in his arms.*

SAM: Where?

BRENDA: Down there anywhere. Find a spot.

SAM *puts down his load and sits on it, puffing.*

SAM: Whew! Jesus they're heavy. [*Grinning*] Well, I reckon a man's made it.

BRENDA: You tried hard enough. [*Smiling*] Mick'll be here in a second.

SAM: Ah, he's been everywhere this arvo, saying goodbye to the mob—all his mates round the place.

BRENDA: [*tidying up here and there*] Mmmnn... I know.

SAM: [*chuckling*] They had a little ceremony up the brush shop, Wocko and them. I was there, Mick pulled his numbers off his coat. Ha-ha, and we helped him say goodbye to them all right.

He laughs.

BRENDA: Oh?

SAM: We put 'em in a bucket and pissed on 'em. [*Gleefully*] We all had a go... bloody near filled the—

BRENDA: Oh shut up, Sam!

  Pause.

SAM: Aw, well I was just telling you... dunno what's wrong with that.

BRENDA: Hmph.

SAM: The whole joint ought to be pissed on—from a bloody great height. That's what I reckon meself.

BRENDA: Oh well, keep it to yourself, then.

SAM: What's the matter?

BRENDA: Nothing. I'm sorry, it isn't you.

SAM: Ah. That's what I thought. [*Pause.*] Man's going out tomorrow, he's entitled to pull his number off and piss on the rotten thing. [*Nodding*] So he did anyway.

BRENDA: I just don't see the point. But never mind.

SAM: [*helpfully*] Yer don't see the point? Oh, well, see, it's like when we was kids. I dunno if you did but where I was when the finish of the year come all the kids used to throw our books in the incinerating thing. Burn 'em, like, 'cos we'd hated 'em all the time and when the time was over for 'em it made yer feel grouse just to throw 'em in the fire and watch it all burn away. Like—

BRENDA: Yes, I understand.

SAM: That was the only time I ever used to turn up, when it was all over and time to do that. Hated school.

BRENDA: Oh.

SAM: Used to wag it all year nearly, I did. Used to go down on the beach where some blokes used to leave their rowboats y'know, fishermen...

BRENDA: Oh, yeah.

SAM: Yeah. They always pulled 'em up on the beach, on the sand up where the tide couldn't get 'em, and they'd turn 'em upside down, the boats, and they all had this little hole—the water was supposed to run out or something, and they'd have a cork in it...

  Pause. BRENDA *is dusting the cupboard.*

Yeah. Well, I used to crawl under some upside-down boat like that, all day, just looking up through the little hole at the sky... all day.

BRENDA: What a mad kid.

SAM: [*laughing*] Yeah! It was just a blue spot, the sky, like when yer look through a long bit of pipe, just a tiny little bit of blue. I must've been mad, lying on me back in the sand with a boat on top of me!

He chuckles.

BRENDA: [*smiling*] You must've wanted privacy.

SAM: Yeah. Might have been that too. [*Pause. Ruefully*] Don't think I ever did know why I did it. I just did it like that... nothing but dark and a little blue bit of light to look at... like a little boob of me own.

BRENDA: [*laughing*] Well, perhaps you were in training.

SAM: Eh? Oh, yeah! For this, yer mean! Ha-ha, yeah.

    BRENDA *smiles.* SAM *chuckles to himself.*

Anyway, I always went at the end of the year and did me bit at the book burning. Never missed that. Made yer feel good, dunno why, but it always did.

BRENDA: You probably felt free afterwards.

SAM: Hnnhn... Yeah, well that's it, that's what I started telling yer—why we all pissed on Mick's number.

BRENDA: [*sighing, smiling*] You win, Sam.

SAM: [*touching his number patch*] When my turn comes, I'm gonna burn this—and then piss on it.

    Pause. The sounds of authority are heard off: voices, bolts banging shut on iron doors, heavy tramping.

BRENDA: Mick had better smarten himself.

SAM: Ah, be on his way now, I reckon.

    The SECOND OFFICER *appears in the doorway and walks in.*

SECOND OFFICER: Right for the night, you two— [*Taking in* SAM *and his bedding*] What's this?

SAM: [*haughtily*] I find that rather obscure.

SECOND OFFICER: What?

SAM: Now there yer go again... What's what?

BRENDA: There's one more to come.

SECOND OFFICER: Oh. [*To* SAM] And what are you doing here, then?

SAM: [*enlightened*] Ohh! Ah, well, now I gather the gist of your interrogation, sir. Yes. Well, yer see, I've just moved in because me mate's going out of here tomorrow and I'm replacing him in the cell.

    He nods.

SECOND OFFICER: I see.

SAM: That's bonzer.

SECOND OFFICER: And who approved this?

SAM: Oh, someone you know. [*Gesturing*] Superior of yours, stripes on his arm and braid on his hat... y'know?

SECOND OFFICER: [*peeved*] Listen, Jenkins...

SAM: [*happily*] I'm all ears, sir.

SECOND OFFICER: Why do you—?

SAM: [*touching an ear*] Yer may have noticed?

SECOND OFFICER: Why do you have to be so bloody smart?

SAM: [*guiltlessly*] Eh? Oh, well, I—Ah!

> MICK *comes in, slow, silent and looking tired. He throws off his hat and coat.*

SECOND OFFICER: Just wondering about you.

MICK: [*ignoring the others*] Oh. Yeah, well, here I am then.

SECOND OFFICER: Waiting to lock the door.

MICK: Go for yer life, then. [*Nodding*] Enjoy it while you're able. Won't be doing it no more, not to this boy.

SECOND OFFICER: [*smiling*] So they all tell me, over and over. [*Nodding*] Got water? Tub? Right. Goodnight.

BRENDA: Yes.

> MICK *and* SAM *ignore his questions. He goes out, slamming the door and clanging the bolt.*

SAM: [*to the closed door*] Piss off.

BRENDA: Sam Jenkins!

MICK: [*grinning*] Really, Samuel!

SAM: Forgot...

BRENDA: Make your bed there for tonight, while I get us a cup of tea.

> BRENDA *goes to a jug already on the table, gets cups and pours tea.* SAM *unrolls his bedding, makes a spot for himself and roughly shoves the sheets and blankets over the mattress.* MICK *sits watching and whistling softly.*

MICK: None for me.

BRENDA: [*firmly*] I've already got it ready.

MICK: Well, I don't want—Oh yeah, well just half a cup then. [*Fishing something out of a pocket*] It'll do to wash down the rest of me little mates here.

BRENDA: [*giving* MICK *his tea*] What is it?

MICK: Sleepers. [*Grinning*] Already took three, half an hour ago.

> *He scoffs the pills from his hand and drinks.*

BRENDA: [*anxiously peeved*] What do you want them for? Where'd you get them? How many are you taking?

MICK: Got 'em off Swampguts. He saves 'em up, the quack puts him on 'em for a month. [*Grinning*] I'm gonna bomb right out in minute and when I wake up again it'll be time to go straight out the gate.

BRENDA: How many?

MICK: [*smugly*] Six. [*Nodding happily*] I'm already half asleep.

BRENDA: But it's our last night! [*Appealing*] Oh, Mick, I thought we'd sit and talk and—

MICK: [*yawning*] Hoh! Yer kidding, aren't yer? What's there to talk about anyway, that we haven't wore out?

He swigs his tea.

BRENDA: Well, we've never said goodbye before.

MICK: Ah. Oh well, goodbye.

He nods and grins. Pause. MICK *drinks.* BRENDA *looks miserable.*

BRENDA: Six sleeping pills. You'll never wake up.

MICK: Oh, yeah, don't worry about me. I already woke up, today, when I seen what I've been away from.

He sits with a reminiscent smirk. SAM *finishes making his bed, and sits on it.*

SAM: Yeah, well come on. Yer gonna tell us about it, what happened?

MICK: What? Aw, well you know it all now, don't yer? I'm going out in the morning, and she'll be there back at the gate to meet me and we're going straight home to bed and I might think about getting up again in a month or so... [*chuckling*] if I'm still alive.

BRENDA: [*giving* SAM *his tea*] Careful you don't spill it.

SAM: Ta. [*Sipping it and smiling*] Grouse.

BRENDA: It's all right. We'll eat later on, when we've settled down a bit and Mick feels better.

SAM: Yeah, I'm starving.

BRENDA: There's plenty to eat... some cheese...

SAM: Not for me, not cheese, I don't eat it.

BRENDA: Oh... well, there's other stuff. Tomatoes, and some devon... an onion too, I think.

SAM: Ha! Devon and tomatoes. [*Grinning*] Yer got me.

BRENDA: [*smiling*] Mick likes devon too.

MICK: No, not me. Not tonight. I'm going to sleep, already told yer that.

He yawns.

BRENDA: But you still have to eat something. You'll be sick with excitement by tomorrow if there's nothing in your stomach. It'll only get wasted... I got it so—

MICK: Will you lemme alone?

He rises, scowling irritably. Although weary, he begins nervously pacing and prowling about the cell.

BRENDA: Oh, but Mick...

MICK: Look, lemme alone, will yer? I don't want no food, I don't want no conversations all night. All I want is for tomorrow to come, quick as it likes.

He flops down on his bed again. Pause.

BRENDA: [*sighing*] Enough sugar, Sam?

SAM: [*winking and nodding*] Sweet as a nut.

BRENDA: Good. I'll have mine.

> *He sits on his bed, sipping tea.* MICK *gets up and begins prowling again.*

SAM: Doing it hard, mate?

MICK: [*tersely*] I reckon I am.

BRENDA: Do some exercises. You haven't today.

MICK: Fuck me exercises. [*Prowling*] What's the time now? Only half past four.

SAM: Ah... about that.

MICK: Jesus. Another fifteen hours... more... can't even work it out... bloody brain's scrambled.

SAM: Uhnhnn. Oh, well, we get out in the morning about quarter past seven. That's, uh...

BRENDA: Nearly fifteen hours.

MICK: Oh, well, I was right.

BRENDA: Fourteen and three quarters.

SAM: Yer got it.

MICK: Uhnnhn. [*Jittery*] I've got it all right... the trouble is I've got to handle it... bloody drag.

SAM: Yeah... I know. Them pills ought to put some petrol in the clock for yer, though. How many yer take?

MICK: Told yer. Half a dozen.

SAM: Oh well, that'll iron yer right out.

> MICK *mutters impatiently. He sits down tiredly on his bed. He droops and responds irritably.*

MICK: Can't feel a thing from 'em. [*Complaining*] Must be near an hour since I took the first lot.

SAM: Uhnnhn.

> *Pause.*

BRENDA: How's your cup, Sam?

SAM: Eh? [*Holding out his mug with a smile*] Oh yeah, well another drop, if yer like.

> BRENDA *gets up and pours him some more, then sits again.*

[*Sipping*] Good drop this.

BRENDA: [*nodding*] It's Bushell's.

SAM: Ah? [*Nodding wisely*] Well, there y'are. I thought it tasted better than bloody usual. I was gonna say t'yer was it the outside stuff.

BRENDA: You can tell the difference.

SAM: Reckon yer can. How'd yer crack it for this?

BRENDA: [*grinning*] Compliments of Mr Higgins. I make his morning tea for him. He brings it in for himself in a little bag, with some cakes for himself.

SAM: The laundry screw? [*Grinning*] Yer obliged him with a boob brew and clout on his Bushell's, did yer?

BRENDA: Fair exchange. I always do.

SAM: [*chuckling*] He'll give yer fair exchange if he catches you at it. Good on yer. Ought to be more of it.

BRENDA: I think he knows. I've been doing it for months. No one could mistake boob tea for that long.

SAM: Oh yeah, an imbecile like him would.

BRENDA: I don't really think he's an imbecile.

SAM: Uh? What are yer talking about? They're all imbos. Wouldn't be screws if they weren't, would they? [*Pause.*] Eh? Well, would they?

BRENDA: Oh, never mind... just enjoy it.

SAM: Ah. [*Grinning*] So I will. [*Slurping*] You just keep it coming, and I'll keep pouring her down.

BRENDA: [*watching him enjoy it*] I can always get plenty.

SAM: Yeah, so Mick's told me. Yer must be a bloody marvel, all the good things he's told me about yer.

BRENDA: Oh? Such as?

    Pause.

SAM: Ah. [*Heartily*] Well come on, Mick, what about today? I bet yer got a shock when he told yer when?

MICK: [*rousing himself*] Uhnnhn? [*Nodding*] Oh, yeah, I suppose I did. Well, you know yerself I wasn't expecting it so soon. [*Brooding*] Nothing to the shock she got, though, when I told her what I thought about her not writing or visiting me properly... all she'd been doing and that. Hmph. I soon fixed her.

BRENDA: I hope you weren't horrible to her.

MICK: Aw no, not horrible. No, I was just sort of firm, and letting her know who wears the saddle and who sits in it.

SAM: She looking all right, though, was she?

MICK: Oh yeah, well she... Ah well, you know what they look like. Beads, bangles and that... bit of a dress...

SAM: Real pretty, eh?

MICK: Uhnnhn... Oh well, yer might say she was... sort of, y'know, like... [*Rising and starting to prowl again*] Well, sheilas are all the same, aren't they? [*Shrugging*] Bangle and bits of this and that hanging off 'em. [*Nodding*] Yeah, well yer could say she looked real pretty, you know, if it's the real feminine sort of thing yer go for. Perfume, and plenty of tit... all that.

SAM: [*appreciatively*] Hnnhn!

BRENDA: What sort of perfume?

MICK: Eh? [*Scowling*] Ahh, well, how would I know what sort of fucking perfume?

> *He sits irritably on his bed again. Pause.* BRENDA *tries not to take offence.*

BRENDA: Well, can I give you some more tea?

MICK: [*sighing*] Jesus. [*Getting up and prowling again*] Listen, will you just have your tea and leave me to know what I want and what I don't? [*He fumbles in a pocket and brings out a rolled cigarette. He pats his pocket then goes to* SAM.] Give us a match, will yer?

> SAM *produces a match and lights* MICK's *cigarette.* MICK *nods a thank you.*

SAM: Yer want to just relax a bit, mate.

> *He glances unhappily at* BRENDA, *who sits, looking miserably at the floor. Pause.*

MICK: [*sighing*] Yeah. [*Smiling*] Ha, you should have seen her, though, Sammy, when I gave her the old evil eye. [*Chuckling*] Terrified, it was. Wouldn't come out from behind the parole bloke till I gave her a bit of a come on. [*Explaining*] In the grip of a guilty conscience she was, see? Not writing when she ought to been, or visiting me right. [*Laughing softly*] And then having to lob today and face a man face to face... poor bitch.

SAM: Hnnhn... poor little bugger.

MICK: Ah. [*Nodding*] Yeah, well she's only a sheila.

SAM: What yer do?

MICK: Do?

SAM: How'd yer work it out, I mean, in the finish, like, when you forgive her and all that?

MICK: Oh, I never told her I forgive her anything. All I done was let it ride, like no point in bunging on a drama in front of the parole rooster here.

SAM: Oh... oh, I thought yer meant that you and her was all sweet. [*Grinning*] Like, when yer said before that bit about going to bed for a month!

> *He chuckles.*

MICK: Ha! Listen, the way she was looking, mate, I might just have to make that six months! [*He pauses and considers, then grins.*] Ah, I might as well admit it, yeah, I did weaken a bit in the finish there... let her off the hook. [*Grinning*] We're all weak mugs, mate, when it comes to that.

SAM: Yeah. Oh, well that's good, mate. I'm glad yers are sweet with each other... yer know what they say.

MICK: What?

SAM: To forget is divine.

MICK: Ah. Well, a man does his best.

> *He yawns.*

SAM: Can't do no more.

MICK: No. Ah, well, that's it. I told her. Far as I'm concerned, I said, I'll give her a go.

SAM: Yeah. Ah well, she'll be feeling better now tonight looking forward to a new start.

MICK: Ah. [*Nodding and standing up tiredly*] Well, I hope she's feeling better tonight than I am.

> *He goes over wearily and sits on his bed. He swings his legs up with a sigh and lies back with his hands behind his head, staring upwards.*

BRENDA: [*acidly*] All those pills. Serves you right.

MICK: Uhnhn? [*Irritated*] Oh, shut up.

> *He scowls, sighs and closes his eyes, relaxing.*

SAM: [*softly*] Yeah. Have a snooze, mate.

MICK: Uhnnhn... [*Pause. He opens his eyes and nods at* SAM.] Your turn's gonna come, mate, same as me.

SAM: Ah.

> MICK *smiles and closes his eyes again.* SAM *eyes* BRENDA *unhappily. He starts to roll a cigarette.*

Aw well, I'll... uh... a smoke.

> BRENDA *suddenly gets up and pulls a blanket from his own bed. He goes over to cover* MICK *with it.* MICK *rouses with a slight start and looks at* BRENDA.

BRENDA: I thought you—might get cold.

> MICK *looks at him silently, sighs, grimaces and rises up on an elbow.*

MICK: I know what you thought... what yer think. [*Nodding*] Yer thought what a bastard I am. Yeah, I know... I am.

BRENDA: No I didn't. You're not. Go on, lie down.

MICK: It's just I want to go off to sleep. [*Trying to explain*] What it is, love, I'm just not here any more. [*Shaking his head*] I'm not here.

BRENDA: [*nodding miserably*] I know. I do.

Pause. MICK *looks tiredly at* BRENDA.

MICK: I'm sorry.

BRENDA: Go to sleep.

> MICK *sighs and closes his eyes again.* BRENDA *stands looking down at him.* SAM *watches, his cigarette unlit.* BRENDA *turns as* SAM *busies himself lighting up.*

[*Smiling wryly*] Hello.

SAM: [*smiling*] Hello.

BRENDA: Got cigarette papers?

SAM: Eh? Oh, yeah, millions of 'em? Yer want…?

BRENDA: No, keep them. I was just wondering. Matches?

SAM: Yeah, plenty of 'em.

BRENDA: Well, [*smiling*] some more tea?

SAM: Yeah!

> *He sits grinning happily as* BRENDA *gets him a drop more tea.* BRENDA *gives it to him, then he sits on his own bed, smiling and gesturing around the cell.*

BRENDA: Well, how do you like us, then?

SAM: [*nodding, grinning*] Yer got it made.

BRENDA: It's clean. The main thing.

SAM: Oh, yeah. I always say.

> *He glances around, worried.*

BRENDA: What's wrong?

SAM: No, she's sweet…

> *He opens a pocket flap and ashes his cigarette in it.*

BRENDA: [*horrified, jumping to get an ashtray for him*] Don't do that!

SAM: [*grinning as he accepts the ashtray*] Ash in pocket good for floor. Ha-ha!

BRENDA: Grub!

SAM: I read that. Confucius say, ash in tray good for carpet. Just changed it a bit.

BRENDA: Yes, well I'm going to change you.

SAM: [*with a slow smile*] I'll be in that.

> *Pause.* BRENDA *shakes his head ruefully, reaches out and gently ruffles* SAM's *hair.* SAM *raises a hand to cover* BRENDA's. *They hold the pose in silence.* BRENDA *smiles and takes his hand back.*

BRENDA: I'll have a quick wash.

SAM: [*happily*] Ah.

> BRENDA *strips to singlet and pants. He organises the wash basin, soap and towel, and sets about having a wash.*

Yer got lovely skin.

BRENDA: [*with a quick grin*] I'm a Lux girl.

> SAM *chuckles happily. He stands up and looks around.* BRENDA *finishes washing, dries himself, empties the water into the sanitary tub. He pours more water into the basin, gets out a clean towel and throws it to* SAM, *who catches it with raised eyebrows.*

For you. [*Gesturing*] Be my guest.

SAM: Oh! [*Stripping off his coat*] Oh, yeah, well I was just gonna ask yer... ah, mmnnn...

> *He goes manfully to the wash basin.*

BRENDA: Take your time. Enjoy it... and don't miss out on those ears. [*With a small grin*] Go on.

SAM: I know how to do it.

> *He proceeds to have a slow, thorough wash, his back to* BRENDA. BRENDA *goes quickly to the cupboard and takes out his orange wig and some coloured material that turns out to be a new dress. He quickly gets into drag, takes the mirror from the cupboard and stands waiting.* SAM *turns smiling as he dries himself. He stares open-mouthed, dropping the towel.*

BRENDA: [*posing*] Look what the cat's dragged in.

> SAM *grins broadly, delighted.* BRENDA *slinks to the table with the mirror and beckons to* SAM, *who follows him.* BRENDA *sits on one chair and gestures* SAM *to take the other.* SAM *sits, entranced.*

Now hold this for me.

> SAM *takes the mirror.*

Where's your cigarette papers? Give us 'em.

> SAM *fumbles his papers out and gives them to him.* BRENDA *rips them open and takes out the cardboard strip.*

Now matches.

> SAM *produces matches.*

Now light this and hold the mirror still.

> SAM *strikes a match, fascinated, and lights the cardboard.* BRENDA *lets it burn down a half-inch, blows it out and tickles the loose ash from it. He nods, satisfied, and leans forward to the mirror.*

Right. Now hang on.

> *He proceeds to beautify his face with charcoal.*

SAM: [*smiling*] Holding it right, am I?

BRENDA: Uhunn. [*Smiling at himself*] You're doing fine. Stay there. Tcha! [*Frowning at the cardboard and gesturing for another match*] More. Light another one.

The cardboard is prepared as before. BRENDA *completes his making up, nods and grins to* SAM.

How's that?

He takes the mirror from SAM *and poses for approval.*

SAM: Aw... aw...

BRENDA: Lovely?

SAM: Incredible.

BRENDA: Say I'm beautiful.

SAM: [*nodding*] Yer beautiful... fair dinkum.

BRENDA: [*gratified, patting his face and rising*] And you look like Rock Hudson.

He puts the mirror back on the cupboard.

SAM: [*staring in wonderment*] I'll be fu—

BRENDA: Ahh! [*Scowling*] Front of a lady.

SAM: Beg yer pardon.

BRENDA: Just remember from now on—handsome.

He poses for himself in the mirror again.

SAM: It's just too good...

Delighted, he watches BRENDA *posing, waiting expectantly. Pause.*

BRENDA: [*pleased with himself*] Mmmnn...

SAM: Uh, what we gonna do?

BRENDA: What do you fancy?

SAM: [*evilly*] You just name it.

BRENDA: All right. [*Slinking over to him, stroking his face with both hands*] I'll tell you what we'll do...

SAM: [*nodding madly*] Ah!

BRENDA: [*giggling*] We'll play...

SAM: Yeah!

> BRENDA *goes to the cupboard and produces the draughts set with a flourish.*

BRENDA: ... draughts!

He puts the set on the table and sits down in a business-like manner opposite SAM, *tipping the counters out and opening the board.*

SAM: [*staring*] Draughts?

BRENDA: [*smiling*] It passes the time.

SAM: Aw.

BRENDA: Come on, help me set 'em up.

> SAM *starts shoving counters around glumly.*

Be good, now—and we'll see.

SAM: [*grinning slowly*] I forgot how to play this.

BRENDA: Oh, I'm not much good.

SAM: I used to be all right.

BRENDA: Mick's too good for me.

SAM: Oh? [*Confidently*] Oh, well then!

He sets up the board swiftly. The prison clock strikes five, each stroke louder than the one before. At the first stroke, MICK *twitches; at the second, he stirs and frowns; at the third, he sits up irritably; he frowns at the final strokes. Then, seeing* BRENDA *and* SAM *at the table, he smiles.* SAM *drops a counter, gropes for it, and puts it back on the board.*

There y'are. Right, now?

BRENDA: Away you go. Wait on.

He turns the board around, black men to SAM. MICK *swings his legs off the bed and sits smiling at them.*

Black to move.

SAM: [*grinning*] No, ladies first.

BRENDA: [*firmly*] Black to move.

MICK: *And win!*

He laughs with delight. SAM *and* BRENDA *turn in surprise.* BRENDA's *shock turns to peevishness at being sprung.* MICK *chuckles fondly.*

That's right, isn't it?

He grins the more for BRENDA's *pained look, and laughs.*

BRENDA: [*rising ominously*] You!

MICK *keeps giggling.* SAM *rises, grinning.* BRENDA *laughs too, then rushes at* MICK, *pouncing on him and pushing him.* MICK *resists, laughing, and pulls* BRENDA *down beside him.* BRENDA *throws an arm around* MICK's *neck and pulls his head against him.* MICK *ceases to resist.* BRENDA *holds him, laughing happily.* SAM *comes closer, smiling uncertainly.* BRENDA *holds out his free hand, and when* SAM *takes it, pulls him down to sit on the other side of him.* SAM *offers no resistance.* BRENDA *throws an arm around* SAM, *and then hugs them both fiercely. They lean against him, as he continues to hug them.* BRENDA *smiles, perhaps cries, it's hard to say.*

EPILOGUE

The yard. Sunday morning. We hear the sound of many feet, voices, the bell, the jingling of keys and rattling of bolts, breakfast dixies being thrown into barrows.

VOICE: [*off*] In the yard, come on, all in the yard!

The sounds fade to silence. Keys are heard rattling loudly. SAM *strolls on, smiling all round. His clothes are impeccably pressed. He carries a newspaper and his mug.*

Come on! Get in your yards!

SAM *breathes deeply, stretches and smiles. He looks at the sky and nods. He looks down at himself, smoothing his clothes and smirking with self-satisfaction. He grins and nods at the audience.*

SAM: Ah, yeah. Bonzer spot this.

He lays the paper down near the fence and sits carefully on it. He sighs, smiles all around and nods as if at some activity in the yard.

They're gonna play tennis. [*Laughing*] I'll have to watch it—bloody molecules. [*Staring downstage, grinning and waving*] Ah there, Wocko! [*Listening with a grin*] Yeah, they tell me I'm looking all right, ha-ha.

He nods again, smiles and waves briefly. He settles back, looks at the sky and claps his hands softly.

Aw, yeah… not a bad day at all.

He picks up his mug and peers into it. Frowning, he blows into it as if to chase dust out. He grins and puts it down.

VOICE: [*off*] Right! All in! [*Pause. Faintly*] All correct, sir!

SAM: Hmph! [*Grinning*] I reckon it is. [*Staring around him, nodding to the audience*] We're all in. Soon be time for—

He breaks off, looking offstage with a sudden smile. He rises.

'Ullo, 'ullo.

BRENDA *rushes on, wearing pants and a shirt. He runs to* SAM *with an excited smile.*

BRENDA: Oh, look Sam, look!

In his outstretched hand, BRENDA *is offering a small yellow flower.*

A flower, Sam!

SAM *stares and smiles hugely. He grins from* BRENDA *to the flower. He puts his arm around* BRENDA's *shoulder and leads him slowly to the front of the stage, smiling from* BRENDA *to the flower as he does so.*

Would you believe that? It was growing out of the wall... out of the stones!

SAM *nods, smiling, his head bowed. Then, with* BRENDA *against him, he looks up at the audience and grins. He takes the flower and wags it at* BRENDA *playfully, touching him on the face with it.*

SAM: Well. [*Grinning*] Mary, Mary, quite contrary...

As they face the audience, the stage behind them fills. The OFFICERS, *the* SWEEPER *and* LEVICK, MICK *and his* WIFE *enter. They all concentrate on the flower.* SAM *chuckles.*

How does your garden grow?

They stand looking at the audience. MICK *moves to stand beside* SAM. SAM *puts an arm around his shoulder. The* WOMAN *moves to stand beside* BRENDA, *who smiles and, takes her hand. The four of them stand together, smiling, while the rest look on. There is music: 'I Wonder Who's Kissing Her Now?'*

THE END

The Cake Man

Robert J. Merritt

Robert James Merritt was born in 1945 and brought up on Erambie
Aboriginal Mission, NSW. *The Cake Man*, written in isolation in Bathurst,
was an attempt to express the root causes of Aboriginal despair. It was
first performed in 1975 by the newly-formed Black Theatre in Redfern. A
season at Bondi Pavilion and an ABC television performance followed and
in 1982 Merritt's Australian Aboriginal Theatre Company production
represented Australia at the World Theatre Festival in Denver, Colorado.
Merritt directed the same company in a revival in Sydney in 1984. He has
since made successful documentary films, including *Eora Corroboree,
Building Dreams* and *Getting Better* and during the 1980s was Chair of
the Aboriginal Arts Board and the first Aboriginal member of the Australia
Council. He was Chair of the Festival of Pacific Arts, 1988.

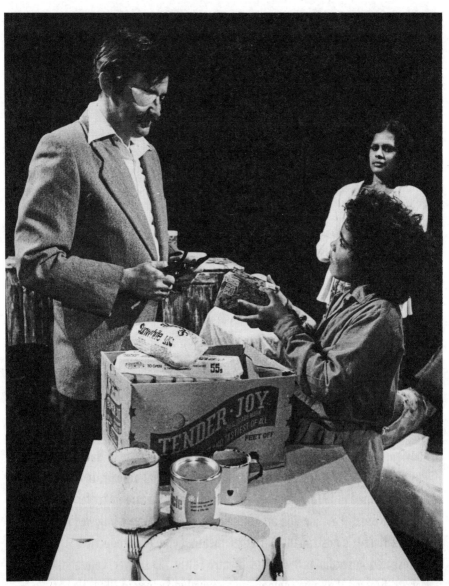

Max Cullen as Mr Peterson, Justine Saunders (background) as Ruby and Teddy Phillips as Pumpkinhead in the 1975 Black Theatre, Sydney, production of THE CAKE MAN. *(Photo: Robert Walker)*

FIRST PERFORMANCE

The Cake Man was first performed by the Black Theatre at the Black Theatre Arts and Culture Centre, Sydney, on 12 January 1975 with the following cast:

ABORIGINAL WOMAN	Justine Saunders
ABORIGINAL BOY	Teddy Phillips and Lisa Maza
ABORIGINAL MAN	Zac Martin
PRIEST	Dan Adcock
SOLDIER	Rob Steele
MR PETERSON	Max Cullen
RUBY	Justine Saunders
SWEET WILLIAM	Zac Martin
PUMPKINHEAD	Teddy Phillips and Lisa Maza
MISSION MANAGER	Dan Adcock
MISSION INSPECTOR	Rob Steele

Directed by Bob Maza
Designed by Nick Hollo and Sandy Gray

CHARACTERS

ABORIGINAL WOMAN
ABORIGINAL BOY, aged about eleven
ABORIGINAL MAN
PRIEST
BRITISH SOLDIER of the Colonial period
CIVILIAN, a Colonial squatter
RUBY, an Aboriginal mission woman
PUMPKINHEAD, her son
SWEET WILLIAM, her husband
MISSION MANAGER
MISSION INSPECTOR

DIALOGUE

Talkin' life with brother Jim,
Tell 'im where's the pain.
Shake 'im word stick at my mind,
Helps me see it plain.

R.J.M.

ACT ONE: GOD AND GUN

A bush scene: a bark humpy, a tree, shrubs, a stream. An ABORIGINAL WOMAN *sits by the humpy working, singing to herself and watching a* BOY, *about eleven years old. The* BOY *is playing with some pebbles, holding about four of them, tossing them up and trying to catch them on the back of his hand. Earth, water, sky: nature at ease.*

The WOMAN *looks off and rises, smiling. The* BOY *pauses in his play and an* ABORIGINAL MAN *strides on, carrying spear and club. He throws two goannas down in front of the* WOMAN. *She picks them up and takes them over to the humpy, expressing her admiration of him. He nods, casual, strong and proud, then lays down his weapons and sits. She fetches him a vessel of water. He takes it from her, nodding, and drinks, then hands the vessel back. She puts it away, embraces him briefly and returns to her chore. The* BOY *approaches the* MAN *from behind while he is drinking, and stands there watching him. The* MAN *turns his head slowly and growls at the* BOY, *who giggles excitedly and runs stealthily behind the humpy. The* WOMAN *stifles a laugh, and the* MAN *grins at her. The* BOY *creeps back, carrying a toy spear and club. He erupts into screeching noise, stamping his feet. The* MAN *spins about, growls and falls to his hands and knees, imitating an animal. They play for some time at hunter and savage beast until the* MAN *grabs the* BOY's *leg, snapping at it with his teeth, and the* BOY *strikes him in the back with the spear three times. The* MAN *gurgles, collapses and falls in defeat. The* BOY *dances victoriously around the 'body', looking to the* WOMAN *for praise and getting it. When he finishes his dance, the* MAN *sits up. All three embrace. They sit contentedly together, requiring no more.*

Pause.

A kettle drum is heard, off. They sit up stiffly, staring in alarm. Three white men march on, dressed in styles of long ago: a PRIEST, *a* SOLDIER, *a* CIVILIAN. *The* PRIEST *carries a Bible and a long crucifix. The* CIVILIAN *carries a bag slung from his shoulder. The* SOLDIER *carries a musket. The drum noise fades away. The* ABORIGINES *stand quietly to face the white men. The* PRIEST *comes towards them waving a blessing with a hand. The* MAN *pushes the* WOMAN *and* BOY *behind him.*

PRIEST: Greetings! And God's blessing. I bring you good news! Here it is, my child, [*offering the Bible*] for you and your little family. And this also I bring to you [*waggling the cross*] and to your people. The gift of love. The promise of salvation. Yours.

He stands offering the book and the cross. The MAN *stands, shielding his family. Pause.*

You don't understand me! No speakee?

The MAN *shakes a slow head, dumb and proud.*

Oh, come now, take these I say!

The ABORIGINES *move backwards together. The* PRIEST *pauses, turns to his companions.*

He doesn't understand me. [*Shaking his head sorrowfully*] Who would dream, in this age, of such ignorance?

SOLDIER: Well, Father, he must be one of the last. I mean, I've heard it told that God's word has been told the length and breadth of the country. So this lot ought to be about the last lot.

PRIEST: Ah! All our black brothers.

SOLDIER: Aye.

PRIEST: Saved.

SOLDIER: God be praised.

PRIEST: From their ignorance and sin.

SOLDIER: Yes Father, indeed.

PRIEST: And from hell.

SOLDIER: Oh, aye.

PRIEST: Through God's mercy and love.

SOLDIER: Amen.

CIVILIAN: Amen.

PRIEST: I notice, however, that this particular fellow is, ah, well he strikes me as being more of a heathen, poor devil, than most heathens.

SOLDIER: It's as you say, Father, aye.

PRIEST: Very backward indeed. Unfriendly, even.

SOLDIER: Aye, very.

PRIEST: Yes, very very very.

They regard the ABORIGINES *thoughtfully. The* ABORIGINES *regard them fearfully.*

CIVILIAN: Here, I'll reach them with my pretties.

He steps forward, reaching in his bag to bring forth bright beads, ribbons, and so on. He offers them in a coaxing way to the MAN, WOMAN, *and* BOY. *They step back and away from his pretties.*

You refuse? [*Angrily*] Well!

He stuffs the pretties back in his bag. Another pause.

PRIEST: [*sighing*] Well. He refuses, yes.

SOLDIER: Savage ingrate.

PRIEST: Alas, yes. Too ignorant for light, too old for change...

SOLDIER: Too stupid for words.

PRIEST: Oh, now they are harsh words.

SOLDIER: Well, it's a brute, Father. So it is.

CIVILIAN: No child is a brute, surely?

PRIEST: Exactly not. We must save the child, by all means we must do that. He is, they are, and we all are God's own children, strange as it is, and we must love one another... or be damned, and lost, and defeated utterly by the power of darkness.

> *The* SOLDIER *hefts his rifle.*

SOLDIER: Never, so long as I live!

PRIEST: Ah! Christian soldier!

> *The* SOLDIER *holds the gun out. The* PRIEST *blesses it briefly.*

SOLDIER: Thank you, Father.

PRIEST: Alas! I have failed.

CIVILIAN: Don't blame yourself, now.

SOLDIER: Aren't the two of us here, Father, both witnesses to your patience?

PRIEST: Bless you, bless you both.

SOLDIER: Aye. Now my duty is plain.

> *He lifts his rifle ominously.*

PRIEST: I must pray!

> *He falls to his knees, praying, head down. The* SOLDIER *shoots the* MAN *dead. The* PRIEST *looks up to see him fall, the* WOMAN *and the* BOY *crying, falling on him in grief.*

Murder! What doest thou? [*Weeping*] Oh, oh, my children! Why killest thou each other? Why murdereth thou each othereth? [*To the* CIVILIAN, *who is inspecting the corpse*] Is it dead? Oh, woe, then, woe to him whose hand obtained the deed! [*Turning to the* SOLDIER] Was I not praying for our answer to this problem? Did you not see me at my prayers? [*Sadly*] Oh, why did you kill this child of God?

SOLDIER: Well, you blessed me rifle.

PRIEST: Thank God for that.

SOLDIER: Anyway there's no law against it.

PRIEST: God's law is against it!

SOLDIER: Well, I wish I hadn't done it.

PRIEST: You confess to the deed?

SOLDIER: To you, Father, aye.

PRIEST: And are you truly sorry?

SOLDIER: Aye. I am indeed.

PRIEST: And was there anything else?

SOLDIER: No, not offhand, Father.

PRIEST: Say three Hail Marys, two Our Fathers. And, mind, before you go to sleep this night.

SOLDIER: Aye. Thank you, Father.

PRIEST: And remember in the future: heathens they might be, ignorant and superstitious they might also be; but they, as we, are God's own sweet children.

CIVILIAN: Amen.

SOLDIER: Amen.

PRIEST: Yes, and make that six Hail Marys.

SOLDIER: Oh, but Father!

PRIEST: 'Thou shalt not kill.'

CIVILIAN: Amen.

SOLDIER: Oh. Well, all right. Six it must be.

PRIEST: And remember again: your duty is one thing, your immortal soul is another.

SOLDIER: Yes. Well, Amen to that as well.

PRIEST: Worms that we are.

CIVILIAN: Aye.

PRIEST: Weakly flesh. [*Sighing*] Yet not a sparrow falls, remember that, nor does a camel go through the eye of a needle. No jot, or tittle, or anything.

CIVILIAN: Amen.

SOLDIER: Will we bury this one now, then?

PRIEST: Yes. Well, first we'll pack up the family, put them in the wagon, prepare them for their journey. [*Smiling*] Ah, yes! And what a journey for them it will be! New life, new love, and a new spirit!

> *The* PRIEST *becomes abruptly businesslike, turning to the grieving but silent* WOMAN *and* BOY *and coaxing them.*

Come, come?

> *They ignore him and sit stonily.*

We must get them in the wagon.

SOLDIER: Leave it to me, Father.

> *He starts a purposeful move.*

PRIEST: No, let me try again. [*Wheedling*] Come? Will you not come now out of darkness into the light? No? [*Shaking his head, smiling sadly*] Oh, you poor savage devils, you don't understand, do you? No, indeed, and how could you know, how could you dream, even, of where you are going—out of your stone-age misery, out, and onwards to every joy of a Christian civilization, with knowledge, and with comfort and enlightenment... ah, yes!

SOLDIER: Amen!

He nods the truth of it at the ABORIGINES. *They sit grieving and uncomprehending.*

PRIEST: Bring them.

He turns and walks a little away.

SOLDIER: Come on, then! Up! Get you up and to the wagon. [*Reaching for the* BOY] Come now!

The BOY *attacks him, sobbing uncomprehendingly with fear.*

So that's it, little brute!

He cuffs the child brutally, knocking him down.

CIVILIAN: Oh, stop it now! [*Moving quickly to restrain the* SOLDIER] It's not to a child I'll see any of that done. Come away, I'll not have that!

SOLDIER: Well, you fetch 'em!

He stands at a distance in bad temper. The BOY *lies hurt and anxious. The* CIVILIAN *tries a smile, reaching out his open arms to the* BOY *and going to pick him up. After a long pause, the* BOY, *watching the promise of kindness in the* CIVILIAN*'s attitude, rises slowly, and slowly reaches up his arms to him. The* SOLDIER *knocks the* CIVILIAN*'s arms down.*

Don't touch it with our own hands! Do you not know of their dirt and how the lice go crawling through their heads, man?

The CIVILIAN *pauses and looks to the* PRIEST.

PRIEST: I should wait till it's washed.

The CIVILIAN *hesitates. He shows every sign of wanting to touch the* BOY *and every sign, too, of fearing the contamination just mentioned. Pause. The* BOY *withdraws.*

We'll try 'em with the old routine. All right now, take up your parts on cue.

They stand apart and cough self-consciously. The PRIEST *winks.*

This'll get 'em for sure!

He claps his hands at the sky and cocks an ear. Music comes from beyond: a piano playing the old Bing Crosby song, 'There's a Happy Land Somewhere'. The PRIEST *sings to the* WOMAN *and* BOY.

Oh, there's a happy land somewhere,
And it's just a prayer awaay.

He carries it through, the others harmonizing.

All you've dreamed and planned is there,
And it's just a prayer awaay!

> There'll be good conditions on your friendly Missions
> Filled with laughing children at plaay.
> Where your hearts will sing for it means one thing
> All your old sins will be passed awaay.

They really sing it up.

> Ohhhh! There's a happy land somewhere,
> And it's just a prayer awaaay.

The music fades away. The PRIEST *stops singing, and holds his arms out wide to the* WOMAN *and* BOY. *They back off in wide-eyed alarm.*

Ohh... didn't you like that? [*Turning sorrowfully to the other two*] Well, they haven't much ear for music, it seems.

SOLDIER: I thought it was rather good.

They look reproachfully at the ABORIGINES. *The* BOY *stands in front of the* WOMAN, *scowling at the* SOLDIER, *who reacts impatiently.*

Ahhh! [*Going for the* BOY] Come with me now.

There is a struggle involving the SOLDIER, *the* BOY *and the* WOMAN.

CIVILIAN: No!

The SOLDIER *is pulled back. The* CIVILIAN *fossicks in his bag and brings out some cake which he shows to the* BOY, *coaxing him.*

Here, little man, lovely cake. [*Pretending to taste it*] Delicious. Mmmm! Lovely cake. [*Backing off, with the* BOY *following*] Ahhh, now that's the clever wee man. Come, I'll give you cake.

The BOY *follows, reaching for the cake, the* WOMAN *following. The* CIVILIAN *coaxes him up to the* PRIEST.

No trouble at all. [*Smiling, offering the cake*] Here it is, then that's a good fellow.

As the BOY *reaches for the cake, the* PRIEST *snatches it away.*

PRIEST: No, mustn't give him that. It would only cause him pain. They are not accustomed to cake, they are not ready for cake.

CIVILIAN: [*confused and angry*] But Father, I promised him the cake.

PRIEST: Oh, promise it by all means.

He eats it. The CIVILIAN *stands back in confusion. The* PRIEST *turns to the* WOMAN *and pushes the Bible into her hands. She accepts it dumbly.*

There, take it and keep it always. Keep it, and from it learn wisdom, and faith, and love.

Together with the SOLDIER, *he starts to shepherd the* WOMAN *and the* BOY *off the stage.*

Come... don't be frightened... put your trust in us... we're going to make you our own.

The kettle drum rattles, off. They exit. After a pause, the MAN *opens his eyes and gets groggily to his feet, coughing a little. He discovers a pile of clothes. He picks up a sandshoe and examines it curiously, then another. He tries them out on his hands, then puts them on his feet. He picks up a pair of trousers and experiments with them, trying them on his head and arms before putting them on correctly. A bright red shirt and a cardigan follow. He walks about unsteadily, and it becomes apparent that he is drunk. He looks up and sees the audience for the first time.*

MAN: Uh, who you? [*Grinning craftily*] Hey, listen, you wanna buy a boomerang? [*He pulls one from under his coat and holds it up for audience inspection.*] Good one, this is. [*Turning it over, reading the back of it*] Made in Japan [*with a grin*] by our trading allies. [*Tossing the boomerang offstage*] There! Now you seen an Abo throw a boomerang. The Australian champeen is a whitefeller now, it's a fact. A Gubba never had a social welfare cheque in his whole life. 'Gubba', that's Koori lingo for whitefeller. Gubbaahhh, is how y'say it if ever y'overseas tellin' someone. I heerd some people in other places is curious about Kooris, an' about our lingo. I know a bit of it, different words an' that. Just ask me an' I'll tell ya. [*He poses proudly now.*] See'n I'm a Koori. The Australian Aborigine, that's who I am and what I am... made in England. [*Pause.*] Oh! Speakin' of social welfare cheques, y'see that in the paper the other day? [*Ponderously*] The Minister said there is some real evidence to the fact... that some blackfellers is spendin' their social on likker. They's buyin' booze. [*With a sigh*] Oh, just like them Red Injuns what ruined 'emselves the same way... at the fire water all the time. [*Sighing, nodding*] I know it's a fact. Hang on there.

He nicks offstage and returns with a half-full flagon of wine. He drinks from it and smiles.

The social cheque came yesterday, thank Christ. [*He laughs, drinks, reflects.*] Ha, that's what she always says. Rube, my missus, she's always thankin' Christ for everythin'... anythin'... nothin'. Her an' that fuckin' book. [*With a laugh*] She heard me say that, I'd be in strife. Christian she is, my old lady, a Mission Chrishyun, the worst kind. [*Scratching his head, mock-serious*] What's that bit again? 'For y'travel over land and sea to make one convert... an' when ya finished with 'im, why, that feller's twice as fit for hell as you are y'self.' [*Laughing gently*] Somethin' like that it goes. In that book of hers. The

Jesus rort... Rort, that's not a Koori word, it's just Australian. It means that whatever ya got goin' isn't exac'ly the genuine article... sort of a swindle, y'see.

He pauses, drinks again, then nods.

But I can't say that t'Rube. I did once, I said the Jesus rort was a rort. Whoo, gahd-jeezus! Nearly hit with that book of hers I was, only she frightened to use it like that. [*Chuckling*] She hit me the other time, though. I got drunk again and things are bad and I'm shakin' my fist at the sky like this. [*Demonstrating*] I'm on at her whitefeller God and I'm singin' out at him real loud. 'You dirty Jesus,' I says, 'Come down here, you dirty little Jesus, and I'm gonna give you a drink a' my vinegar with me. Ha! You white bastard, you Jew bastard, you gunjie little Jesus... gunjie bastard...'

He pauses to drink again.

Gunjie is a Koori word... means policeman. We say gunjie, it means a white copper animal. Down there at Victoria, now, they got this different word, they say he a berrimaja, the white copper a berrimaja. [*He sits down by his flagon.*] It's all the same what the words is. Only me, I don't talk much real words to my missus... have to pretend a thing, have to live it and hide it all the time, anyway I got no strength to put behind what words I say to anyone... just a fuckin' blackfeller, me.

Pause. He drinks, loses interest for a few seconds, then regards the audience with mild surprise.

You still there? I still got somethin' that you want? What you want from me that I got? [*Leaning forward and coaxing*] Don' be scairt, jus' say it. That's what I wanna know too... [*He stares out dully.*] The Australian Aborigine—that's me—stands in danger of losing his identity... [*Nodding solemnly and drinking*] I read that in an old paper, all about how gubbas is very interested in Dreamtime stories. Uncle Foley's an old blackfeller lives around here and he's about a hunnert years old—he was one of them I been gettin' drunk with t'day, only they gone home now—well, Uncle Foley can tell you them Dreamtime stories. Oh, gahd-jeezus, he knows how everythin' started off once. [*Pause. He drinks.*] I know one. [*Shyly*] I could tell yuh... 'bout how the emu lorst 'is wings so can't fly no more. It was on account of this other bird, the curlew...

He stares upwards and recites.

Long time ago the emu had wings and he could fly real fast and he used to show off. The curlew was jealous. One day he came up to the emu and said: 'I betcha I could beat you running.' The big emu looked at the little curlew and laughed: 'You can't beat me at runnin', 'cause I can run just as fast as I fly.' Curlew said: 'We'll just see about that, we'll have a race you and me. What did y'said t'that, Mr Emu?' Well. That big flyin' emu said yes. Curlew said: 'Listen, one other little thing is that, your wings bein' so much bigger'n my wings, it wouldn't be fair if you was to start flyin' 'stead of runnin'.' Emu said, 'No.' The curlew said: 'We'll both cut our wings.' [*Laughing*] Hhmm, that silly big prick of an emu said all right. [*Chuckling*] 'Come on, we see who's the smartest runner 'round this claypan.' Curlew said give him the knife first and he'd cut off his own wings. So the emu gave the knife to curlew and the curlew went off in the bush with it and pretended to be cuttin' off his wings, all yarmbul-cryin' real loud so the emu would hear and think the curlew was really hurtin' himself cuttin' off his wings... Yarmbul-cryin' means what y'might call foxin' a bit. Anyway, that curlew went on with his cryin' and yowlin' and makin' a noise... an' he got a dish of clay—that was filled with blood, and he poured all the blood over his wings and rubbed in some dirt and then he come out again to the emu and give him the knife and said, 'Now it's your turn.' And the silly emu was tryin' to be fair so he took it an' cut off both his own wings straight away there right in front of everybody... and then he said was curlew ready to race, and the curlew said, 'Yes, let's go,' so they lined up and the race was off—Go!

He pauses and chuckles.

Well, that big emu took off fast as hell, and when he thought he must be far enough in front he peeked back but he couldn't see him anywhere. He heard laughin' and he stopped right there, and he just looked up at the curlew flyin' over the top a him, and he didn't know what to do. [*Drinking again*] Poor old emu, he just put down his head right there, and he sneaked off into the bush... stayed in there a long time. [*Pause.*] That's how emu lost his wings. [*Pause.*] That make any sense, y'reckon? [*He shakes his head, wryly.*] That Killara Station... fuck workin' there. [*Smiling*] Social fixed all that anyway. An' wogs. Wogs come in the door, Koori flies out the window. [*Shrugging*] Prob'ly ain't true, that, but a man's gotta blame things on somethin'. Wogs'll do. They end up buyin' big houses an' runnin' the joint.

He shrugs and sighs. He gestures around.

This is it, here with me mates... few flagons, then back to the Mission an' bein' Sweet William for me missus. She calls me that, Sweet William. [*Chuckling*] Ain't so sweet, not inside, but no use of lettin' her know what's the inside of the outside of things. If y'know what I mean. I s'pose y'don't... I'm fuckin' sure I don't. [*He drinks.*] Most of

all I don't know what I got any more that you want. What about a
song? Yeah, you like that.

He stands up, prancing, and sings.

Oh, my girl's a high-born lady.
She's dark but not too shady...

He pauses and falters, forgetting the words.

Feather like a peacock... just as gay... just as gay...

He sits down and drinks.

Sorry... I'm not used to this... only want to please—to pleasure you
all, as my 'Merican cousins'd say. Militant little buggers they are, tch,
tch, tch. Nothin' seems to work for them over there... started off tryin'
to please a long time ago too, when the white mens was doin' it to the
black womens. Then they changed it round, so the black mens was
doin' it to the white womens. What next, I wonder? [*Grinning*] Know
what happens when y'cross a black crow with a white rooster? Y'get a
magpie. That's why we got so bloody many magpies in Australia and
parts elsewhere. [*He pauses and drinks.*] Uncle Foley's grandfather
was Irish. He didn't stay but returned to his estate over there. He was
what they call a black Irishman, borne out by the fact that his grandson,
Uncle Foley, is also black... black... black-black-black! That was my
famous imitation of an Aboriginal duck—black-black-black... [*He
grows silent, then stern. He drinks. Pause.*] I suppose this shits you as
much as it does me?

He stands.

Look, actually I'm here to make an inquiry, to discover, if possible,
what it is I have that you now want. [*Whining*] Please, boss, you bin tell
'im Jacky, then him plurry happy! What is it? [*Pause. He gestures in
appeal.*] No? Well, there y'are. Me boomerang won't come back. [*He
drinks again, now awfully drunk.*] Well, I'm as sick of this as you are.
[*Sighing*]... I thought I might be able to say somethin'... not to no
gubbas what wear uniforms of any kind, but come along here an' had a
yarn. We might of got together and made a magpie. [*Pause.*] Nothin'
wrong with magpies, not really. But it has to be black one part an'
white another part so it makes one whole bird. It's hard t'splain. If
you'll sit there a bit longer [*picking up his flagon*] I'll try show y'
somethin'.

*He exits with his flagon, staggering. The next Act begins
immediately.*

END OF ACT ONE

ACT TWO: THE HAPPY LAND

SCENE ONE

Inside a house on a Mission for Aborigines, it is night. The walls are wooden below, fibro on top. A wood stove with a pot and a billy on it, hardly any fire in it and no fuel in sight; cupboards; a table; a battered leather armchair with a Bible lying on it; a baby's cot; an upside-down kerosene tin and an upturned box by the table—no sign of normal kitchen chairs.

RUBY, the woman from Act One, now 'civilised', stands using a flat iron over brown paper to iron a child's shirt dry. Three candles in old sauce bottles provide her light. She sighs, looks at the iron and spits on it, then goes and puts the iron on top of the stove, but a glance into the fire box disappoints her. She goes back to the table, picks up short pants and a school jumper, folds them neatly and lays them aside. She is careworn, greying and sad. PUMPKINHEAD, *the* BOY, *also 'civilised', sits playing on a blanket on the floor, tossing some pebbles and catching them on the back of his hand. In the cot a baby starts crying.*

RUBY: Oh, that's Bubby, Pumpkinhead. You be my good boy and see him a minute, while I'm doin' your school clothes dry for tomorrow?

PUMPKINHEAD: Yeah, I get Bubby, Mum.

> *He goes to the cot, looks in and reaches a gentle hand to do something with the baby.*

He got his eyes stuck again, Mum. Sores is stickin' 'em all shut. Can' open 'em.

RUBY: [*anguished*] Oh! [*Wringing a cloth in a bowl of water*] Look here, do it with this, good boy, do it soft.

> *She throws the cloth.* PUMPKINHEAD *catches it and turns to reach into the cot, gently wiping the baby's eyes.*

PUMPKINHEAD: Hey, I'm fixin' you, Bubby. No cryin'.

> *The crying ceases.*

RUBY: Oh, you're my good boy.

> *She retrieves the iron and quickly finishes the shirt, frowning at the iron.* PUMPKINHEAD *returns to his blanket and pebbles.*

Oh, dear, ain't enough fire in the stove to make it hot enough. Be lucky you get your stuff done for school.

PUMPKINHEAD: [*rising again*] Be orright, Mum. Don' care I can't go to school.

RUBY: Pumpkinhead, love, you be a good boy and go see for some coal, maybe a little piece, a bit of wood maybe, to make some little bit of fire?

PUMPKINHEAD: Ain't no coal, Mum, no wood, nothin'.

RUBY: Maybe you find some chips then, good boy?

PUMPKINHEAD: It's dark. Get you coal tomorrow, Mum.

RUBY: Mum'll stand right at the door.

PUMPKINHEAD: No, birriks might get me. Sweet William said, birriks get me I go out in the dark.

RUBY: You don' call your father Sweet William.

PUMPKINHEAD: Birriks.

    He jibs obstinately, afraid.

RUBY: Listen, you think you get out of school 'cos no hot iron, boy, you got another think comin'. Now come on, I stand at the door, talk to you all the time while you try find me some chips. Pumpkinhead...

PUMPKINHEAD: I ain't goin' no school, I ain' got no dinner. Gubbas look at you. Eat their cakes and make me see 'em when they know I ain't got nothin'... no dinner.

    Pause.

RUBY: [*pained*] You know what the Welfare said.

PUMPKINHEAD: Don' care.

RUBY: You don' care—I care! Welfare said you miss any more school, they put you in the home for bad boys.

PUMPKINHEAD: Don' care.

RUBY: They do that to my baby, I'll die. [*Coaxing*] Oh, Pumpkinhead. Come on, you find Mum some chips.

PUMPKINHEAD: Mum, there ain't no chips out there. The birriks is out there, can' go out there.

RUBY: [*sighing*] Oh, I'm a poor woman.

PUMPKINHEAD: Ain't goin'. [*Pause.*] Gubbas ain't gonna send me to no home. I'll run away in the bush, I will, when they try and get me for the home.

RUBY: They just catch you again... take you.

PUMPKINHEAD: No. I'll get a spear, stick it in 'em. Then when I come back I'll take you and Bubby down to big Sydney and buy a big red house and have a TV and Bubby can take sandwiches and cakes to school for his dinner and gubbas can't look at him.

    He frowns, dreaming defiantly. RUBY *goes and puts her arms around him.*

RUBY: Son, you're my good boy, but can't run away in the bush, can't figure things with no spears.

PUMPKINHEAD: I'll be a bushranger.

RUBY: They hang you sure then.

> *But she smiles and rubs his head. Then she goes to put away the clothes, hanging the shirt for drying.*

PUMPKINHEAD: I get you some bits of coal, Mum, where I get it from the railway. Tomorrow after school, if I go to school, get the coal any rate.

RUBY: You careful on that railway line. I'm happy for the coal you find there, good boy, but won' be happy you're not careful and train get you.

PUMPKINHEAD: Not when I'm gettin' coal, no train get me.

RUBY: Oh, that's good then. Now there's all your wearin' for school tomorrow. All clean again. Soon be time for your bed, gettin' late like it is.

PUMPKINHEAD: Um. Pub shut soon. Sweet William comin' home.

RUBY: Don' call your father that, I tol' you!

PUMPKINHEAD: Your husban' be home soon then.

RUBY: [*angrily*] You call your father your father. [*More angrily as he ignores her*] You hear me, you cheeky little bugger. Now see you made me swear, and all because you damn hatin' your good man father who loves you. Your good man father, you hear me say that, Pumpkinhead?

> *He stands obstinate, pressing his lips tightly together and starting to breathe emotionally. She sees his tears coming.*

Oh, now why you gonna cry? Ain't you my big boy? My good brave boy what's maybe a bushranger soon?

> *She goes to embrace him. He pulls away, trying to defeat his own tears. But as she stands, helplessly he starts to sob with great heaves, turning away with his back to her, then sobbing more and more. Pause. Watching him, she reaches gently with a hand, and the boy suddenly turns to bury his face in her and hold on to her with his hands, crying into her.*

There... I know... your Ruby understands, yes she does... my good boy... there...

> *She strokes him, his shoulders, his hair, and he starts to subside. She leads him to the armchair, and sits down. He slides down to the floor, with his body against her knees and his head leaning close.*

All right, now come on, we'll have a nice story before our bedtime comes. Nearly time now, we have a Jesus story to get happy, hey?

> *He sniffs. He recovers. He raises his face to her.*

PUMPKINHEAD: Cake Man. I like the Cake Man.

RUBY: [*jollying him, smiling*] Oh, the Cake Man! We'll tell about the Cake Man, will we?

>   *He looks up, nods, trying a smile.*

Well come on, you gotta laugh first!

>   *She reaches suddenly to prod and tickle him. They wrangle a second, then he giggles and is recovered.*

There! You my funny man again!

>   PUMPKINHEAD *smiles, and waits.* RUBY *settles herself, a hand on his head, stroking, and there begins a story session in which* PUMPKINHEAD *becomes altogether involved, forgetting his worries.*

Ready, now see if I remember. You have to help me. [*Beginning*] Long time ago, when Dreamtime's ending, Jesus, he sent the Cake Man over the sea to find the Koori children. And he come...

PUMPKINHEAD: With the cake. With the cake Jesus put to carry in his heart. Plenty!

RUBY: He come, with the cake, the cake that was love from Jesus, and he's lookin' 'round then for good children to love and give cake to...

PUMPKINHEAD: Only the bad men stuck a stick in Cake Man's eyes!

RUBY: That's the truth, the bad men, the wicked men done that...

PUMPKINHEAD: And then the Cake Man lose his way, and can't see because his eyes is blind, and he can't see the Koori boys, only the gubba kids he kin see ever since them bad men done that! Cake Man's a blind man...

RUBY: Yes, and all the time since then, the Cake Man been walkin' around the bush lookin' for somethin' he's forgot about what it was...

PUMPKINHEAD: But he still got all the cakes, and we gotta find him and tell him!

RUBY: He still got all the cakes, that's right, but he don't know any more about who told him to give 'em to—

PUMPKINHEAD: He forgot! He don't even know he is the Cake Man! His eyes gone blind, and he forgot even who he s'posed to give the cakes to, and he forgot even about havin' to do it. He don' know who he is... gotta tell him!

RUBY: Pumpkinhead, who's tellin' this story? [*Pause.*] Well then, what we got to do, we got still to wait for him, got to keep lookin' till we see him there, and then we tell him about the cakes that Jesus sent to Koori children, make him know himself, remember he is the Cake Man...

PUMPKINHEAD: Got to stick him in the heart with a spear! Story says that... a spear!

RUBY: Yes, story says that, but I don' know about that part.

PUMPKINHEAD: Yeah! That's the best part, Mum! [*Relishing the idea*] When the Koori boy finds the Cake Man, then he got to stick a spear in the Cake Man's heart, right in his heart, and then the Cake Man remembers, and he knows who he is, that he's the Cake Man Jesus sent one time...

RUBY: Well, that's the story... my Daddy told me... yes it is.

> *Pause. They sit quietly. She strokes his hair.* PUMPKINHEAD *sighs and looks up at her.*

PUMPKINHEAD: Arr, ain't no Cake Man, Mum.

RUBY: There is so too! [*Pretending to be cross*] Now you stop that, little Pumpkinhead, there is so.

PUMPKINHEAD: No, there ain't.

RUBY: [*firmly*] Ain't no birriks, is what there ain't. You sayin' believe in silly ghosts, but no Cake Man?

PUMPKINHEAD: Gubba kids said there ain't. They tol' me and Collie and Noelie and Collie's Sissy...

RUBY: Gubba kids! How they know, them kids?

PUMPKINHEAD: No Father Christmas, they know that. They knows, 'cos they's gubba. That Ralphie knows.

RUBY: I ask you how? Gubba kid just a kid, same as you are and Collie and Noelie.

PUMPKINHEAD: Ralphie knows. He said you buy toys from the shop and when mothers got no money, ain't no Santa gonna come to no Koori kids.

RUBY: Oh!

PUMPKINHEAD: An' I seen the money name tickets on all the toys too, I have, and me and Bubby ain' got no toys, so that's why no Father Christmas... only got birriks I can see.

RUBY: You fibber! Can't see no birriks either! Where you seen birriks, you bugger of a boy?

PUMPKINHEAD: Seen 'em. Me and Collie and Noelie seen 'em. Two of 'em, all dressed in black down the church, and we were scairt and we run all the way to the Mission and we told Uncle Foley and he said they was so! He said they holy birriks and he knows 'cos he's wise!

RUBY: Uncle Foley! That liar ol' man! [*Softening*] Oh, now don' you listen to no gubba kids or no silly old men. [*Reassuring*] Your Ruby tellin' you there sure is a Cake Man. Jus' gotta find the feller.

PUMPKINHEAD: We all been lookin' to find him. We been lookin' all in the bush, everywhere, and we been up the streets in the town, lookin' to see the man who can't see us. [*Sighing*] But they see us.

Pause.

RUBY: No, they don' see you.

PUMPKINHEAD: Huh! They chase me and kick my arse damn good for no seein' me.

RUBY: You wash your mouth.

She hits him a light slap on the head.

PUMPKINHEAD: [*hushing her suddenly*] Listen.

They cock their heads, listening. A dog starts to bark outside. We hear, getting louder, the sound of a man singing.

SWEET WILLIAM: Ohhhh, Ned Kelly was born in a ramshackle hut,
      He battled since he was a kid.
      He grew up with bad men and duffers and thieves,
      And learned all the things that they did.

He breaks off, cursing the dog. The barking stops. Pause. SWEET WILLIAM, *the man from Part One, enters, resuming his song.*

Oh, Ned Kelly was born with duffers and— [*Nodding drunkenly as he closes the door behind him*] Ah, you sittin' up late, Rube?

He stands swaying.

RUBY: You see, Sweet William. I got some nice tucker on that stove.

She pulls the upturned kerosene tin over to the stove, gently pushing him to sit down. He sits and looks drunkenly at PUMPKINHEAD, *who looks at him sullenly and turns away.* WILLIAM *opens his mouth to speak to* PUMPKINHEAD, *then sighs and hangs his head tiredly.* RUBY *takes an enamel dish and tips a little vegetable food from a pot. She gives the dish and a spoon to* WILLIAM. *He eats slowly. The baby cries in its cot.* WILLIAM *stands, muttering with concern. He puts his plate on the floor and heads for the baby.* PUMPKINHEAD *shoves at him bitterly.*

PUMPKINHEAD: Git away. I do that.

SWEET WILLIAM *stands drunk, hurt, and uncertain. Then he stumbles back to his tin and plate, sitting dejectedly and staring down.* PUMPKINHEAD *wets the cloth. He goes to the cot and repeats his performance of bathing the baby's eyes. The crying stops.* RUBY *looks on reasonably. She goes to sit in her armchair, stroking the Bible.*

RUBY: Pumpkinhead.

He looks to her from the cot.

You're my good boy.

He smiles at her sadly and attends the baby.

Time for your bed now.

She regards PUMPKINHEAD *and* SWEET WILLIAM *anxiously.*

PUMPKINHEAD: I know, Mum.

He concentrates on the baby. WILLIAM *drops the plate and spoon. He starts to talk in a dull tone, not looking at either of them.*

SWEET WILLIAM: Ahhhh, you're a good woman, Rube, too good for me. [*Laughing dully*] Sweet bloody William, they call me, huh, the jacky with the 'baccy... 'n the wine. Ha, cigareeeeets 'n whisky.

He pauses tiredly. RUBY *fidgets anxiously and looks to* PUMPKINHEAD.

RUBY: Bubby's good now, good boy. Come on, it's time for your bedtime. You go now, Mum'll come in in a minute.

She gestures to the bedroom door. PUMPKINHEAD *nods, goes slowly to stand by her, and touches her as she touches him, both miserable.*

SWEET WILLIAM: [*shaking his head*] That's what I'll do. That's the place. Nobody cares what colour, long as he works. Can work any gubba in the ground any damn day, done it before today...

He muses. RUBY *carries the cot off to the bedroom. She comes back to* PUMPKINHEAD. *She stands quietly, regarding* WILLIAM, *then gently pushes* PUMPKINHEAD *before her and they go into the bedroom, taking a candle.* WILLIAM *sits alone, muttering to himself.*

Arr, yeah Rube... [*Nodding, affirming it to himself*] Used to do it, till they went 'n brung them Balt bastards in—bastards. [*Explaining*] Not that I got nothin' personal 'gainst no one.

Pause. RUBY *comes back and looks at him sadly.*

That's it, Rube. Bring the light back.

RUBY *puts the candle down. She goes slowly to sit in her old chair. She sits stroking the book, and opens it during his next lines.*

But a man's got nothin', not even the little bit used to be there. Got to get a quid, same as anybody. Arr, but Jesus, [*sighing*] I mean there used to be a bit of a go once. Damn it, Rube, those bloody Balts the ones that took it all.

Pause. RUBY *looks at him. She shakes her head and sighs, then reads quietly again.*

The fruit season, they were the good old days. Man could go to town them days, hold his head up, Rube. [*Thinking* PUMPKINHEAD *is still there*] Y'hear that, do ya, Pumpkinhead—Your ol' man used to hold up his head them days. Jist ask your mother.

RUBY *starts to look emotional at his words. He focuses on her again, catching her eye. She nods gently, agreeing with him. He loses focus again. He talks at his feet.*

But there's work still down the city. [*As something appeals he starts chuckling*] Hah, hah! Sydney's the place! Got their own bloody pub, the Kooris have... [*Amazed*] Fancy that. Man can stand up at the bar and have a good go. [*Living it*] Hey, your shout, mate! Sweet William, it's your bloody shout! [*Grinning*] And with your own damn money, too, that y'earned all by yourself.

He falls silent. She reads on, the same page, glancing at him once or twice as he sits starting to sway on the tin. He falls to the floor and lies there like an old rag. She sighs. She puts her Bible down and goes to raise him up, pulling as he climbs to his feet.

RUBY: Now just you easy, my Sweet William.

She leads him to her armchair and sits him in it. He slumps. She pulls the ironing blanket off the table and throws it over him. She stands sadly. Gradually growing louder, until the curtain, we hear Janis Joplin singing 'Mercedes Benz'. She pushes the pots and billy off the stove. She blows out one candle and fusses about. She picks up the other candle, carries it to the door, where she pauses, looking sadly at SWEET WILLIAM. *She blows out the candle. In the dark, Janis Joplin is ending the song: 'Oh, Lord, won't you buy me a Mercedes Benz'.*

SCENE TWO

Next afternoon. The backyard of a house: clothes line; various bits of junk lying about; a fairly high fence with a gate shut with an inside bolt; a wood box; a coal bin.

The CIVILIAN, *dressed in modern work clothes, is pottering about in the yard. There is a noise at the gate. He hears it and backs off, quietly waiting. A small black hand comes through the gate and fiddles to open the bolt. The* CIVILIAN *hides. The gate opens and* PUMPKINHEAD *enters stealthily, dressed neatly in school jumper, with his socks pulled up. Quickly and quietly he goes straight to the coal bin, plucks five or six lumps of coal and shoves them inside his shirtfront. As he turns to leave, the* CIVILIAN *jumps out of hiding.*

CIVILIAN: Gotcha!

He blocks PUMPKINHEAD'*s exit, then advances on him slowly.*

Right, now put back my property.

> PUMPKINHEAD *looks about, hesitating. The* CIVILIAN *gestures abruptly.*

Go on, you little spook bastard!

> PUMPKINHEAD *turns, defeated, reaches in his shirt to pull out a piece of coal. He hesitates.*

Go on, go on, you little swine. Put it all back. [*Nodding in nasty satisfaction*] Got you this time, haven't I?

> PUMPKINHEAD *makes as if to throw the piece of coal back in the bin, but instead he suddenly lobs it over the* CIVILIAN's *head.*

Whaaa?

> *He dodges, and tries to catch the lump of coal.* PUMPKINHEAD *reaches swiftly to grab another lump, dodges around him and flies from the scene. The* CIVILIAN *chases him with a shout of anger and dismay.*

You sneaky—! Come back here! Come back with my property! Black bastard! Mission rat!

> *He halts at the empty gate. The bird has flown altogether.*

Right, well that's it. I'll just get my coat on, and we'll see about you thieving lot of dirty...

> *He mutters and glares out the gate. He then stomps resolutely off.*

SCENE THREE

The same afternoon. The house on the Mission. RUBY *is sitting in her chair, reading her Bible. The door opens and* SWEET WILLIAM *comes in. He looks at* RUBY, *gets a smile, sighs and goes to sit by the stove.*

SWEET WILLIAM: Huh. You prayin' again, Rube?

RUBY: Now don't you go talkin' like that, Sweet William. That's why we never have no luck all the time. Do you good, it would, to read this book, that's where I get my strength from in every day, truly is.

SWEET WILLIAM: Couldn' do me no more good than a smoke would right now, Rube. Or a little drink.

RUBY: Don't want you talkin' like that in the presence of this here good book, Sweet William!

SWEET WILLIAM: Huh! [*Reaching*] Give it here then, Rube, and I'll get me strength back. [*Grin and sigh*] I been all over the bloody Mission, haven' I, tryin' to get a draw, an' I'm plain buggered.

RUBY: You're a sad man, Sweet William.

She gets up and takes the Bible to the bedroom.

SWEET WILLIAM: Humph. I say I am. [*He gets up and starts to wander about the room.*] I don' know, Rube, buggered if I do. Man's been all around, everywhere... nothin' bloody doin'.

RUBY: [*off*] You try your Uncle Foley?

SWEET WILLIAM: Course I did. First. Thought I'd be a sure thing. 'Specially I said it was for you.

RUBY: [*entering*] You damn devil of a man. Shouldn't do that, sayin' things is for me.

SWEET WILLIAM: [*wryly*] I know it. Old bastard give me a lecture, that's all, 'bout bringin' your nerves on again.

RUBY: He give you a smoke?

SWEET WILLIAM: Uh. Said he smoked his last bumper this mornin'.

RUBY: Oh. What else he say?

SWEET WILLIAM: Nothin'. Oh, yeah, he said give you this.

He fishes out a small paper packet.

RUBY: [*opening it*] Tea!

She smells it, smiling.

SWEET WILLIAM: Yeah, I know, just what you need.

RUBY: Just what I need.

SWEET WILLIAM: That's what I said.

RUBY: [*delighted*] Start right now!

She grabs the billy off the stove and leaves the room. SWEET WILLIAM *prowls about, muttering aloud.*

SWEET WILLIAM: Old bastard... can't mind his own business... tellin' me I should pack up and get out of this damn stinkin' place. Go to Sydney, get work, get a decent place for Ruby and the kids. All you need is spirit, just put your shoulders back, take a good job and get some good money, bring Rube and the kids to a—ah, damn shit! Sydney! [*He paces slowly in peevish thought.*] All right for Uncle Foley, old bastard, he ready for his grave with nothin' to care about no more. [*Scoffing*] Him and his shit talk about the Dreamtime.

RUBY: [*coming back, putting the billy on the stove*] What you sayin' to yourself, Sweet William?

SWEET WILLIAM: Ah, nothin'... nothin' Rube.

RUBY: You never mind. Feel better when I make this nice tea. We'll have it, you and me.

SWEET WILLIAM: How would I get to Sydney!

RUBY: What's that?

He shakes his head and sits down. She shakes hers and goes to the cupboard. She takes out two Golden Syrup tins, puts them on the table, then goes to stir the fire in the stove, adjusting the billy.

Get you nice tin of tea.

SWEET WILLIAM: You good, Rube.

He sighs and looks at the floor. She looks at him, fond and sad. She goes behind him and starts to massage the back of his neck. He sighs and relaxes gratefully.

RUBY: Never you mind, Sweet William.

SWEET WILLIAM: Ah, Rube. [*Miserably*] Ain't nothin' but to mind... Your Sweet William ain't so sweet, just what they say, he's a no-good nigger.

RUBY: No, he is not.

SWEET WILLIAM: Why not, Rube?

RUBY: Well... niggers is Americans.

SWEET WILLIAM: Ah.

RUBY: My William ain't no 'Merican.

SWEET WILLIAM: No, but he ain't no use either, Rube.

RUBY: Oh, never mind. You don't worry with me. I know what's your fault and what isn't. I know how you're feelin'. I know you tried a long time.

SWEET WILLIAM: Oh, yeah, Rube... [*Sighing, enjoying his massage*] But, Rube, there ain't nothin' now I know to do. Just hopeless, and no price I can pay because there ain't no price I've got to give that anyone wants. I got nothin' they want!

RUBY: Got to have faith. That's what God wants.

SWEET WILLIAM: God wants!

RUBY: Sit still. Something will turn up, I know.

SWEET WILLIAM: Even Pumpkinhead, even my own son hates me. He blames me for all this. And it's not my fault, it isn't, Rube, you know it ain't my fault. You know I'd give my right arm—If there's a God he can have my right arm if he'll let me give you and the kids everything and make Pumpkinhead proud of me. [*Sighing*] But he ain't proud of me like this... I wouldn't want him to be.

RUBY: He will, Sweet William. He's only eleven, one day when he understands... be proud of you then.

SWEET WILLIAM: If he could just know what it does to me, when I have to beg... when I don't want to.

RUBY: Well... you wait, one day when our boy, Pumpkinhead, looks back on life, then you just see how he knows who was the man and he'll have the right one who's his father... yes.

Pause.

SWEET WILLIAM: Make the tea then, Rube. And I'll go into town... see if I can get... what I can get.

RUBY: You mean credit?

SWEET WILLIAM: I said try, Rube.

She smiles, stops the massage, strokes his hair, then moves away to the billy.

RUBY: Can't do no more than try, Sweet William.

SWEET WILLIAM: Trouble is, Rube, credit is hard.

RUBY: [*busy at the stove*] Mmmmnnn?

SWEET WILLIAM: All the shops, they know me.

RUBY: Oh.

SWEET WILLIAM: It's wrong, it's back to front, Rube, see? Credit's supposed to be when you come from their town and they know you.

RUBY: [*looking at the water*] It won't be long.

SWEET WILLIAM: Uncle Foley, he says I should go down to the city, and make something, and take you and the kids after me when I done it.

RUBY: That's for you to think, not Uncle Foley.

SWEET WILLIAM: He says nothin' here in Cowra, never will be, nothin' but the Mission and like this.

RUBY: Sydney is a long way, Sweet William.

SWEET WILLIAM: Henry, he walked there.

RUBY: Well, you ain't got no train fare neither.

SWEET WILLIAM: Can walk as good as Henry.

RUBY: [*smiling*] To Sydney? Why, Sweet William, that Henry already had brothers and sisters waitin' for him in Sydney when he got there. Different for you, and where would you go even when you got there?

SWEET WILLIAM: I know where I'd go.

RUBY: Where then? [*Pause.*] I ask you where?

SWEET WILLIAM: There's a place... I know.

RUBY: And I know what you know, Sweet William! You thinkin' of that dirty pub! That low-life, no-good, stinkin' pub in that Sydney where all stupid country boys go when they get there, 'cause they don't know anywhere else to go, and then they get nothin' but mad with the booze in 'em and no work and no money and in the gaol before they knows where they are!

SWEET WILLIAM: All the brothers and sisters go there, Rube, even Uncle Foley said that to me. He did, today, you just ask him. He says if a cousin come there from the bush, why, they gonna help him along and see him right pretty soon...

RUBY: How they see him right? How? What they've got to see him right
with? [*Lecturing knowledgeably*] I tell you, Sweet William, they ain't
all stayin' in that pub 'cause they want togetherness, now! Oh, no, they
all there because them white people don' allow no black people to
drink any other place! That's why!

SWEET WILLIAM: You been there, Rube?

RUBY: You don't be smart with the questions, Sweet William. I don't have
to been there, it's everybody knows about that dirty pub... it's everybody
knows that they don't do nothin' but get drunk and go to the gaol.

> SWEET WILLIAM *nods and sighs*, RUBY *shakes the tea into the billy.*

Now we just let that stew a minute.

SWEET WILLIAM: I been stewin' all my life. Ain't made me no better, Rube.

> *He grins.*

RUBY: You always tasted good to me.

> *They smile at each other.*

SWEET WILLIAM: I'm goin' sour now though, Rube. Time's gettin' along,
and I ain't got nowhere, ain't got you the things we used to plan on. I
don't get a leg on, Rube, gonna be too late.

RUBY: Never too late, Sweet William. [*She brings the billy, holding it with
a cloth in one hand, and pours tea into the tins.*] We just got to trust in
God, don't I keep tellin' you? And you see how good it comes one day.

> *She returns the billy to the stove; she picks up the old flat iron and
> puts it on to get hot; she goes to sit with* SWEET WILLIAM *and drink
> some tea.*

SWEET WILLIAM: You puttin' the iron on early, Rube?

RUBY: Got to wash the clothes for school and iron 'em dry. Must be
gettin' late now, send Pumpkinhead for the bread ration, don't let me
forget... Got some spinach they not gonna want for their tea.

SWEET WILLIAM: Rube, I'll just go down to that Sydney, I'm gonna be
lucky and get a job and find somewhere that's gonna be ours, and soon
buy a big red house like Pumpkinhead wants and clothes and a 'lectric
iron for you, 'lectric light, too, and plenty of tucker for the kids that we
could buy out of my good job I'll get. I can work, Rube, you know I
can. Job, that's all it needs.

RUBY: [*pausing*] You keep sayin' it a lot today... makin' me think you
might be meanin' it.

SWEET WILLIAM: I am meanin' it, Rube. I got to try.

RUBY: Sweet William, you have to think about what you want... got to
decide, and you don't ask no woman of yours what you gonna do, but
you can tell me what you gonna do and I'll know that's right and you
gotta do it and I know you will too.

SWEET WILLIAM: You really think that, Rube? You do?

RUBY: I tell you so.

SWEET WILLIAM: Ah, Rube, you tell me so. [*Wryly*] But you don't tell me what you know, about how you feel, I never heard you tell the truth about me yet.

RUBY: Yes, you just did.

SWEET WILLIAM: I just heard you tell what a good woman you are, Rube... pretendin' I'm not no good.

   Pause.

RUBY: You sayin' I told a lie, Sweet William?

SWEET WILLIAM: Just a white lie. But I know, Rube.

RUBY: How do you know what I think, huh?

SWEET WILLIAM: Just been married to you for years, Rube. [*Smiling*] I know you say things.

RUBY: You know my good book, Sweet William?

SWEET WILLIAM: Not as good as you do, Rube.

RUBY: Well, I swear on my good book, that's what I do. I swear what I said is sort of true.

SWEET WILLIAM: Rube, I'm sick of hearin' you tell the kids damn stories that ain't never comin' true. All about Jesus loves us, and how one day we're gonna find the Cake Man...

RUBY: Jesus is true. Cake Man is true. Shut up.

SWEET WILLIAM: Ah, Rube... ain't no Jesus, ain't no man who... They just stories.

RUBY: Shut your wicked mouth, Sweet William!

SWEET WILLIAM: Sick of it, Rube, tired of knowin' that Pumpkinhead makes me tell him stories too. You know that, Rube, about the bushrangers, about Jimmy Governor, how the Kooris used to be brave, and how we'd fight and run and fight again...

RUBY: What's wrong with you, you stupid man? You forgot what you liked when you was a little boy? You don't want your own boys to have some stories from their own father? They got no 'spensive books like the gubba boys got, no one but you and me to have stories for 'em... and you too tired?

SWEET WILLIAM: Rube, will you stop pretendin'?

RUBY: What you're sayin', you fool of a man?

SWEET WILLIAM: Pumpkinhead... he don't want no stories about the Koori bushrangers... not 'cause he likes me tellin' him stories, Rube. No, that boy he makes me tell about when the Kooris were brave, and he's only meanin' to make me know about myself.

RUBY: What?

SWEET WILLIAM. You know what, Rube… about me, I ain't never stuck up no white man, and I ain't done not one thing in my whole life is brave. All my life, all I ever done was be a jacky-boy.

RUBY: You done your best!

SWEET WILLIAM: And my son wouldn't spit on me.

RUBY: He would so!

SWEET WILLIAM: [*laughing sadly*] He would damn so. I know.

RUBY: He's only eleven, a baby boy.

SWEET WILLIAM: He looks at me sometimes, I get the feelin' our baby boy is a hundred years old.

RUBY: I don' know this fool talk.

SWEET WILLIAM: I'll go to Sydney, Rube, and I'll make everything right before it's too late. Right now, tomorrow, and I'll make good—

> SWEET WILLIAM *waits for* RUBY *to answer.* RUBY *goes slowly to get herself more tea.*

RUBY: Some more tea, Sweet William?

SWEET WILLIAM: No, you keep it, Rube.

> *She comes back and sits down.* SWEET WILLIAM *avoids her eyes.*

RUBY: What you say is good, Sweet William.

SWEET WILLIAM: [*encouraged*] You think so, Rube?

> *She nods.*

I tell you what, I go down there to that city. I'm gonna do like Uncle Foley said, get me some spirit, hold my head up with my shoulders back. You won't hear from nobody that they ever seen me drunk like you been used to.

RUBY: That's happy talk you're sayin'.

SWEET WILLIAM: A good job. Rube, you know I'll get us that red house, in just a little while down there.

RUBY: Well, I'll… be waitin' for it.

SWEET WILLIAM: You believe that? Me?

RUBY: I believe.

SWEET WILLIAM: That I won't get drunk?

RUBY: Course.

SWEET WILLIAM: And the red house?

RUBY: I'm plannin' the furniture.

SWEET WILLIAM: Why you believe me?

RUBY: Well, I been lovin' you a long time, Sweet William, don't you know that already?

SWEET WILLIAM: I mean it, Rube…

RUBY: So do I... and we'll be waitin' here.

The baby starts crying in the cot.

Oh, Bubby.

She goes to the cot, reaching a hand in gently, then turns and goes swiftly for a cloth, dipping it in some water, visibly upset as she talks.

Oh, Will, his eyes are stuck shut again.

She reaches in to bathe the baby's eyes gently, crooning to the child, and it stops its noise.

He sleeps all the time, and when he sleeps the sores run. Then his eyes get stuck.

SWEET WILLIAM: [*hovering near her*] Can I do somethin', Rube?

RUBY: No, I'm used to it. Haven't I had it with both of them? Just have to clean it away all the time. [*Beseeching him*] Do you mean it, Will? You'll go, and you won't get drunk, and you'll get us out of here... William?

SWEET WILLIAM: I mean it, Rube... you'll see, you wait.

He goes to her and holds her gently. She puts her arms around him, the cloth hanging wetly against his trousers. She sobs a little, but then forces a laugh and leaves him.

RUBY: Well! You'll think I'm a sook.

SWEET WILLIAM: You know what I think about you, Rube.

RUBY: Well, you do it for us then. Try, even.

SWEET WILLIAM: Rube, all it'll depend on is them whitefellers lettin' me have the chance. You don't worry about my bit, because there ain't nothin' I want so bad as to make us a good life family.

RUBY: You're a good man for wantin' it, Sweet William. No matter anythin' else comes.

SWEET WILLIAM: It'll be like I say, Rube. Just wait.

RUBY: I told you, fool man, we'll wait.

The door flies open and PUMPKINHEAD *enters quickly, heading directly to unload coal from his shirt in front of the stove.*

Pumpkinhead!

PUMPKINHEAD: Arr, Mum. Gotcha some coal... railway.

RUBY: [*with mixed feelings*] My good boy. Look at your bloody shirt.

SWEET WILLIAM: [*scoffing*] Railway!

PUMPKINHEAD *gives him a filthy stare.* SWEET WILLIAM *weakens and shuts up.*

PUMPKINHEAD: [*playing the happy hunter*] Six lumps, Mum, keep you warm.

RUBY: Could I do without you? [*Giving him a quick hug, then complaining*] Oh, you wicked boy, lookit what you done to your clothes that I wash. Take 'em off, quick, and put your shorts on. Go get the bread ration.

> PUMPKINHEAD *grins and disappears to the bedroom.* RUBY *turns to* SWEET WILLIAM.

You shut up. I know ain't no railway coal left since years ago.

SWEET WILLIAM: [*a dig*] Thought stealin' was a sin.

RUBY: What stealin'? Hey? How's it you know, Sweet William, that maybe he ain't got a coal mine he's diggin' for himself? Clever boy like that...

SWEET WILLIAM: Wish he'd find a gold mine.

RUBY: Well, he might. But you leave him be, don't say nothin'll spoil what he thinks I think.

PUMPKINHEAD: [*entering in just a pair of shorts*] I'll run get the bread, Mum.

> *She smiles and nods. He goes out the door.* RUBY *goes off into the bedroom.*

SCENE FOUR

The garden of the MANAGER'*s nice white house on the Mission. The door of the house has a few steps leading up to it. A large rubbish bin stands at the bottom of the steps, with a lid. Two men come out of the house. They are the* MANAGER *and the* INSPECTOR *of the Mission, played by the same actors as the* PRIEST *and* SOLDIER *respectively. They pause in front of the house, chatting good-humouredly.*

INSPECTOR: Well, I must say Mrs Moreton really knows how to make scones.

MANAGER: She loved to hear you say so, Mr Gigg. Oh, yes, ha ha, she always says I married her for her scones.

> *They share a nice little laugh.*

INSPECTOR: Marvellous little housekeeper, always whenever I come to this Mission, Mr Moreton, I'm always glad because I know your good wife will be here to set a civilised table, that, in your home, I'll find the sort of example that should be always shown to these poor devils that you're caring for, yes indeed.

MANAGER: Thank you, Mr Gigg. I know I can speak for my good wife, too, that she'd appreciate your remark there.

INSPECTOR: Well, she's doing a fine job. Now then, I suppose before it gets too late I'd better have a look about the place. Would you care to lead off?

MANAGER: Yes, well, we'll just poke about wherever the fancy takes us, eh? Make a few surprise raids? Ha ha!

INSPECTOR: Ha ha! Yes, catch 'em on the hop. Oh, ha ha!

They have fun considering their inspection. The CIVILIAN *stomps on. They pause, regarding him affably.*

MANAGER: Hello, sir.

CIVILIAN: You the trump around this rat's nest?

MANAGER: I beg your pardon?

CIVILIAN: Are you responsible, I mean, for keeping these black bastards on this reservation and away from decent people's property?

MANAGER: A Mission, sir, not a reservation.

CIVILIAN: It's a rat's nest. Now, you listen to me, I'm only one of the people of this town who're sick and damn tired of your blacks and their thieving and damn vandalising and making a filthy nuisance of themselves around this town. And I'm here to see it stopped.

MANAGER: Well!

CIVILIAN: That's right! Damn right!

He stands there angrily. Pause.

MANAGER: Well, sir, Mr... ah...?

CIVILIAN: Peterson.

MANAGER: Oh. How do you do?

They nod at each other. He indicates the INSPECTOR.

This is Mr Gigg.

The CIVILIAN *nods at the* INSPECTOR, *who nods.*

Mr Gigg is, ah, our Inspector, y'know, just about to have a look around the Mission.

CIVILIAN: Yes? Well then, I'd suggest he just has a look in their nests for half the private property in Cowra. Thieving, destroying, filthy nuisances!

MANAGER: [*tut-tutting*] Ho, now Mr Peterson! Really, it's plain you're rather upset, but do be a little more explicit.

CIVILIAN: Explicit?

INSPECTOR: Something to go on, you know.

CIVILIAN: Oh, something to go on, is it, you want? Well then, a little while ago, you see, I went out into my own backyard—my own backyard—and just in time to catch the little animal at it again.

MANAGER: The little animal?

INSPECTOR: Doing what again?

CIVILIAN: At my coal box, pilfering it again, that's what the little animal was doing again. You know how many ton of coal he's got from my box this year?

MANAGER: Who?

CIVILIAN: The little black bastard who comes and takes it, of course! Aren't I telling you that?

MANAGER: Well! Mr Peterson, I—

CIVILIAN: Now, look! Let me say it another way. Look, your job is to run this... this Mission, right? Keep the blackfellers two miles from the town, right? On this reservation, away from decent people and their property and their wives and their town, right?

MANAGER: Oh, well, in a way... yes. But, you know, it's...

CIVILIAN: Oh yes, I know! But do you know, do you know, that instead of doing your job, sir, you're allowing them to run absolutely riot? Oh yes, staggering all over the town, around Cowra, drunk and filthy and an embarrassment to the whole community.

INSPECTOR: Drunk, you say?

CIVILIAN: Drunk. Filthy drunk. And it's getting so that decent women working in the shops simply dread to open their doors, for fear of the unpleasantness of having to refuse them credit, these drunken filthy blacks and their whining at the shop doors, stinking of metho, stinking of themselves, stinking the town out.

MANAGER: Well, surely you exaggerate. I mean, it's true we get complaints from time to time, but—

CIVILIAN: Hah! Time to time. It's all the time, blacks doing what they like all over Cowra. Not a day's work in the lot of 'em. What's the good of giving 'em welfare money, eh? What use, when all it does is load 'em with wine and metho and degrade a decent town?

MANAGER: That is not my responsibility, sir.

CIVILIAN: Oh, it isn't?

MANAGER: The Government pays out social service, Mr Peterson, not me. Nor would I, if you want to know, but in fact I've just got a job to do and I do it. I keep this Mission clean.

CIVILIAN: Oh, you do?

MANAGER: Yes, I do. The outside, at least.

CIVILIAN: Oh. Well, that's not good enough, not as from today. No, now look, I'm just a plain citizen and I want no part of running the affairs of men like yourself. No, that's right, but what I do want and what I am entitled to is your attention to your own job, you understand me? What I mean is, I mean to say that all this that's been going on has to damn well stop and stop right now, today.

INSPECTOR: [*making a note in his book*] Going on...

MANAGER: Going on? What, uh, exactly...?

CIVILIAN: You know what I'm going to do? I'll tell you what I'm going to do. What I'm going to do, I'm going to hang a blasted rabbit trap where his black thieving hand comes through my gate to open it and steal my property. My coal! My wood! Anything that will burn, obviously, that his low-life parents send the little snake to thieve, obviously, in order to warm their blasted wigwams with my coal!

MANAGER: You've been missing some coal...

CIVILIAN: Ah! I've been missing some coal! And what of the golf course, tell me that? What do you mean by their vandalism there? Tearing up the green... And the gangs of 'em by the railway line, throwing rocks at decent people in their carriages. Not a fowl safe in its coop, not anywhere in the town or for twenty miles around! Our hens are stolen, our golf course destroyed, our fuel filched, our trees and gardens laid bare, sheep taken in broad daylight, goats, any damn thing dead or alive that they can eat, burn, or throw rocks at. Blasted lot of delinquent black baby bushrangers. Now what are you going to do?

MANAGER: The devil you say.

CIVILIAN: Yes, exactly. The devil I say. Black bastards!

MANAGER: Well...

INSPECTOR: Yes, well, we'll look into it.

CIVILIAN: Black bastards.

INSPECTOR: Oh quite. Quite, Mr Peterson.

CIVILIAN: I call a spade a spade.

INSPECTOR: Oh, ha ha ha... that's very good.

MANAGER: Yes, Well I'll...

CIVILIAN: Yes, well, I know you will... what?

MANAGER: Well, I'll investigate it. I'll... inquire.

CIVILIAN: Oh, you will?

MANAGER: Indeed I will.

CIVILIAN: Hmph. Yes, well, while you're doing that, I'll tell you what I'll be doing... what every decent man in the town will be doing from now on.

MANAGER: Oh?

CIVILIAN: The next time I corner my particular piece of the Stone Age in my yard, well, I'll be taking a gun and putting a bullet in his black arse. You hear?

> *Pause.*

INSPECTOR: The next time you corner it—him?

MANAGER: You mean you already have... caught him?

CIVILIAN: I had the little thief today, an hour ago. I told you that, he was there in my own yard.

MANAGER: Well, Mr Peterson, why on earth didn't you grab hold, take him in hand, and bring him to me?

CIVILIAN: [*pausing, horrified*] Take it in hand. D'you suggest that I'd actually touch one with my hands? Do you not know of their dirt, the lice of them? [*Scoffing*] I'd as soon dip me hands in the plague.

MANAGER: Yes, well... well look. You say, sir, that you'd recognise your tormentor?

CIVILIAN: Would I!

INSPECTOR: Yes?

MANAGER: You would?

CIVILIAN: I would.

MANAGER: [*to the* INSPECTOR] He says he would.

INSPECTOR: Remarkable... yes.

MANAGER: [*to the* CIVILIAN] Well, perhaps you'd care then to accompany Mr Gigg and myself...?

CIVILIAN: Where to?

MANAGER: Mr Gigg is just about to inspect 'em.

CIVILIAN: What, all of 'em?

INSPECTOR: Oh, no no no... just here and there.

MANAGER: Never know, you might just see yours.

CIVILIAN: Right, well, I'll come then.

MANAGER: Good... good... well, let's away!

As they are about to leave, PUMPKINHEAD *arrives.*

Ah! It's Ruby's little fellow. What is it, then, my little man, your Mummy's bread, is it?

He takes the lid off the rubbish tin, gets out a loaf of bread and gives it to PUMPKINHEAD.

PUMPKINHEAD: Ta, boss.

He runs off with the bread. The CIVILIAN *does not recognise him.*

MANAGER: I dislike the way they all call me boss... [*Sighing*] Doesn't sound the best. Ah, well, Rome wasn't ruined in a day. Let's away then!

They walk off to inspect the Mission. Faintly, off, we hear the kettle drum.

SCENE FIVE

RUBY's *house.* WILLIAM *still hangs around in the room.* RUBY's *at the stove. She puts down a pot, moving it from the heat to the side of the stove.*

RUBY: There, that's nice spinach.

> *She goes to set the table with spoon, syrup tin, and bowl of dripping for* PUMPKINHEAD. *She returns to the pot, takes it from the stove and proceeds to the sink where she strains water from the spinach into a bowl. Then she puts the pot back on the side of the stove, leaving the bowl of spinach water on the side of the sink.*

There. Let that cool. Put some in the bottle for Bubby. Good for 'im.

SWEET WILLIAM: Oh Jesus. I got to do somethin', Rube.

> *He sits dejectedly on the upturned box.*

RUBY: I hear Pumpkinhead.

> *She cocks her head, listening, and nods.* PUMPKINHEAD *arrives back with the bread.*

PUMPKINHEAD: Y'are, Mum. Mr Moreton's around with that Mr Gigg, and there's a bad gubba with 'em.

SWEET WILLIAM: [*rising in some agitation and dismay*] Inspector?

PUMPKINHEAD: I got the bread and then sneaked back an' watched 'em. They comin' around the place, they are.

RUBY: Bad gubba? Who's a bad gubba?

PUMPKINHEAD: Ohhhh... I don' know 'im.

RUBY: How's he a bad gubba then?

PUMPKINHEAD: He's worse'n Mr Moreton. I know.

RUBY: They not comin' here, anyway. Now come on you sit down, boy, eat your good spinach up.

PUMPKINHEAD: [*pulling a face, but sitting at the table*] Ain' no good, spinach.

RUBY: Shut up. Eat.

> *She cuts some bread for him, spreads it with dripping and puts it by him.* PUMPKINHEAD *starts to wolf the bread. She gets him a bowl of spinach. He pulls another face but eats it. She pours some spinach water into the syrup tin and takes it to him.*

Drink. All the goodness in it.

> *He sighs, nods and drinks some. There is a loud knock at the door. As* RUBY *goes to answer, it is pushed open, and the* MANAGER *and the* INSPECTOR *enter. The* CIVILIAN *pauses in the doorway.*

MANAGER: Well, Ruby. William. Here's Mr Gigg come along to see how we're going. Oh, come in, come in, Mr Peterson. [*Pulling him in*] Ruby, now this is Mr Peterson, from the town. He's paying us a visit. William, this is Mr Peterson.

SWEET WILLIAM: Um.

> *The* CIVILIAN *gives a dirty nod. His eyes flick around the room. He sees the coal. The* INSPECTOR *snoops about slowly. He stands behind* PUMPKINHEAD *and pokes a couple of fingers in the boy's hair, prying and poking as* PUMPKINHEAD *squirms.*

INSPECTOR: [*satisfied*] Yesss... not too bad.

> PUMPKINHEAD *scowls at the* INSPECTOR. *The* CIVILIAN *looks from the coal to the familiar scowl.*

CIVILIAN: Him. [*Pointing dramatically*] He's the one! [*Pointing to the coal*] And that's my coal. Right there.

> *He starts picking up his coal.* PUMPKINHEAD *leaps up and fights him.*

PUMPKINHEAD: You leave that coal down.

> *He knocks the coal back onto the floor and kicks ferociously at the* CIVILIAN'*s shins.*

That coal's my muvver's!

MANAGER: Hey hey hey! Enough of that!

> *He grabs* PUMPKINHEAD *and shoves him away.*

RUBY: [*getting between the boy and the men*] You leave that boy be!

INSPECTOR: Well!

CIVILIAN: My property. The coal is mine.

PUMPKINHEAD: Coal's not yours. Our coal!

CIVILIAN: Thief!

PUMPKINHEAD: [*scowling from behind* RUBY] Gubba! Git from our house!

MANAGER: Now, now, now! [*To* SWEET WILLIAM] William, it's quite obvious to me, and to Mr Gigg, that this coal belongs to Mr Peterson here. Plainly it was stolen, as Mr Peterson says, by this boy of yours. Now it must be returned at once. I mean for a start... and then we'll have to see about this dreadful business of a boy from this Mission stooping to theft.

> *He assumes a shocked air.*

PUMPKINHEAD: [*to the* CIVILIAN] I send birriks on you now.

MANAGER: You be quiet, boy!

RUBY: Don' you tell my boy quiet! You callin' him thief, then tellin' 'im be quiet soon's he don't like it! [*To the* CIVILIAN] You git! Git from my house! Sweet William, make 'im git!

They turn in a body to SWEET WILLIAM. SWEET WILLIAM *swallows nervously.*

SWEET WILLIAM: Um… well, you're doin' good, Rube.

He nods his approval of her efforts. She is disappointed.

RUBY: You're sayin' it's your coal. How you knowin' it's your coal? You show me where it says on that coal it's your coal.

CIVILIAN: Ah! [*To the* MANAGER] It's my coal.

The INSPECTOR *is roaming about. He opens cupboards and peers about here and there. The* MANAGER *hovers around after him. The* CIVILIAN *moves after them.*

Well, what are you going to do about it?

He sees past the INSPECTOR, *notes the empty cupboard. He frowns uncertainly, and begins to look around him, taking in the poverty of the place. His frown deepens.*

Good lord. What's all this?

The baby starts crying.

RUBY: Oh!

PUMPKINHEAD: Orright, Mum.

PUMPKINHEAD *gets the cloth. The visitors watch as he reaches into the cot with the cloth. The* CIVILIAN *peers in.*

CIVILIAN: God!

PUMPKINHEAD: [*grimly*] No. It's Bubby.

The CIVILIAN's *eyes are widening. He turns to the* MANAGER, INSPECTOR *and* RUBY. *The crying stops.*

CIVILIAN: That's a baby…

He looks aghast at RUBY. *She nods silently.*

But, her eyes… What is it?

PUMPKINHEAD: Not her. Bubby's a him.

MANAGER: [*peering into the cot*] Ummm… lot of that.

CIVILIAN: A lot? Where?

RUBY: [*gesturing to the Mission outside*] Here.

The CIVILIAN *takes in the syrup tin and the remains of the spinach, bread and dripping. He looks more unhappy.*

CIVILIAN: God Almighty.

He moves a hand abruptly to his chest, as if a pain has struck him there. They all look at him and he looks at RUBY.

I've made a mistake. [*Shaking his head*] It's not my coal. Sorry. [*Nodding at the* MANAGER *and* INSPECTOR] It's not my coal. [*He goes quickly to the door, turns to* RUBY.] Sorry.

RUBY *gives him a bemused nod.*

PUMPKINHEAD: Told yuh.

CIVILIAN: Yes. I didn't see.

Abruptly he turns and is gone. Pause.

INSPECTOR: [*to the* MANAGER] Well!

MANAGER: I thought it was a heart attack.

They smile confusedly together.

RUBY: It was. That man just had little heart trouble.

PUMPKINHEAD: Pity it weren't big knock-'im-down sort.

MANAGER: Now, now! [*To the* INSPECTOR] Still… most strange.

INSPECTOR: Um. Well, there you are.

They shrug off the incident. Pause.

But, I'll still have to report this business, I'm afraid, soon as I get back to Sydney. [*Gesturing at the coal*] The point is, Ruby, William, it's my job to see things are in order here. This business of possible theft…

MANAGER: [*nodding righteously*] I'll have to make a report myself.

They assure each other with righteous nodding.

It's a question of doing our jobs

INSPECTOR: Or of not doing our jobs.

MANAGER: That's what the whole point is.

INSPECTOR: Of course. The whole point.

They nod in unison at her.

RUBY: Oh.

INSPECTOR: But… [*Winking at* RUBY] Well now, the other thing is this… we have to consider…

He pauses wisely. They wait on him.

I mean, now, I wouldn't want to be the sort of man who's not willing to overlook one mistake. I mean every man, every boy, for that matter, as we all must agree, is entitled to a second chance. And, uh, the thing is, if I go back Sydney and report about a thief of a boy on this Mission, well, the thing is that boy could easily end up being put in a home for bad boys, you see, and we wouldn't want such thing to happen, would we? Over a boy's first mistake. So, ah…

He pauses, regarding them.

RUBY: No. Man said the coal not his now.

PUMPKINHEAD: I never done it.

MANAGER: Well, I suppose not. Not the first time.

RUBY: Pumpkinhead won't do it no more. I promise.

INSPECTOR: No. Well… [*warning*] but thieves are put in gaol, my boy, and other nasty places.

PUMPKINHEAD: Won't do it no more, Mr 'Spector.

INSPECTOR: [*looking satisfied*] Promise?

PUMPKINHEAD: My father's honour.

RUBY: He's promised.

MANAGER: Good boy.

INSPECTOR: [*pleased*] Ahhh… father's honour! Ha ha, that's a new one. Very good too, yes.

>   SWEET WILLIAM *looks pretty glum.*

What do you say, William? [*Joking*] When a boy swears on his father's honour, is that good enough for the world?

SWEET WILLIAM: Oh…

>   *He looks to* PUMPKINHEAD. PUMPKINHEAD'*s expression mocks him.*

RUBY: Good enough for me.

MANAGER: Good.

INSPECTOR: Yes, very good.

>   *They make their fun, unaware of a conflict between* SWEET WILLIAM *and* PUMPKINHEAD.

Well then, we'd best be getting along, Mr Moreton…

>   SWEET WILLIAM *has been trying to make up his mind on something. He does.*

SWEET WILLIAM: Mr Gigg, sir, 'fore you go…

INSPECTOR: Yes…?

SWEET WILLIAM: [*hesitantly*] Mr Gigg… don' wanna ask no favour to offend…

INSPECTOR: Something I can do, William?

SWEET WILLIAM: Maybe, Mr Gigg. If— [*Suddenly firm*] Pumpkinhead, you run outside, play for little while while I talk somethin' with the grown-ups.

>   *Pause.*

PUMPKINHEAD: Don't feel like playin'.

>   *He turns his back on* SWEET WILLIAM *and stands by* RUBY. WILLIAM *straightens his shoulders, moves quickly and plants the side of his boot against* PUMPKINHEAD'*s backside, knocking him to the floor.*

SWEET WILLIAM: [*firmly*] You play when I tell you.

>   PUMPKINHEAD *looks up, amazed and hurt. He feels his backside and appeals to* RUBY.

RUBY: You just heard your father, boy.

PUMPKINHEAD: [*scrambling up*] Ma!

SWEET WILLIAM: Out.

RUBY: Your father talkin' to you.

SWEET WILLIAM: [*waggling his boot suggestively*] Out.

RUBY: [*pushing him to the door*] G'wan, skit!

> PUMPKINHEAD *goes out in miserable defeat.*

MANAGER: [*interested*] Well!

INSPECTOR: I hope this isn't a rude joke, William!

> *He cackles.*

SWEET WILLIAM: No, sir, it's... Well, Mr Gigg, you said before you gonna go back down to Sydney soon—tomorrow?

INSPECTOR: Well yes, William.

SWEET WILLIAM: Me too?

INSPECTOR: You too?

SWEET WILLIAM: I got to go down to Sydney. [*Making it up*] Got a message, I did, Mr Gigg, my sister's awful sick and cryin' for me down there. Have to get down there soon's I ever can, 'fore she dies.

INSPECTOR: Oh?

> *He looks to* RUBY. *She nods sadly.*

SWEET WILLIAM: I'm thinkin', Mr Gigg, won't mind if you say no, but I got to ask 'cause of m'sister...

INSPECTOR: You want a lift down, is that it?

SWEET WILLIAM: 'Zactly it.

INSPECTOR: Well, of course. You know where you're going, I mean when you get there? Where is it?

SWEET WILLIAM: Town called Redfern, that's it. Suburb...

INSPECTOR: [*amused*] Ho, Redfern. Of course.

> *He exchanges a smile with the* MANAGER.

SWEET WILLIAM: Well... got to get there.

INSPECTOR: All right. I'll take you there!

> *He nods and smiles in good humour.*

SWEET WILLIAM: [*smiling*] You will? Tomorrow?

INSPECTOR: Leaving at noon.

SWEET WILLIAM: Um. Well, then what'll I do, Mr Gigg, I mean where will I come... to go?

MANAGER: Mr Gigg will be leaving from my house, William, you can find your way there all right.

INSPECTOR: Yes, that will do.

SWEET WILLIAM: [*nodding*] Twelve o'clock.

INSPECTOR: Have you in Sydney tomorrow evening. How will that do, not too late for you?

SWEET WILLIAM: Never too late, Mr Gigg.

He smiles at RUBY.

RUBY: [*nodding smugly*] Told you so.

INSPECTOR: And you'll be all right, Ruby, and the boy, while the man's away down there?

RUBY: Pumpkinhead'll mind us here.

MANAGER: I'll bet.

INSPECTOR: But who'll mind Pumpkinhead?

They take the excuse to end with a laugh. She goes to the door with them. They pause.

Twelve o'clock, William!

SWEET WILLIAM: I'll be there. Thanks.

INSPECTOR: Don't mention it. 'Bye, Ruby.

They go out together.

RUBY: [*softly*] 'Bye, 'Spector, Mr Moreton. [*Calling out the door*] Pumpkinhead? You come back now. [*Coming back to* SWEET WILLIAM] I'm gettin' your clothes pressed later, after Pumpkinhead's in bed and we talk.

SWEET WILLIAM: [*posing, the hunter about to go hunting*] Maybe I'll let 'im stay up.

RUBY: Oh. Well, if you say so, Sweet William.

She smiles. SWEET WILLIAM *smiles back at her.*

SWEET WILLIAM: Soon have you and him down after me, Rube, give you some surprise seein' what house you've got to live in. All the things we'll have then.

RUBY: You remember be careful, that's all, don't go forgettin' all what you said. Drinkin'...

PUMPKINHEAD *enters. He prowls about, ignoring them.*

SWEET WILLIAM: [*loudly*] Well, no, 'course I won't, Rube! Soon as I get to Sydney [*eyeing* PUMPKINHEAD] ... tomorrow... I'll be gettin' to see some brothers an' sisters, then sure I'll find out where's the work, and where's a red house with 'lectric light... for us.

PUMPKINHEAD *turns, not believing his ears.*

RUBY: [*nodding to* PUMPKINHEAD] Your father's goin' to Sydney now, goin' down in the big car with Mr Gigg tomorrow.

Pause. PUMPKINHEAD *looks to* SWEET WILLIAM.

PUMPKINHEAD: Down there? [*Smiling*] Down Sydney?

SWEET WILLIAM: [*casually*] Arr, gettin' a good job, movin' you an' Mum an' Bubby down the city... pretty soon.

PUMPKINHEAD: An' a red house... you said.

SWEET WILLIAM: Um. New clothes an' things.

PUMPKINHEAD: Pretty soon?

SWEET WILLIAM: Um. Damn soon. You got to mind your mother for me an' Bubby... an' hang on just a while.

PUMPKINHEAD *looks happily at* RUBY.

RUBY: I'll see where's some clothes, Sweet William, have to clean that suitcase in there.

She exits to the bedroom. SWEET WILLIAM *regards* PUMPKINHEAD.

SWEET WILLIAM: You'll do that... be lookin' after things for me till I'm sendin' for you?

PUMPKINHEAD: Oh yeah.

He smiles at SWEET WILLIAM, *who smiles back and opens his arms.* PUMPKINHEAD *rushes to embrace him. Embarrassed,* WILLIAM *laughs and pushes the boy away lightly, then aims a playful jab at him.* PUMPKINHEAD *blocks it and throws a playful punch back. They box each other, laughing.*

SWEET WILLIAM: Jus' watch the ol' left, now.

He feints, and jabs a left, laughing. PUMPKINHEAD *boxes him back furiously.* WILLIAM *suddenly surrenders, pretending to collapse from a blow. He lies, beaten.* PUMPKINHEAD *stands above him, fists in the air. They laugh.* WILLIAM *reaches up and pulls* PUMPKINHEAD *down. They sit pushing each other happily.* RUBY *enters, sees them and smiles.*

RUBY: Well!

She grins and leaves again. Pause.

SWEET WILLIAM: Now you don' get in no trouble, not now.

PUMPKINHEAD: No.

SWEET WILLIAM: Anythin' you've stole, you put it back... you do that? [*Nodding*] An' let me get us things.

PUMPKINHEAD: [*reluctant, then nodding*] Yeah.

SWEET WILLIAM: Like that coal. You put it back.

PUMPKINHEAD: Um. [*Sighing*] You say so, Dad.

SWEET WILLIAM *nods that he does say so.*

END OF ACT TWO

ACT THREE

SCENE ONE

Next afternoon. The CIVILIAN's *backyard. The scene is as before, except that on the coal bin sits a large deep box filled with goodies: groceries packed high; all sorts of packets and bottles, etcetera. The small black hand comes through the gate and slips the bolt.* PUMPKINHEAD *pushes the gate open, pokes his head in and enters the yard. He carries the coal in a small hessian bag. He proceeds quietly towards the coal bin, then pulls up, staring in astonishment at the box of groceries. He is confused because the box is on the coal bin, preventing him from lifting the lid; then he is tempted. He hesitates, then shakes his head at himself. He takes the pieces of coal from his bag one at a time, laying them in front of the bin. Holding the empty bag, he picks out a few articles from the box. He fights off the devil reluctantly, trudges slowly to the gate and, after a lingering look at the groceries, leaves. Pause. The* CIVILIAN *appears quietly from the house. He looks with surprise at the groceries and at the returned coal. He runs after* PUMPKINHEAD, *and stands in the gate calling after him.*

CIVILIAN: Hey, wait a minute! Come back. Boy! Come on. I won't hurt you. Come on, here. [*Coaxing*] Want to show you...

He nods and steps back to allow the returning PUMPKINHEAD *into the yard.* PUMPKINHEAD *pauses inside the gate, pointing.*

PUMPKINHEAD: Din' take nothin'. See? Put it back...

CIVILIAN: No, come on, that's for you. Take it now.

He points to the goodies. PUMPKINHEAD *looks astonished and confused.*

Take it to your mother. Go on. [*Lifting the box, offering it to* PUMPKINHEAD] I mean it, go on, take it.

PUMPKINHEAD *nods. He smiles a little. He tries to pick up the box. It is much too big and heavy.*

Oh. [*Gesturing*] Go on, get that end... out the gate now... I'll show you, just out here... we'll get it in the car... lift it up now...

PUMPKINHEAD *grins in astonishment, but he lifts.*

Right. Now you walk backwards.

They tote the box between them out the gate. The yard stands empty again. A car door slams, off. A motor starts up.

SCENE TWO

RUBY's *house. The table is bare.* RUBY *sits in her chair reading, of course, her Bible. The door is knocked open and* PUMPKINHEAD *comes in backwards with one end of the box, the* CIVILIAN *following on the other end.*

PUMPKINHEAD: Mum! Look, Mum!

> *Poor* RUBY, *she stands and drops the Good Book.* PUMPKINHEAD *and the* CIVILIAN *stand smiling with the box.*

CIVILIAN: Where do you want it? It's for you.

> RUBY, *speechless, indicates the table.*

Right. Lift it, boy.

> *They heave the box on to the table.* RUBY *and the* CIVILIAN *stand there looking at each other. He shrugs, indicating the box. His tone asks acceptance.*

It's just some things...

RUBY: [*solemnly*] That's... you're kind.

> *Pause.*

CIVILIAN: Well, you see... I didn't know.

> RUBY *nods, and she smiles a little smile.*

PUMPKINHEAD: [*dying to get at the box*] We gonna see?

> *He looks from* RUBY *to the box.*

CIVILIAN: Why, sure we're gonna see! [*Ruffling the boy's head, and pointing at the box*] Come on, let's get it out of there.

> *He begins to pull everything from the box. He gives each item to* PUMPKINHEAD, *who grins wider and wider, accepting each item, grinning at* RUBY, *piling things on the table. The scene is a very excited and happy one.* RUBY, *hesitating, picks up a big tin of milk, looks at it, smiles, looks at the cot, smiles. The box is emptied, apparently, and the* CIVILIAN *lifts it off the table, puts it on floor and reaches in.*

And last, but not least...

> *He pulls out a cardboard box.*

PUMPKINHEAD: [*eagerly*] What's it?

CIVILIAN: [*winking*] Ah, ha!

> *He opens it and lifts out a great big cake, which he puts on the table.* PUMPKINHEAD's *eyes open wide. He stares open-mouthed at*

the CIVILIAN, *at the cake, at* RUBY, *and points suddenly in recognition.*

PUMPKINHEAD: [*awed*] Awwww! You d'Cake Man!

The CIVILIAN *smiles. He looks to* RUBY *in puzzlement.* RUBY *smiles at him and nods to* PUMPKINHEAD.

Cake Man!

He rushes at the CIVILIAN, *embracing him excitedly. The* CIVILIAN *hugs him back, pleased and affectionate.*

Got to tell Collie! [*Dancing happily*] Got to tell Noelie! Tell 'em all!

He runs out the door. His voice can be heard screeching, off.

Hey, Collie, the Cake Man! Found the Cake Man! Noelie! Cake Man! Robbie! Come on, come an' see what's in here. The Cake Man!

The CIVILIAN *looks puzzled, smiling at* RUBY. *She shrugs. They both look to the door and kids come streaming in one after another as* PUMPKINHEAD *shows them the cake, the big, beautiful cake, and the 'Cake Man', who has trouble embracing all those kids as they run to him.* RUBY *gives him a knife. He gives cake to all the children.*

SCENE THREE

This scene could be a brief film sequence. Evening. A street in Redfern, outside a pub. We hear traffic, a juke box from the pub, voices and laughter and all the pub noises. SWEET WILLIAM *walks along quietly and stands outside the pub door. He has a battered suitcase in his hand. He pauses, looking in. Out the door staggers a drunk. He is an Aborigine. A few others like him are pushed out the door. The* PUBLICAN *appears behind them in the doorway.*

PUBLICAN: Now g'wan get on your way! Back when you're sober.

They mutter and mumble and call abuse. They bump into SWEET WILLIAM *and crowd about him.*

Go on, piss off. [*Warning*] The police were rung for five minutes ago. Better get.

They give him some more abuse, and linger. We hear the roar of a police van pulling up. The PUBLICAN *nods. The Kooris look on in alarm. Two* POLICEMEN *run on with batons.*

POLICEMAN: This the trouble, Mr Pott?

The PUBLICAN *nods. He turns and goes inside his pub. The* POLICEMEN *proceed to arrest the lot. They run them off to the van, and at last the pair rush back at* SWEET WILLIAM.

Right you, get your arse in that wagon.

SWEET WILLIAM: Who, me? Oh, no boss, I'm down from the bush.

POLICEMAN: Don't you bloody well answer me back!

They grab WILLIAM. *They give him the bum's rush offstage. We hear the wagon's back door being slammed and locked. The other doors slam. The motor starts, roars and fades. The* PUBLICAN *appears in the doorway. He smiles, satisfied, after the wagon. Music: 'There's a Happy Land Somewhere'.*

END OF ACT THREE

EPILOGUE

SWEET WILLIAM *enters, in different clothes, and speaks directly to the audience.*

SWEET WILLIAM: No? Ah, well it don't matter. Please don't give it another thought. Forget all that shit they say about giving me back my culture. That's shit. It isn't what I'm really after, not really. What I want, what I'm here for… it's something else again, if I could get it across what I mean…

Pause. He sits down.

Look, I'll tell you something. No laughing, you're not allowed to laugh, but you got to try and listen and not call me a liar or laugh. I'm no liar… ask Ruby, ask my missus, she'll tell you that's one thing about me, that I ain't a liar… one thing I'm not. [*Pause.*] You ever heard of eurie-woman? You say it like that, eurie-woman. No? Never heard of one a' them? Well, listen, then. I'll tell you what's a eurie-woman, and what it is I want here.

I was working at Killara Station… after I had me feed, I went an' laid down on me bed an' started readin' this gubba book I had… [*wide-eyed*] … an' all of a sudden I heerd this emu drummin' somewhere close. I got up and wen' outside an' stoked up the fire, and all the time this emu was still drummin'. I's trying to hear 'zactly where it was so I could find that nest… then the drummin' started closer to the tent. I was sort of curious, like, y'know? [*Pause.*] I thought, I won't have no trouble findin' that nest in the morning… but this time it was right behind the tent. [*Pauses dramatically*] Sooooo… while I was turnin' 'round, I got the biggest fright of me whole fuckin' life! It weren't no emu, it was a woman. And she had hair that was shinin' black, an' it hung down over her backside. She was the prettiest woman I ever saw…. yeah… she was a eurie-woman… I fair bolted out of there! You'd a thought I had wings, the way I flew out a there… [*Shaking his head slowly*] Didn' do no good, must have run easy a mile… but just as I ducked through the fence wires, there she was again, right in front of a man… between me an' the road… an' it was summer, hot as fuckin' hell, but I had the freezin' cold sweat all over me… an' then I took off again, runnin' for my life, scairter than ever I was before… runnin' fast… but didn't matter how or where, she was always there in front of me, and at the same distance away from me... her hair shinin' and swirling like it was made out of water, an' her skin like black lightin', if you can imagine that... so beautiful she couldn' ever be bad... but she was scary anyway, an' always there in front of me... but somewhere else.

He pauses in reverie.

Well, all I remember then is a gubba I was workin' for, was sayin' to me what was wrong, what happened... an' just the way he looked at me, I knew he never had, that he never would or never could see that eurie-woman... a gubba. Ain't no eurie-woman for gubbas, she came to tell me so I'd know. [*Pause. Smiling*] Y'know what? He said: 'Come on, William, ain't no eurie-woman... come back to reality.' [*Pause. Smiling sadly*] Exac'ly what that eurie-woman was sayin' to me... [*Pause.*] Two realities. [*Pause.*] An' I've lost one. [*Pause.*] But I want it back... I need it back. [*Pause.*] Not yours... mine.

THE END